CROSSING THE LINE

CROSSING THE LINE

AN ISRAELI-PALESTINIAN LOVE STORY

MYA GUARNIERI

RED LIGHTNING BOOKS

This book is a publication of

Red Lightning Books
1320 East 10th Street
Bloomington, Indiana 47405 USA

redlightningbooks.com

First printing 2025

Cataloging information is available from the Library of Congress.
ISBN 978-1-68435-236-4 (hdbk.)
ISBN 978-1-68435-242-5 (pbk.)
ISBN 978-1-68435-237-1 (ebook)
ISBN 978-1-68435-238-8 (web PDF)

This book is dedicated to everyone *who lives between the river and the sea or who considers the place their home.*

It is also dedicated to the two children Mohamed and I have together, living proof that Jews and Palestinians can exist in one body.

ACKNOWLEDGMENTS

First and foremost, I want to thank Mohamed Jaradat. This book wouldn't have been possible without your encouragement and support and without you spending long stretches alone with the children so I could write.

I also want to thank our two children for sacrificing time with me so I could go out and create this book. This is my story, yes, but it's also the story of how you came to exist.

There are so many other people to thank: Noam Sheizaf, who asked me shortly after I left Bethlehem if I would write something "longish" for +972 about my experience living there. "Two thousand words," he said. That two thousand words became a six-part series that was well over ten thousand words. And then that six-part series was translated to Hebrew for +972's sister site, Sikha Mekomit (Local call). Following publication, the emails and messages I received were, by and large, positive, particularly from Sikha Mekomit readers, many of whom asked me: "You're turning this into a book, right?" And that's when I thought for the first time, huh, yeah, maybe I will turn this into a book.

Big thank-yous to Michael Schaeffer Omer-Man and Edo Konrad for editing those initial +972 essays; I also want to thank Joseph Dana for bringing me into +972, giving me and my writing a home way back in 2011. Another early +972er, Noa Yachot, has always supported my work. I am also grateful for the whole +972 crew, old and new. That this website still exists and you all are still doing what you're doing is a spot of light in these dark days.

Other thank-yous: Nat Sobel, who championed this project and helped me with early iterations of the proposal.

Steve Almond: Genius and saint. This book wouldn't have made it over the line without you.

An enormous thank-you to Dan Crissman, formerly of Indiana University Press, who commissioned *Crossing the Line*. I also want to thank Gary Dunham and Anna Francis.

The following people supported me in various ways through the decade it took me to write this book. They are, in no particular order, Leslie Bogart and Bruce Kritzler, Valerie Bogart and Jerry Wein, Sam Freedman, Marilyn Williams, Tania Hary, Ashley Petkovic (you didn't know what you were getting yourself into when you put that striped shirt on!), Barrington Smith Seetachit, Cate Malek, Rana Mousa, Rebecca Granato, Akin Ajayi (narrate harder), Clare Needham, and Patti Ezratty. Love you all.

AUTHOR'S NOTE

A note about the cover art: Mohamed took this photo in Beit Jala or Al Walaja while this portion of the wall was still under construction. The door was most likely used by the Israeli army; Mohamed took the photo with the thought that soon even this door would be closed and the segmentation of Palestine would be complete. The wall would become his horizon.

While the image could be interpreted as a sign of hope, to Mohamed it was the opposite: it was a sign to him of diminishing prospects and an increasingly dark future living in the West Bank under Israeli occupation. Israel's control over the door also reminded Mohamed of the fact that, ultimately, it is Israel that controls Palestinian movement and every aspect of Palestinian life. This image made salient for Mohamed the unescapable feeling that he had little control over his own fate.

There aren't many doors like this in the separation barrier, and this door should not be mistaken for something that Palestinians can freely use. While there are some access gates for Palestinian farmers whose land has been cut in two by the separation barrier, it is hard for these farmers to obtain the necessary permission from Israel to reach their land on the other side. Even when they do get the necessary permit, they still do not have unfettered access to their land and are often subject to the whims of a schedule imposed by the army.

In regards to the text: this book is a memoir. As such, it is vulnerable to the issues that always come with the act of remembering and reminding: the current moment and our perceptions invariably color our recollections of the past. Memory is a dynamic act of reconstruction, not replication. So is this book.

While I have endeavored to stay as true as possible to the story as I experienced it between 2007 and 2014, some changes—both intentional and not—have been made. For narrative's sake, I have made some adjustments to the timeline of events. Most names have been changed to protect, as much as possible, the privacy of people who didn't know they would turn up in a book I didn't know I would write. Mohamed has retained his name, as has his father; additionally, interviewees who appeared in my Al Jazeera English stories and other people I reported on are named, as well.

None of the people in these pages are composite characters. They are not characters. They are real people.

A small portion of the final chapter was previously published on +972, where I first offered multiple accounts of my time in Bethlehem. Otherwise, while writing this version of the story, I avoided looking at most of my previously published pieces. This was intentional as I was trying to avoid self-plagiarism. As this book is a retelling of the same period that was covered in previous essays that were published in a variety of outlets, some of the content might be the same. I might have duplicated aspects of previous tellings, which would be unavoidable; conversely, I might have changed aspects of previous tellings, which would also be unavoidable. At some points, dialogue rendered in this book might be different than I'd recorded it in previous essays. However, the spirit of those conversations remains the same.

Lastly, this book includes both historical references and snippets of stories I reported. I believe these bits of history and journalism to be error-free; however, any errors that might have been introduced into either are unintentional and are my own.

CROSSING THE LINE

Prologue

September 2013, The West Bank, Occupied Palestinian Territory

As the minivan rounded the corner and the Israeli military checkpoint Palestinians call "the Container" came into sight, the driver hit the brakes. The breeze flowing through the open windows came to a sudden stop, as did the boisterous conversations of the Palestinian men around me. All of us passengers on this *servees,* or shared taxi, to Bethlehem fell silent as we looked ahead toward the guard tower, with its slit of an unblinking eye, looming over us like a malevolent, all-seeing God.

Beyond that stood steel and spikes and booths and Israeli soldiers.

The *whoosh* of fabric gliding through metal filled the air as, all at once, we pulled our seatbelts on. As we drew nearer to the first set of tire spikes, the driver reached for the radio, and the Arabic love song pumping through the speakers ended with an unceremonious *click.*

The only sound now was the gentle *tick tick tick* of green prayer beads, the strands bumping together as they swayed from the rearview mirror.

The driver exhaled and wiped the sweat from the back of his neck with a washcloth—it was hot and this old minivan-turned-taxi was unair-conditioned. Putting his hands at ten and two, where the soldiers would be able to see them, the driver gripped the steering wheel tight as he eased the *servees* forward. The front tires bounced over the spikes—*ca-duk ca-duk*—and the green prayer beads responded, lurching from side to side, ticking frantically.

There was no going back. If the driver hit reverse, the spikes would blow the tires.

Then I heard it again: *ca-duk ca-duk*. The back tires. We were completely inside the checkpoint now.

An Israeli soldier stood before us in the middle of the road, his baggy, ill-fitting olive-green fatigues rolled up to the elbows, a semiautomatic rifle slung across his narrow torso. He looked like a child playing dress-up in his parents' clothes; still, adrenaline shot through my arms and legs. I'd been through the Container countless times—I passed through this checkpoint every day en route from the Palestinian city of Bethlehem, where I lived, to the Palestinian village of Abu Dis, where I worked at a local university—and I'd never seen a soldier standing in the road like that. Usually, they're in the booths or off to the side, milling about, chatting with each other or texting their girlfriends. Sometimes they sit in the shelter—a single bench topped by a sliver of corrugated tin, its shade useful only to the wild, sand-colored dogs who drift into the checkpoint, tumbleweed-like, from the surrounding Palestinian villages, seeking relief from the heat, oblivious to the politics of the place.

This soldier standing in the road could mean one thing and one thing only: we were being stopped. The soldier would check IDs. And if he caught me here, I could end up in jail because, as an Israeli, this checkpoint was legally off-limits to me. Never mind that I was born in Florida and have an American passport; while US citizens *are* allowed to pass through this checkpoint, to the Israeli government and army alike, I had been nothing but an Israeli since the moment I'd taken citizenship over five years before. Whenever I entered or exited the country,

I was required, by law, to use my Israeli passport. Legally speaking, it was the same situation out here in the West Bank: my US passport was irrelevant. To this soldier, I would be an Israeli popping up at an internal checkpoint, that is, a military checkpoint that divided one Palestinian area from another. To this soldier, I would be an Israeli who was somewhere she wasn't supposed to be.

That I was a journalist wouldn't help either. Though a press pass would allow me to move freely through all parts of the West Bank, as a freelancer, I didn't have one. And I wasn't passing through the Container for work. I was on my way to Ramallah to meet my Palestinian boyfriend, Mohamed—a detail this soldier probably wouldn't find endearing.

There was another problem with handing over my Israeli ID—all the passengers around me would see it. Because Israeli IDs are blue and Palestinian IDs are green, they would know, right away, that I was Israeli. That could be risky. Maybe the Israeli army had demolished the home of one of these men. Maybe the army had killed a family member. Maybe the Israelis had held one of these men in administrative detention, detaining him for years without charge or trial. Maybe one of these men was in Hamas.

I leaned forward, clutching the black backpack on my lap, my legs tense, my breathing shallow, my body ready to explode out of the minivan, to run. I looked out the window, searching for an escape route but there was none. To our left, the face of a mountain; to our right, the steep drop-off to Wadi Nar, "the Valley of Fire." I imagined myself opening the sliding door, leaping out of the van, and sprinting out of the checkpoint, back to the Palestinian village where I'd boarded the *servees* just a few minutes before.

Trying to run out of a checkpoint, I realized, would be a great way to get shot.

Riding the brakes, his hands still at ten and two, the driver inched forward toward the soldier, who flicked his fingers downward and to the side, signaling to the driver that he should pull into the bay next to the small shelter. Yes, he was going to check IDs. My stomach flung itself into my spine.

I sent Mohamed a frantic text: *I'm at the Container. They're pulling us over.*

And then another: *I love you.*

Worried that any movement might call the soldier's attention to me, I didn't wait for Mohamed's reply. I slid the phone into the front pocket of my backpack, my fingers grazing the edge of my *teudat zehut*, my Israeli ID. Behind that was my American passport, which I could give to the soldier instead in hopes that he would open it, glance at the photo, and hand it back without checking for a visa. But that was risky: because if the soldier looked for a visa and didn't find one, he would know that I was local, and he would also know that I was trying to hide that fact from him.

Handing him my American passport instead of my Israeli ID was also a tacit admission that I knew this place was off-limits. If he checked for a visa and didn't find one, the soldier would know that I knew that I was breaking Israeli law by going through this checkpoint. His suspicions aroused, he wouldn't just ask me what I was doing here, in a servees full of Palestinians, at a checkpoint that was off-limits to me. He would ask me: *Why didn't you hand over your teudat zehut in the first place? What game are you trying to play?*

And then I'd *definitely* be going to jail.

Getting arrested would strip me of the courage to continue living in the West Bank. Fearful of being caught again, I would move back into Israel and, with a wall between us, that would be the end of my relationship with Mohamed—the love of my life, the man who would eventually become my husband and the father of my children.

Mohamed.

I thought of his eyes, that particular shade of hazel that Arabs call *asal*, "honey." I pictured his dark hair and skin, the color of toasted almonds. I thought of his smell, so familiar from the start, as though we'd already been together all our lives. I remembered our first kiss, how Mohamed had been too shy and sweet to go for it, how he'd nuzzled my cheek as we sat on a boulder in an olive grove, listening to the call to prayer. I thought of the weekends we'd spent together in Bethlehem: long afternoons in bed, our bodies wrapped in white sheets, balcony doors flung open, billowing curtains parting to reveal gentle hills glowing red in the bright Mediterranean light before snapping shut again. Wrapped in that cocoon two floors above the Old City, hidden but looking out at the world flickering beyond us, I had the sense that we were the only two people on the planet, that time and place no longer existed. It was only this and us.

I remembered the first time we'd met, two years before: I'd gone to Ramallah to report a story and a mutual friend had introduced me to Mohamed, who was also a journalist. We'd ended up spending a day working together, sparks flying. But we'd both pushed those feelings aside. And then we'd spent a year and a half circling each other, working together occasionally, pretending our interest in each other was strictly professional.

But then, about six months ago, unable to deny our feelings any longer, we'd decided to give dating a try, despite the fact that I'm Israeli and he is Palestinian; despite the fact that his father had been in the Palestine Liberation Organization (PLO), which Israel had once deemed a terrorist group; despite the fact that his family would never approve of our relationship. I'd been living in Jerusalem then, and we'd tried dating with the wall between us, with me sneaking into and out of Palestinian areas of the West Bank, avoiding the Israeli soldiers who might detain me, and Mohamed crossing into Israel without a permit, risking arrest or death.

Because circumventing the wall could be lethal for Mohamed, and because it was impossible for him to move into Israel, I decided to use the privilege afforded by my American passport to move to a Palestinian city in the West Bank, Bethlehem—a place that was legally off-limits to me according to Israeli law. Now Mohamed could reach me. But, out here, we faced other challenges: the West Bank was fragmented, broken into parts by the Israeli checkpoints that stood between one Palestinian area and another, including the Container. And at the end of the day, I was still an Israeli, something I had to keep secret from most of the Palestinians I lived among as well as the Israeli soldiers I ran into.

Like the one pulling the servees over now.

My fingers still in the pocket of my backpack, I touched the edge of my Israeli ID. *What if I was honest?* I wondered. *What if I outed myself?* I imagined stepping out of the servees and calling the soldier *achi*, "my brother," leading him to the shelter, sitting down together on the bench, and telling him our love story. Would he be sympathetic and let me through the checkpoint?

No. I would have crossed too many lines as an Israeli. Political lines. Cultural lines. Personal lines. Friendship with a Palestinian was one thing. But romance? That was the ultimate taboo: I'd betrayed the Jewish people. This soldier would call me a "leftist traitor" and arrest me on the spot.

The soldier opened the van's sliding door and peered inside at all of us. I looked out the window, pretending that I could render myself invisible by not looking at him. If I didn't see him, maybe he wouldn't see me.

"*Hawiyah* [ID]," he said in Arabic. My heart fought against my ribs as the other passengers surrendered their green Palestinian IDs. I did nothing. I would play dumb foreigner as long as I could, pretending that I didn't understand or that his words didn't apply to me.

The soldier collected the IDs, lining the edges up, making a neat stack of green. And then he began to open them, one by one. Not taking his eyes off of the IDs, he said, "*Gam at*," in Hebrew, using the feminine form of "you." I was the only woman in the servees. It was unmistakable—he was talking to me. Was he speaking Hebrew to me because he'd guessed me to be Israeli? Or because he didn't know how to say "You, too" in Arabic or English? I had no idea. I stared at him but didn't move.

"Gam at," he said again, looking up at me this time.

Bringing my hand to my chest, which was covered by the black turtleneck I wore for modesty's sake, I said, "Who me?" in English, simultaneously pretending not to understand and making it clear that I did.

"*Ken. At.*" (Yes, you.)

I carefully slid my American passport out of the pocket, making sure the Israeli ID stayed hidden, and handed the passport over. The soldier opened it, looked at the photo, looked at me, and passed it back.

My insides melted in relief.

Green Palestinian IDs still in hand, the soldier told us, in Arabic, to close the windows. Then he slammed the minivan's door shut and walked away, and the sun began its furious dance on the roof, sending the temperature inside the servees skyrocketing, leaving me wondering if I would make it to Ramallah, to Mohamed, wondering if, instead, I might die here, wedged between a mountain and a cliff, at a checkpoint manned by my own countrymen.

1

I wouldn't have ended up at that checkpoint, trying to reach Mohamed in Ramallah, if I hadn't had a visceral reaction to Israel the first time I visited in 2006. At the time, my physical response to the place, which would eventually put me into direct conflict with my political leanings, surprised and confused me. But almost twenty years later, I see a clear chain of events—a domino effect—that led me to Israel, rooting me in that troubled land.

The short version goes something like this: I grew up in the Deep South with a strong sense of both my Jewish identity and the fact that I was a minority and an outsider. Then, when I was seventeen, I was date-raped by a friend at a Fourth of July party, an attack I later came to believe was antisemitic. To make things worse, in the days immediately following the rape, my friends doubted my experience, and my mom, unintentionally, abandoned me emotionally, leaving me feeling isolated, embattled, alone.

Enter Miguel.

When Miguel, who would become my first husband, came along, I leapt into the relationship, taking refuge in him and his big, warm family. But by the time we married, I'd realized I was going to give up too much of myself to make things work. As our marriage was collapsing, I happened to take a trip to Israel, where I was bowled over by the profound sense of safety and belonging I felt from the moment I stepped off the plane. Here, I was no longer the Other. My experience was no longer discounted. I would no longer be dependent on a man who didn't want me to have my own identity.

In Israel, I was free. I was safe. I was home.

That's the short version. You can either bear with me as I get you up to speed—I'll do my best, dear reader, to keep it brief—or you can work this book Choose Your Own Adventure style and skip to chapter 2.

* * *

How does a Jewish girl end up in the Deep South? That story starts with my mom, who was born and raised in New York City, the daughter of first- and second-generation Jewish Americans. Though my grandfather had Orthodox roots, my mom was raised secular, save for Hebrew school and occasional visits to the synagogue, where my grandfather urged my mom to put all her spare change in what she thought of as "little blue boxes," donation boxes for the Keren Kayemeth LeIsrael Jewish National Fund (KKL-JNF). The money was being collected to plant trees in the young state of Israel, my grandfather proudly told my mother, and at some point, he had an olive tree planted somewhere in Israel in my mother's name.

But my grandfather was a complicated man. On the one hand, he was a Zionist—that is, someone who believes in a Jewish state. On the other hand, he took my mother and her brother out to distribute flyers protesting the Vietnam War.

A young hippie, my mother went to college in upstate New York only to promptly drop out. Trying to figure out her next move, she called a hippie friend who was like, "Hey, why don't you move down here to Gainesville?" Apparently, in the 1970s, there was something of a scene there despite the fact that this was the Deep South. How Southern? Let me put it this way: Gainesville is just ninety miles from St. Augustine, where Martin Luther King Jr. and a group of rabbis marched in 1964 to protest the racism and segregation endemic to the place. And fifteen years later, when I was born, racial tensions remained in North Florida.

While I was a social child who always had friends, in elementary school I was usually the only Jewish kid in class, and I often found myself struggling to explain my holidays, with their strange-sounding Hebrew names. Then there were the classmates who were not so nice. Pointing at my *chai* pendant dangling from a thin gold necklace, they would laugh and howl, "What's that? A dog? Why are you wearing a *dog* around your neck?!" (To be fair to these classmates, I can see now how the word could resemble a dog to eyes unadjusted to Hebrew. Look here and decide for yourself: חי.)

I would try to explain that this pendant—an heirloom handed down from my maternal great-grandmother—was the Hebrew word for "life." But the teasing continued no matter how many times I tried to translate my *chai* and myself.

When I was a child, my mother also made me aware of our outsider status every time we drove through town in her little blue Ford Pinto. "Look at this place," she would say, pointing out the window, her silver bangles jingling as they slid down her olive-skinned arm. "There's a church on every fucking corner!"

There were two or three small synagogues in town, but we didn't go. Jewish life is expensive in America, and we were poor. My mother had divorced my biological father when I was three; though she'd remarried, my stepdad, who adopted me and who I call Dad to this day, was a janitor at that time. My mother was going to community college to get an associate's degree in graphic design. With no money to spare on a synagogue membership or Hebrew school, we did our own thing at home: Hanukkah candles in the winter; in the spring, my mom always added matzah to the dinner table, putting it alongside the baguette she loved. I also came to understand bagels and lox to be part and parcel of our American Judaism, but I wasn't sure why.

My aunts all sent me lots of books about Judaism and strong Jewish women, books I hid in my closet where my Christian friends couldn't see them. Occasionally, Mom and I visited our super Jewy extended family. My mother's aunt and uncle had been founding members of their synagogue in Cleveland, Ohio, and most of our gatherings revolved around Jewish holidays or life-cycle events. And when we went to synagogue for a bar mitzvah and I saw everyone's lips moving in time to the Hebrew prayers, including my mother's, I wondered: What is this language, these words, that everyone in my family knows except for me?

* * *

Now let's fast-forward to 1997, to the summer between my senior year of high school and my freshman year of college. On July 4, I was at a party with a group of my girlfriends when a guy I'd been friends with since our freshman year of high school—someone I trusted—peeled me off from the group and led me into the woods behind the apartment complex where the party was held. There, among the trees, he pressed his lips to mine. Because I had feelings for this friend but not those kind of feelings, I didn't kiss him back. Hoping to preserve the friendship, I turned my head away.

He pressed on, and, next thing I knew, I was on the ground, in the dark, and my friend was shoving my shorts and underwear to the side. I told him "no," more than once—before he penetrated me and after, as he pinned me down and groaned while he raped me. I said "no," and he didn't listen. I thought for a moment of trying to push my friend—who was a full foot taller than me and at least 60 pounds heavier—off of me. But if I got out from under him, where would I go? He'd led me into the woods, and I didn't know my way out.

When I realized that I had no say in what was happening to my body, when I realized that my friend was going to continue until he was done, when I realized that my only way out of the woods was to lay there and let him finish, that's what I did. I held completely still, like I was dead. Unable to process what was happening to me, I unhooked my soul from my body and let it fly away to the tops of the trees.

Obviously, I was traumatized; this trauma was only compounded by how the people around me reacted. The next morning, when I told my best friend what had happened, she insisted on telling the guy's girlfriend, who didn't believe me and who spread the word to all of our friends that I was a bitch, a liar, a slut. My phone started blowing up as everyone called to berate me. I was devastated but did my best to hide my feelings because I didn't want to explain to my parents what had happened. My mother knew something was up, though; she sat me down on the couch one afternoon and asked: "What did you do?"

Sitting there with her, looking down at the cushion beneath my legs, tracing the black-and-white patterned fabric with my finger, I thought, for a moment, about telling her the truth. But no one else believed me. Would she?

As young women in these circumstances often do, I had begun to doubt and blame myself. And I worried that my mother would, too. After all, I'd been wearing a halter top that night. How many times had she warned me against going out dressed too skimpily? How many times had she told me that my shorts were too short? How many times had I been told that giving it up would get me nowhere? How many times had she shared that old cliché with me, which she, undoubtedly, had heard from her mother: "Why buy the cow when you can get the milk for free?" Only several years later, after my attacker called me and told me that I'd always been "different" than our other friends, would I understand that the attack had been tinged with antisemitism. Because what was the one thing that had always set me apart from my classmates and everyone in my social circle? The fact that I am Jewish.

But I hadn't yet put it all together that July afternoon when I sat on the couch with my mom. In shock, I hadn't put anything together, really. So when my mother asked me "What did you do?" I didn't respond. I clenched my teeth tight. I stayed silent.

As my mother's eyes scanned me for an answer, she realized I was no longer wearing my chai. "Where is your chai?" she asked.

I looked up at her then and saw her dark brown eyes narrowing, her thick black eyebrows collapsing inward, onto themselves. I thought about telling her how, when I'd gotten home on July 4, I'd taken off every single thing that I'd been wearing, even my chai, and I'd buried it all deep in the garbage.

"I took it off," I said.

She looked at me suspiciously.

Here I feel the need to pause and defend my mother, who didn't know that I had just undergone a major trauma. Her intentions were good. But that conversation opened up a chasm in what was already a complicated relationship. It would take me years to realize how that talk on the couch had shattered my ability to trust my mother. It had also left me unable to trust myself. The attack and its aftermath are issues too big for me to deal with fully in this book and this isn't a memoir about sexual trauma. But that night shattered any sense of belonging I felt in my hometown, my community, in my family, in myself and it set into motion the events that would lead me first to Israel and, eventually, to Mohamed. Suffice it to say that the assault had robbed me of the sense of physical safety that I would find later in Israel. Suffice it to say that Israel was the place where I felt my soul returned, finally, to my body. But before Israel, the assault left me reeling, looking for something stable to latch onto, and that was what propelled me into my first marriage.

* * *

Miguel and I met two years after I was assaulted, when I was nineteen, at a get-together hosted by his brother. Miguel, twenty-one, had curly black hair, these John Lennon–type glasses, and a strong Roman nose. A psychology major minoring in criminology, Miguel was squeezing in creative writing classes whenever he could. I'd wanted to be a writer since the moment I'd learned to read and was double majoring in English and psychology. When we met, I was taking a poetry workshop, and Miguel, a junior, was in advanced fiction writing with Harry Crews, the renowned Southern novelist. Because students had to apply to that fiction class and not everyone made the cut, I was immediately impressed. Our first date, which took place a week later, ended with us sitting together in front of his computer, scrolling through Miguel's short stories.

Intellectual soulmates, we dove into the relationship headfirst. Three weeks after we met, Miguel took me home to meet his parents.

There, at their house in Tampa, I found the big, stable, intact family I, an only child, had always wanted. Not only did Miguel have another brother and a sister; his parents were still married. His Italian American father was a successful attorney; his Puerto Rican mother was a stay-at-home mom. Considering me something of an orphan, Miguel's family embraced me as one of their own, and I enthusiastically folded myself into his clan.

Still, I had doubts about my future with Miguel. Fairly early on, I realized that we were looking for different things. But I brushed those concerns aside, and five years into the relationship, despite my growing ambivalence, I went through with the wedding. I wasn't just marrying him, after all. I was marrying his family, who I didn't want to lose because they offered me the feelings of safety and belonging I craved.

But all that safety and belonging came with some serious conditions, expectations that left me feeling confined and suffocated: Miguel and his parents wanted me to be a traditional wife. At twenty-four, I wasn't ready to be that woman. I wanted my shot at life: I wanted to go to graduate school and get a Master of Fine Arts in Creative Writing. I would write books; I would have a career; I would have a life of my own. I would be more than someone's wife.

* * *

So, just a year after we'd married, I left Miguel in St. Augustine, Florida, where we'd moved for his first job, so I could go to graduate school on the other side of the state, in Tallahassee. My identity as a member of this big Latin family crumbling, I began to shore up my sense of myself as a Jewish woman. In Tallahassee, I attended synagogue, where I went to services and a study group. I quickly found, however, that while I enjoyed exploring Judaism intellectually, I couldn't leave my secular roots behind.

And then, one day, a guy I'd become friends with in grad school, this Jewish guy from Brooklyn, told me about something I'd never heard of: Birthright, a program that offers young Jews from the diaspora a free trip to Israel.

That I balked at the name (Birth*right*?! What right do I have to this place that I have never set foot on?) but signed up anyway tells you everything you need to know about my politics at the time. Because I'd grown up firmly outside the framework of mainstream American Jewish life, I had no opinion about Israel. I wasn't a Zionist. Neither was I an anti-Zionist, someone who opposes an independent Jewish state. Sure, I had family in Israel—distant relatives on my mother's side—but I didn't feel that the country represented me. I didn't feel a need to form any kind of opinion about the place and what was happening there.

Warning that the tour guides would try to brainwash me, my anti-Zionist friend advised me to ignore them, which is exactly what I planned to do.

But even before the tour guides started yammering away about our forefathers and our home and all of that, something weird happened when I stepped off the plane in Tel Aviv, something I hadn't expected: I had a visceral reaction to the place.

The moment I set foot on the tarmac, I got goose bumps all over my body.

Today, almost twenty years later, I *still* can't work out why my body had this physical reaction to its first arrival in *eretz yisrael*, "the land of Israel." Though I'd always had a strong sense of myself as a Jew, my mom had never said much about Israel. But presumably, at family gatherings, someone had. Or maybe it was that, at every family gathering, an aunt would unzip a purse and produce the latest photos of our Israeli clan, including pictures of my cousin Rotem, who I hadn't seen in the flesh since she was seven and I was eighteen months old. Despite the years, every photo I saw of her—Rotem, in her army uniform, auburn curls just like mine spilling over her collar; Rotem in civilian clothes, standing in front of the Old City in Jerusalem with her father, Aviram—evoked an older image of us, frozen in my mind, a photo from a family wedding showing Rotem squeezing a little, chubby me with a crooked grin on my face. Although Rotem and I didn't share blood, there was a strong physical resemblance, a fact I found unnerving. These images of Israel as a place where the people looked like me must have made their way into my subconscious, settling there.

I had probably been exposed to the idea of Israel as the Jewish homeland more than I'd realized and the thought must have taken up residence on the ocean floor of my brain. I have rummaged through my head, trying hard to pinpoint a moment when someone overtly articulated this concept to me, and I can't find one. The messages were so subtle and so many that they became an organic part of me, and my body was responding to finally being in this place that was lodged in the most unreachable recesses of my mind.

But when I look back, I think the biggest reason I got goose bumps when I arrived in Israel was because the place imbued me with a profound sense of physically safe—a feeling that had been stolen from me on July 4, 1997.

Whatever the causes, the second I set foot on that tarmac in Tel Aviv, I was gripped by the feeling that I'd come home and that I never wanted to leave.

I was also, almost immediately, thrown into a conflict with myself. Regardless of how my body responded to the place, I didn't completely buy the ideology the tour guides tried to sell us, maybe because I was on the trip with students from Yale. As the tour guides did their best to indoctrinate us all, those Yalies pushed back with hard questions that gave me a crash course on the conflict. I learned that in 1947, the United Nations voted to partition Palestine, which had been under British rule at the time, into two states—one Jewish, the other Arab—and that fighting had broken out in the wake of that vote. I learned that in 1948, on the eve of the May 15 British withdrawal from Israel, Zionist leaders declared independence, and the civil war escalated into a regional conflict as the armies from five neighboring Arab states—Egypt, Jordan, Syria, Lebanon, and Iraq—attacked the nascent Jewish state. I learned that the war had ended in 1949 with armistice agreements that delineated what is called the "Green Line" (supposedly because it was drawn with a green marker), a boundary that, today, serves as a de facto border between Israel and the Palestinian territories.

I learned that the Green Line basically split Jerusalem into two, dividing the city into the Jewish west side, which was part of Israel, and the Palestinian east side, which fell under Jordanian administration in the years immediately following the 1948 war—that is, until 1967, when there was another war.

Israelis call that 1967 war the "Six Day War" because of their lightning quick victory over the Arab armies; when fighting was over, the Israeli military held onto the Palestinian territories of East Jerusalem, the West Bank, and the Gaza Strip, as well as the Syrian Golan Heights, marking the beginning of what is referred to as "the occupation," which continues today. Initially the occupation was only a military presence; however, shortly after the 1967 war, Israeli civilians began building settlements, Israeli communities outside the Green Line that stand on Palestinian land, oftentimes privately owned Palestinian land.

Of course, some of the Yalies mentioned the First Intifada, the first Palestinian uprising against Israeli rule, a rebellion that spanned 1987 to 1993, as well as what came after: the Oslo Accords, the provisional agreement that was supposed to culminate, in five years' time, in a binding, lasting peace. But "Oslo," as it was known, had been a failure, and in 2000, the Second Intifada had broken out. That Palestinian uprising had only ended about a year before I was there in 2006.

To be honest, back then, none of this history interested me. What stuck with me was that completely visceral and totally unexpected connection I'd felt to the place when I'd stepped off the plane. In Israel, I felt myself breathing; I felt myself *here*. For the first time in years, I felt myself alive.

* * *

Just days after I got home, the Israeli soldier Gilad Shalit was captured from Israeli territory by Hamas during a cross-border raid, sparking a conflict on the southern border. In the north, on the border with Lebanon, war broke out with Hezbollah, a conflict that was viewed very differently by a Lebanese classmate than it was portrayed by the Western and Israeli media I consumed. And I didn't argue with this Lebanese classmate. Open, always, to other viewpoints, I listened.

Amid the war, I tried to go to lunch at a place called Ali Baba, a restaurant that was owned by Samir, the Palestinian husband of one of my classmates. I arrived to find Ali Baba closed, however, a sign on the door. Samir hailed from a small village in the far north of Israel, close to the border with Lebanon; he had lost a family member in the fighting and was staying home to grieve, the sign said.

When Samir reopened, he edged the wooden patio with white flags. As we sat together one afternoon there, in the sun, Samir gestured to the cloth flapping in the wind and said, "I surrender. I don't care who wins. I just want the fighting to stop." He went on to explain that during this short war, he'd lost family members in both Israel and Lebanon.

How could he have family on *both* sides of the border, in enemy states, I wondered aloud.

He explained: The 1948 war hadn't just given birth to Israel; it had also turned approximately 750,000 Palestinians into refugees, an event referred to in Arabic as the *nakba,* the "disaster" or "catastrophe." Amid the fighting, his extended family, including his grandparents, had packed up and fled the village. But when they were halfway to Lebanon, they realized that—amid the chaos and panic—they'd left one of their children behind. So Samir's grandparents had turned around and gone back to the village where, eventually, Samir was born. And that's how his family had ended up half in Lebanon, half in Israel—separated into two enemy states—and that's how he'd lost relatives on both sides in the past month.

Samir knew I was Jewish and that I'd just been to Israel, and he missed the place, which he called Palestine, keenly. So rather than talking politics, Samir asked me to share my impressions with him. I told him about the Mediterranean, about how, one day, as the bus was leaving Tel Aviv, we'd been driving along the water and everyone had started chanting, "*Yam! Yam! Yam!*" Hebrew for "sea." It was an unscheduled stop, but the guides told the driver to pull over anyway. With our swimsuits packed in the luggage tucked under the bus, we ran toward the shore, pulling off our clothes as we did so, crashing into the water in bras and underwear.

I told Samir that there was something about that color of blue: mesmerizing, so beautiful you couldn't tear your eyes from it even though it made you wince with longing and left you aching. But I'd run toward it anyway, and as I floated in the Mediterranean, I closed my eyes. My breath and my pulse and the water's hush filled my ears, and as I listened, the sea soothed me, putting my broken heart back together again, sealing the cracks with that brilliant blue. It was like the water, that place, had returned me to myself, and I was finally whole and complete again.

And *that* was the feeling I had to go back for.

Samir nodded wistfully, sighed, took a sip of his beer, lit another cigarette, pumped me for more details. He just wanted to talk to someone who'd been to the land, who had breathed the air, who understood how he ached for the smells and the soil.

That conversation made the issues tangible for me in a way that reading Edward Said, the preeminent Palestinian intellectual, as an undergraduate English major never had. I understood from Samir's story about 1948 that having our Jewish state—having the place where I felt physically safe and emotionally free—had come at others' expense. And I understood that maintaining a state with a Jewish majority meant that Palestinians are still paying the price.

* * *

Here I could offer you a simple story about my relationship with Israel that goes like this: my starter marriage over, I—a newly minted Zionist—head to Israel. But that's not what happened.

For one, despite the fact that I'd already told Miguel that I wanted a divorce and despite the fact that he'd moved to south Florida and we were now living five hours apart, we hadn't filed the papers. We'd been together for seven years; in many ways, his family had raised me. So we both seesawed constantly as to what we should do about our faltering relationship. Couples' therapy? (He said no.) Salsa dancing classes? (No again.) A baby? (I said no. I wanted a house full of kids someday but not yet.)

What we *did* agree on, though, was that I would go abroad for my third year of my master's program, my thesis year, so we could both have some space to figure things out. It would be a trial separation, during which we would both be free to see other people. At the end of my thesis year, we agreed, I would return to Florida, so we could either work on our marriage or file for divorce.

Initially, I wasn't going to go to Israel. Because I spoke decent Spanish—better than Miguel's, ironically—I thought about spending the year in Argentina or Spain. But we'd honeymooned in the former, and Miguel had family in the latter. While both places might give me the physical space I wanted, neither would give me the psychological distance or the sense of self I needed.

I thought about India for no reason other than the fact that it would be cheap to spend a year there. And whatever I did needed to be cheap because I would use student loans to pay for my living expenses; Miguel hadn't helped me with the cost of graduate school, and he definitely wasn't going to help me stay afloat while I was abroad.

And then I remembered: at the end of Birthright, I'd learned about all these heavily subsidized Israeli volunteer programs. I began hunting for one that would be a good match, ideologically speaking. Though I'd come back from Israel thinking I might be a Zionist—and I'd flirted with the idea for a few months—by the time I was researching volunteer programs, I'd learned enough to put me back into the undecided camp. Already, I was ambivalent about the place; some of those doubts were rooted in my understanding of Jewish values. A lot of the things the state was doing to the Palestinians contradicted Judaism's core beliefs, as I understood them.

With Samir's family history fresh in mind and my politics leaning left, I found a social-justice-oriented volunteer program called Tikkun Olam, Hebrew for "world repair," a foundational Jewish value. The program billed itself as part-time, meaning I would be able to finish my master's thesis. Ten months long, it would start in September, at the beginning of the fall semester, and end in June, when my thesis happened to be due.

Perfect.

The idea of the program was that participants would live in the same neighborhood they volunteered in. My heavily subsidized apartment would be in south Tel Aviv, an impoverished part of the city with pressing social issues. The program also offered the option of volunteering in the neighboring Palestinian area of Jaffa. Under the 1947 UN Partition Plan, Jaffa was supposed to be part of an Arab state; however, Israel had conquered this historically Arab place during the 1948 war, and in 1950, the city of Tel Aviv annexed Jaffa and Hebraicized its name to Yafo.

Among the many papers I had to fill out when I signed up for Tikkun Olam was a list of places where we would be able to volunteer.

From the various options in both south Tel Aviv and Jaffa, I committed to volunteering at a Palestinian school in Jaffa—a choice I likely made because I had grown up outside of the Jewish mainstream.

Because I wasn't going to Israel for the usual ideological reasons, I was primed to understand the place differently than a lot of the American Jews who end up there. (I was also primed to feel deeply conflicted about the place, and eventually I did.) Politically speaking, I wasn't pro-Israel, but I wasn't anti either. And because I didn't feel that Israel represented me—Judaism and the Jewish people predated the state of Israel, and both would outlast the state, should it fail to survive—I didn't feel the need to decide where I stood on things. I was only going to be there for ten months.

Or so I thought.

* * *

Tikkun Olam began by whisking us through the first steps taken by the early Jewish settlers who built the country. Although we would be living in south Tel Aviv, we started the program on a kibbutz, a collective farming community, in the south of the country. Agricultural settlements had formed both the ideological and physical backbone of the early Zionist movement, which began in the late 1880s, and there, on the kibbutz, we got a little taste of the Jewish pioneers' lives: we spent our mornings in the fields, digging up sweet potatoes, and our afternoons in *ulpan,* Hebrew school.

After six weeks on the kibbutz, we moved to Tel Aviv. Before we started volunteering, however, we were required to visit the different volunteer sites the program offered, despite the fact that we'd already committed to a place before we'd arrived in Israel. So one morning, I went and saw a place called a *gan*. Though the word was Hebrew for "kindergarten," it wasn't a kindergarten in the proper sense of the word. It was a black market daycare for the children of Southeast Asian migrant workers and African asylum seekers, and it existed for one reason: the state of Israel didn't recognize these children before the age of three. When I got a look at that gan and saw one caregiver and dozens of toddlers, with no toys or books, running around an almost completely bare room or sitting on the bare cement floor crying, when I saw the line of silent cribs in the corner—the babies quiet because they learned that no one would come when they cried—I was heartbroken.

I was so shocked by what I saw in the gan that I decided, in that moment, to switch tracks. I wouldn't volunteer at the Palestinian school in Jaffa. I would devote myself, instead, to these children.

This moment also led me to question everything about the place. The Israeli government had no security claims against these children, and yet it was violating their human rights. Why? Simply because they weren't Jewish. Because I soon learned that Israel was deploying some of the same policies and tactics against the foreign, non-Jewish community as it did to the Palestinians, I began to interrogate the state's treatment of the Palestinians even before I first set foot in the occupied territories. Were Palestinians' human rights being violated because of the state's security claims or was it just because they weren't Jews? This led me to another question: Could the state be both "Jewish and democratic," as Israel's founders had declared? This goal seemed contradictory to me. This wasn't a view I developed in the West Bank. Rather, it was the understanding that I brought to the conflict with the Palestinians, which I would come to write about extensively as a journalist.

* * *

Although the volunteer program had billed itself as part-time, it came with a lot of obligations. In addition to volunteering, we attended a secular yeshiva—a secular religious school (yes, it's a contradiction in terms)—where we studied Jewish religious texts through a cultural, political lens. We joined a seminar at Tel Aviv University and went to Hebrew and Arabic classes; there were program meetings and weekend trips, too. All of this left little time for my thesis. So I dropped out of the program.

But I continued volunteering at the black market kindergarten, which older children also attended when they got out of the municipal schools in the early afternoon. Spending time with these kids—the Hebrew speaking, Israel-born children of Filipino migrant workers—did more for my Hebrew than any class had.

I was also learning Hebrew from this guy I'd started hanging out with, Oded.

A mutual friend had introduced us just after we both moved to Tel Aviv. Oded was what Israelis call a *yeled tov Yerushalayim*, "a nice Jerusalem boy": he came from the standard two-parent, three-children Zionist home. In the prestate days, when the British had been in control of the place, before the state of Israel was founded in 1948, Oded's paternal grandmother had been in the Irgun, a Jewish paramilitary organization the British had deemed a terrorist group. But her son—that is, one of Oded's uncles—would end up being a founding member of Shalom Achshav, "Peace Now." When I met Oded, the range of political ideologies inside his family was a perfect mirror of the country itself.

Oded had moved to Tel Aviv to study industrial design at the prestigious Shenkar College. We'd exchanged numbers because I'd liked his dark sense of humor, and as we were both new to the city, we thought we'd explore Tel Aviv together. Though we'd liked each other from the start and did eventually get romantic, we did so under the premise that our relationship had very defined boundaries and a shelf life: Oded knew that I was only in Israel for ten months, that I was separated from Miguel, and that I'd head back to Florida after the volunteer program was over. This all suited Oded, who wasn't looking for a relationship and who never wanted to get married or have children. Even back then, when my first marriage was falling apart, I already knew that, in the future, I wanted to give marriage another try. I knew I wanted children. Five to be exact: a big family, a tangle of arms and legs, a chorus of voices, to make up for how alone I'd felt as a child.

We were incompatible in other ways: Oded was a drummer in a metal band, and metal is the only genre of music I can't stand.

Even though we weren't destined for a serious relationship, we had fun together and Oded helped me assimilate in ways I never would have without him. Oded's English was good but labored, so he basically spoke Hebrew with me from the get-go; a lot of the language I picked up came from him, including colorful expressions like *al hazayin sheli*, which translates to, pardon me, "on my dick." It's just a really strong way of saying "bullshit" or "I don't give a fuck." Later, after I'd been in Israel for several years, as we debated politics with Oded's parents over dinner at the family home in Jerusalem, I accidentally dropped an *al hazayin sheli*, and the roar of laughter that erupted around the table broke any tension that had gathered around the weightier issues at hand.

From Oded, I also got a crash course in the books, music, and culture that I wouldn't have gotten otherwise. I learned that, in Israel, curls like mine—that big hair that my classmates had made fun of and that I'd tried, for years, to tame—were so ordinary they had a name: *bakbookim*, "bottles." In Israel, my hair was no longer a defect, a thing that made me stand out; here my curls were admired, they drew compliments, they helped me blend in. I learned that there was an old Israeli folk song that just so happened to bear my name, which is pronounced "Maya," and that Maya is an extremely common name in Israel. At Oded's parents' house, where we celebrated holidays—oftentimes with Oded's maternal uncle, a reform rabbi who would eventually depart for America—I learned how to do Judaism in that quasi-secular, quasi-observant Israeli way.

Whether it was a holiday or a Friday night dinner, after we cleared the table, we would crowd into the small living room where Oded's father would sit, perched on the end of the piano bench, a guitar resting on his knee, Oded's sister next to him, fingers poised over the black and white keys, Oded seated on the couch, ready to tap out a rhythm on his thigh. And then they would make music and lift their voices and sing, like an Israeli version of the Von Trapp family. I remember sitting there in the living room on some cold winter night, huddled next to a space heater, a lamp casting a warm glow over us all as I sat listening to Oded's family, melting into the couch, falling asleep there, Oded waking me up and steering me toward his childhood bedroom, which had been converted into a guest room, tucking me into the twin bed he'd once slept in himself.

From Oded, I got a sense of comfort and belonging.

Over the years, as I worked on my Hebrew, he also brought me books. In the beginning, there was *Tiras Ham* (Hot corn), a beloved children's book, and then, as my Hebrew improved, a Hebrew translation of Dr. Seuss's *Oh! The Places You'll Go*. "My little bird is leaving the nest," he inscribed in Hebrew, making a reference to one of the Arik Einstein songs his family sang in the living room. But it was also a nod,

I realize, to the temporary nature of our relationship. By giving me the language, like a parent, Oded was giving me the tools I needed to fly and thrive on my own.

Obviously, there were some parallels to my relationship with Miguel and his family. But there was a crucial difference—Oded imparted me less with a sense of belonging to a couple or his family and more of a sense of belonging to the place. Israel came to mean warmth and comfort. The place itself began to feel like a second skin to me.

* * *

For the sake of finishing my thesis, I'd dropped out of the volunteer program and pulled a small writing group together; one of the writers just so happened to be a journalist. When I told her about the gan, she suggested I pitch the story to her editor, with whom she connected me.

The editor took the story and then, even before it was printed, sent me out on assignment to do another. I will never forget the thrill of holding a newspaper in my hand and seeing my byline for the first time—I felt like I was really doing something. I was giving voice to the voiceless. I was making a difference in the world.

My byline also felt like a rebuke to those former classmates who hadn't believed that I'd been assaulted; it felt like a rebuke to Miguel's attempts to dictate the terms of my life to me. Although it wasn't the type of writing I'd dreamed of doing, I was hooked and threw myself into this career.

Almost overnight, I had fairly steady work as a journalist. With my volunteer visa expiring soon, I began to toy with the idea of taking citizenship, not out of ideological motivations but, rather, for the pragmatic reason of staying and continuing to write about south Tel Aviv and the injustices I saw there. Under the Law of Return, anyone with one Jewish grandparent would be automatically granted Israeli citizenship upon request. But I wrestled with the decision to take citizenship for the same reasons I balked at the word "birthright." Law of Return? What return? Sure, there was archaeological evidence that the ancient Hebrews had, indeed, been here. But in my mind, none of that translated to a right to come back and claim the place as my own, especially at the expense of the native inhabitants, the Palestinians.

I was also acquainted with the argument that taking citizenship legitimized the state of Israel and, by extension, Zionism and therefore harmed Palestinians. But I saw some flaws with this reasoning. Whether or not I chose to take citizenship wasn't going to make or break this state. The place was a fact.

But there was another problem: even if there was an ocean between us, I was still legally married. However, Miguel, who had given up on his own literary aspirations, encouraged me to stay in Israel for the sake of pursuing my writing career.

So, without fanfare, I took citizenship by filing the necessary paperwork and picking up my newly issued Israeli ID a few weeks later. And then I went all in on journalism—going to Hebrew-language press conferences, scribbling new vocabulary into my notebooks, pitching, reporting, often in Hebrew, and then laboring to translate and transcribe those interviews.

Because I'd also done a little bit of reporting about Tel Aviv's art scene, my inbox was constantly full of Hebrew-language press releases about gallery openings. I translated those, too, and at night, Oded and I went to art openings and drank for free. Waltzing into galleries all over the city, it felt like Tel Aviv was ours. When there were protests, I dragged Oded along to those. The two of us walked everywhere, me with my recorder and notebook, Oded sometimes pointing at things and naming them, me making up silly little rhymes and beats so the new words would stick.

"*Safsal*," he said, pointing at a bench, as we left a protest at Rabin Square one evening.

I liked this word safsal and so I threw it into a rhyme.

"*Sof sof, ani yoshevet al safsal*!" Finally, I'm sitting on a bench! I shouted as I sat, ecstatic to be able to spontaneously forge a sentence without a dictionary.

And then I climbed up and stood and cried, *Sof sof, ani omedet al safsal!* Finally, I'm standing on a bench!

I began to dance and, as I stomped my feet, I announced, *Sof sof, ani rokedet al safsal*!

Laughing, I jumped down. I jotted *safsal* into my notebook, and, as we walked through the city, I practiced conjugating Hebrew verbs by chatting excitedly about all the things people could do on a bench, Oded grinning as he listened.

* * *

The more Hebrew I learned, the better I understood the place, the better my pitches, the more work I had. My work as a journalist, of course, necessitated that I learn more Hebrew, so this was all a self-reinforcing cycle by which my sense of myself as both a journalist and an Israeli became inextricably linked. Quit one and I would lose the other. And I didn't want to lose either. My career seemed to take on a life of its own, and it felt to me like there had been this path waiting for me all along and I'd just stepped onto it. Soon I was writing for Al Jazeera and making the occasional appearance on BBC Radio and television. Amid all this, I found that I was no longer translating Hebrew. I was thinking in Hebrew, I was dreaming in Hebrew; I began to find that sometimes, when speaking English, words would escape me. It was shocking not to be able to recall something in my mother tongue. But it solidified my sense that I'd forged a new self here. This new self was confident and strong in all the ways I hadn't been as a seventeen-year-old or as a young married woman. And there was no way I was going back to America and to the person I'd been there.

But the combination of my politics, my journalism, Israeli citizenship, and Hebrew all had a paradoxical impact, too. The disillusionment I felt about the place colored my journalism, which connected me to a community of Israeli dissidents who, ironically, made me feel more at home in the country. The more integrated I became and the more attached I felt to the place, the more I felt the need to take a stand on what Israel was doing and the more I felt the need to speak out publicly about Israeli policies and actions. So I became an outspoken critic of Israeli policy. I went head-to-head with an Israeli government spokesperson on BBC Radio, arguing against the government's plans to deport Southeast Asian migrant workers' children, the same children I'd volunteered to help in south Tel Aviv. One of the pieces I published in *The Guardian* about protests against the planned deportation was so sharp, in fact, that the Israeli ambassador to the UK emailed my editor to complain. But I was undaunted, and I continued with unflinching coverage of the place.

Journalism also kept me afloat financially. Though my career was humming along, my personal life was a mess. I was living in limbo: while Miguel and I were informally separated, we *still* hadn't filed for divorce. In the meantime, Oded and I had moved in together—less for romantic reasons and more because we'd found an amazing place in the city center that neither of us could afford alone. If we split the rent, though, it was cheap. But I didn't really want to live with Oded. It felt inauthentic and dishonest. And by hiding out inside a transactional, dead end relationship with all these predetermined limits (no marriage, no kids), I was forestalling real intimacy with someone who could be a real lifelong partner.

But the Arab Spring would change all of that.

* * *

The Arab Spring started in Tunisia, in December 2010, when a twenty-six-year-old produce vendor set himself on fire to protest poverty and governmental corruption. In the wake of his death, demonstrations erupted in Tunisia that would eventually force the president to step down and flee the country. Emboldened by their Tunisian counterparts' success, demonstrators in Libya and Egypt took to the streets to protest repressive regimes, as well. Then the Arab Spring spread further, to Syria.

As media organizations diverted their resources towards covering these uprisings, there was less money for and interest in coverage of Israel and the occupied Palestinian Territories, a conflict that seemed, at the time, like it was on a low burn. Overnight, my work dried up as my editors pulled the plug on stories that they'd already greenlit; a major outlet owed me thousands of dollars and dragged its feet on payment as it threw money at freelancers in Egypt instead. I sent polite but increasingly desperate emails to my editor begging for the sum. To no avail.

Because Miguel and I spoke often, he knew what was going on and he tried to swoop in to save me. "Looks like your big career is over. Why don't you come on home, little lady?" he said. And though he'd said it somewhat tongue in cheek, I knew that he was passing off his true feelings as a joke. I hated the way he condescendingly called my work "big" and me "little." It felt patronizing. If this was what I was "going home" to, well, I didn't want to go at all.

As for my parents, they loved Miguel, and though they were proud of my journalistic work and the short stories I'd published, they didn't approve of our prolonged separation. My mom articulated her disapproval. Not knowing what had happened on July 4, she didn't realize I'd entered the relationship looking for refuge. My parents didn't know that my actions were a typical trauma response—a combination of fight, flight, and freeze. They didn't understand that I'd fled into marriage and then frozen and that I'd fled to Israel, only to freeze again.

Regardless, they disapproved, and I wasn't about to reach out to them for help.

With rent as my top priority, I tightened my belt. For food, I scrounged through the leftover produce vendors dumped onto the pedestrian walkways of the Shuk HaCarmel, Carmel Market. I also familiarized myself with bakeries that put their unsold bread out in plastic bags on the sidewalk on Friday afternoons.

When my Israeli bank account went into overdraft, someone from the bank called to ask me if I would like to raise the limit on my minus, allowing me to go deeper into debt. Or perhaps I wanted to take out a loan? I wanted to do neither. But feeling that I had no choice, I walked over to the branch where, three years before, I'd opened the account using the first check I'd received as a journalist. Back then, I'd entered the bank with a dictionary and a script I'd written, in Hebrew, to get myself through the interaction. Now I had control over the language but no checks to *lehafkid*, to deposit.

Sitting before a clerk with long black hair that reminded me of my mother's and a chai like the one I'd worn as a child—the necklace I'd taken off and buried in the garbage along with my clothes on July 4—I cried as I signed the papers to raise the limit on my minus. However tortured my political relationship with the state of Israel, the place was home. But I wasn't sure how I would stay.

* * *

Late one afternoon in June 2011, just three months before I would meet Mohamed for the first time, I was at the *shuk*, picking through a mound of half-rotten vegetables, when an editor called from Ma'an News Agency, a Palestinian outlet I'd been writing for during the past couple of years. They wanted to send me to Athens to cover the flotilla: international and Palestinian activists' attempt to break the Israeli blockade of the Gaza Strip by sailing a fleet of ships to the besieged Palestinian enclave. Though the boats would carry various supplies, and cards children had handmade for the people of Gaza, the action was largely symbolic. It was intended to shed light on and protest the Israeli policies that isolated Gaza from the world and that prevented the most basic, most innocuous items from reaching residents there.

I'd written about the previous year's flotilla, which had departed from Turkey and made international headlines after Israeli forces conducted an overnight raid on the *Mavi Marmara*, the largest of the group of half a dozen ships, killing nine activists. As the Israeli navy towed the boats into the port at Ashkelon, I'd raced to the south of the country to report. But, this time around, I would be on a boat covering what could be another violent confrontation between the army and activists. If Israeli forces didn't raid the ship, we would make it to Gaza, where I could finally do some on-the-ground coverage of the blockade, an issue I'd only covered from my apartment in Tel Aviv via phone.

The budget was small, and I would have to pay for everything upfront and get reimbursed. So in a bid to save money, I split a hotel room with an American Israeli friend and fellow journalist, Jacob. But when we went to check out, my card didn't work. I'd exceeded my minus, and the bank had shut it off. Jacob ended up footing the bill for my entire trip: hotel, food, and the cheap beer we drank at bars with other journalists.

In the end, we didn't even make it out of Greek waters.

After I returned to Tel Aviv, there was Miguel to contend with. I'd chosen the flotilla over reconciling, which made it crystal clear to both of us that our marriage was beyond over and had been for a long time. We agreed, finally, after four years of separation, to file for divorce.

I was devastated. And because this had all been a long time coming, my own devastation took me surprise. As I turned everything over in my head—as I sifted through the rubble of my first marriage and my life—I understood for the first time just how much July 4 had impacted me. I'd run to Miguel so I could hide out, but then when things had gotten too real, too intimate—and that intimacy threatened to bring me closer to myself and my feelings, including the ones I'd buried the night I was raped—I'd run away, all the way to Israel.

Though I had felt a profound sense of belonging and safety in Israel, and I loved working as a journalist and giving voice to the voiceless, telling other people's stories, I realized, was also an elaborate way of avoiding my own. My dead-end relationship with Oded was another way of hiding out, too, because being with him effectively cordoned me off from the intimacy that might bring me closer to both another person and myself and all those feelings I was still trying to repress.

I realized that on July 4, when I'd unhooked my soul from my body, when I'd shut down all my emotions to survive a moment that felt unbearable, I'd also shut down my ability to love and that I still hadn't recovered that feeling. Love, and all the vulnerability that came along with it, felt too risky, too scary, too dangerous.

While I'd tucked my heart away, I had tested my physical safety over and over again. Not only had I ended up in Israel but, after I'd taken citizenship, I'd traveled to Lebanon and Syria, enemy states where I could have been arrested or taken hostage. I'd covered protests in the West Bank where Palestinian and international demonstrators were sometimes injured or killed by the Israeli army; just a few months ago, I'd run from live fire myself during a protest at Qalandia checkpoint.

Time and time again, I'd proven to myself that, physically, I was fearless and I was capable of keeping my body safe. But when it came to emotions, I was so scared of confronting the feelings of shame, anger, and powerlessness I'd had when I was attacked that I'd buried everything. Because unearthing the good feelings—love, joy—risked pulling up all the things I didn't want to deal with, I'd become frozen, emotionally. I could and would take physical risks, but I was incapable of taking the emotional risks that true intimacy and love demanded. If I couldn't be emotionally vulnerable, I realized, I would never love or be loved. So I decided I would take to wearing all black because I was mourning the love I could never give or receive. And what is a life without love? It's no life at all. I would wear black, I decided, because, on some basic level, I was already dead.

* * *

At the same time that these epiphanies had thrown me into mourning, I was also doing my best to tell myself that they weren't true. It was easier to inhabit the simple story that I had thrown my marriage away for my career. But now, thanks to the Arab Spring, that career was faltering, and if my career fell apart, I wouldn't be able to live inside this fiction. So I doubled down, pitching frantically, broadening the net even beyond paying publications. I needed bylines to prove to myself that I really was a journalist and that I really had abandoned my marriage and stayed in Israel simply because it was where I worked, not because it had been some sort of giant escape hatch.

A Palestinian American friend connected me to an editor at the *Boston Review* who wanted coverage of an upcoming event. Until that point, Palestine was an observer state in the United Nations. But in September 2011, the Palestine Liberation Organization was going to the United Nations to ask that they grant Palestine full membership. The president of the Palestinian Authority, Mahmoud Abbas, would present the request to UN chief Ban Ki Moon; Abbas, aka Abu Mazen, would also give a speech to the UN General Assembly. Should the UN grant the Palestinians full membership, it would be tacit recognition of the Palestinian state that still didn't exist, almost two decades after Oslo and sixty-three years after the UN had voted in favor of the creation of two states, one Jewish, the other Arab.

But the editor didn't want a straight-up news story, which I could write from my apartment in Tel Aviv. I would need to go deeper. How did Palestinians themselves actually *feel* about the PLO's move? To find out, I would go to Ramallah, the seat of the Palestinian Authority (PA), to interview Palestinians on the street. Even though I feared going to the West Bank, in general, and Ramallah, in particular, I was desperate for a byline. And it was that story that brought me to Mohamed.

2

Dread.

That was the feeling I woke up with on the day that I would meet Mohamed for the first time. I didn't want to get out of bed, so I lay there, alone, listening to the buses rumbling up King George Street. I could smell the coffee Oded had made for himself and the cigarette he was smoking in the living room. I looked at my phone. It was nine o'clock already. I had to get going, or I wouldn't get my reporting done.

As much as I wanted to do this story and as much as I wanted the byline, I didn't want to go to Ramallah. No matter how many times I went to the West Bank, I was scared to go for so many reasons: the soldiers, the settlers, the checkpoints. I was scared of getting lost, of being detained or even arrested.

Or worse. I was scared of getting killed. In May, I'd covered a protest at Qalandia refugee camp, where the army had used live fire. I'd run when the sound of bullets rang out. And I had no illusions about the Palestinians—being occupied doesn't make one a saint. So I'd come up with this rule for myself: I had to be out of the West Bank by sundown (a rule that, in retrospect, seems stupid and arbitrary, seeing how October 7 happened not under the cover of night but in broad daylight).

Another complication: I didn't have a car, and using public transportation to get from Tel Aviv to Ramallah would take a lot of time. As the crow flies, it should only take about forty-five minutes—on a clear day, Tel Aviv is visible from Ramallah. But back then, in 2011, the journey usually took me about two and a half hours.

The trip is long because, beyond the Green Line, the Israeli system is built around privileging Israeli movement while keeping Jews and Palestinians apart. So getting to Ramallah from Tel Aviv meant going first to the Central Bus Station in south Tel Aviv. From there, I would take either a *sherut* (the Israeli equivalent of a servees) or a bus to Jewish West Jerusalem. And then, because transportation to and from the West Bank is segregated, I would have to cross the Green Line that divides Israel from the occupied Palestinian Territories and enter Israeli-controlled Palestinian East Jerusalem, where I would board a Palestinian-only bus that would take me to Ramallah.

Leaving Ramallah and making my way back to Tel Aviv was even more of a pain in the ass because Ramallah was technically off-limits to me as an Israeli.

The West Bank is carved up into three noncontiguous areas: A, B, and C. All the major Palestinian cities, including Ramallah, are marked as Area A, which is under Palestinian administration and is, according to Israeli law, legally off-limits to Israelis. Area B is under joint Israeli and Palestinian governance and can be accessed by both Israelis and Palestinian. Area C, which comprises about 60 percent of the West Bank, is ruled completely by the Israelis.

If it's mind-boggling and confusing to read about this on paper, imagine navigating this in real life. Moving through the West Bank meant I needed to be constantly aware of what area I was in and whom

I might run into there. And because certain areas were legally off-limits to me, I had to be extra careful when I was going through checkpoints to exit the West Bank, which also complicated my trip.

In short, I had to get moving, or I wasn't going to be back before sundown.

I got out of bed. The second my bare feet hit the tiled floor, I felt the black film that covered everything in our apartment, soot that blew in from the windows we kept open 24/7 for most of the year because we didn't have air conditioning. Rushing to the bathroom, I contemplated taking a shower. Because the drain didn't work, that would mean flooding the bathroom and then using a *sponja*—a squeegee-type mop—to corral the pool of water, steer it through my bedroom and onto the balcony, where I would then push it out between the wrought iron bars.

Recently, tired of the whole showering ordeal, I'd asked my landlady to call a plumber to fix the drain; when he'd finally shown up, he shined his flashlight down the hole and then beckoned me to look. Peering into the pipe, I'd remarked that I saw something gray. "A tree," the plumber had explained, adding, "*Ein ma laasot*" (There's nothing to do). Removing the trunk and branches that were inching their way up through the pipes would necessitate taking apart the entire building, he said. That was exactly how I felt about myself and my life—like there was an enormous block inside of me, growing, taking over, and that I needed to dismantle the entire building around it if I wanted my insides to work properly.

For the sake of saving a bit of time, I'd skip the shower.

After brushing my teeth and washing my face, I hurried back to the bedroom, where I stood before the small wardrobe, hunting through a pile of clothes, looking for a pair of black pants, a black shirt, a black sweater. My black backpack. I was still mourning the self I'd lost on July 4, the self who was able to love and be intimate with other people; everything had to be black.

I picked out a pair of black pants I'd found draped on a bench outside my old apartment on Reines Street. Then, I put on a black spaghetti-strap tank top, a piece I'd picked out of a pile of clothes I'd found on another bench here on Sheinken Street. Even though it was hot in Tel Aviv, I also grabbed a thin black sweater to take with me. I would need to cover my chest and arms for modesty's sake once I arrived in Muslim-majority East Jerusalem, and I would need to continue to do so in Ramallah.

Before making coffee, I remembered to put on a pair of rubber-soled shoes—the wiring in the kitchen was messed up, and touching a metal surface without shoes meant getting shocked. So I slid my feet into a pair of black Mary Janes, made some Nescafé in a to-go mug, and headed toward the living room, where Oded sat at his desk by the window, shirtless and slumped over his laptop, a fan blowing on his back, already glistening with sweat. Next to him, the avocado seeds I was sprouting and the basil I'd planted in tin olive canisters—throwaways from the shuk—stood on the windowsill. The plants had grown so big they reminded me of sails; I imagined the basil floating away, taking the apartment and me with them.

"Bye," I said, as I stood at my desk, which was next to his, stuffing the black sweater into my backpack.

"You don't have to go," Oded said, still facing his laptop. He was angry about this trip; to him, it seemed like I was taking an unnecessary risk.

"I need the byline," I reminded him.

"You know, they lynch Jews in Ramallah," Oded said, fidgeting with his auburn beard, worrying that same invisible spot on his face as always. Oded was referring to the murders of two off-duty Israeli soldiers who, in the early days of the Second Intifada, had taken a wrong turn and ended up being detained by Palestinian policemen just outside of Ramallah. Word quickly spread among Palestinians that two Israelis were being held in the police station, and a mob broke in and killed and mutilated the men, with one of the murderers taking to a window on the second floor and displaying his bloody hands to the cheering crowd below. Then, Palestinians dragged the mutilated bodies to Manara Square. It was after this event that Israel declared it illegal for Israeli citizens to enter Area A.

Mentioning this horrific event was Oded's last-ditch effort to get me to stay, I knew. He was worried about me and my safety. I could have—should have—turned toward Oded with compassion. But the comment just pissed me off. At the time, I thought his comment angered me because it was racist. Looking back, I realize it also bothered me because it felt like an attempt to tamp down my ambitions.

"They don't lynch *Jews* in Ramallah," I shot back. "They lynched two *Israelis. Two.* Like ten years ago."

Hearing myself, I cringed. It sounded like I was justifying or dismissing the death of those two reserve soldiers. I wasn't. I hated this about the conflict, the way it backed me—the way it backed everyone—into ideologically indefensible corners, the way it often pushed people into taking sides they didn't, in their heart of hearts, actually support or believe in.

"At gam yisraelit [You're also an Israeli], Mya," Oded said, knowing just what to say, just where to hit.

In many ways, Oded had come to know me better than I knew myself. When he'd sat alongside me at my desk, helping me as I labored to translate and transcribe interviews I'd painstakingly conducted in Hebrew, he knew—without me asking—exactly what words I didn't know. He would pause and then, fiddling with his beard, turn to me and begin, *"At yodaat mah zeh"* (Do you know what is), and then he'd fill in the blank with the unfamiliar Hebrew word. Oded's grasp of my vocabulary was astounding—it was like he lived inside my mind. And oftentimes, when I spoke Hebrew, it was his voice I heard in my head. There were other clues that Oded inhabited the inside of my skull: one day, I had music on as I worked at the desk next to him, and he turned to me and said, "You like a 9/8 tempo." He'd spotted the pattern, and he'd had the vocabulary for this thing that I didn't have words for—this thing I didn't even know about myself.

So when Oded said, "You're also an Israeli," he was appealing to the part of me that, he knew, craved those words, that validation that was sometimes denied me by other Israelis because I spoke Hebrew with an American accent, because I hadn't been born here, because I hadn't served in the army. Oded knew exactly where to hit, and he'd hit hard.

But because I was going to Ramallah and doing that story whether he wanted me to or not, I punched back: *"Ani lo b'emet yisraelit"* (I'm not really Israeli). "I have an Israeli passport. There's a difference."

"Not to the Palestinians there's not."

"Oded, no one will be able to tell that I'm Jewish or Israeli or whatever. They'll all just think I'm a *foreigner*. And if someone does think I'm Jewish, they're not going to kill me. And it's *racist* for you to say they will."

He shrugged. "OK. So I guess I'm a racist. At least I'm still alive."

Oded's words only made me more determined to go and come back safely to prove him wrong. But there was more than that: every time I went to the West Bank and returned in one piece, I was showing him not only that he was wrong about the Palestinians but that the situation in Israel wasn't as hopeless as he thought, that the conflict wasn't quite as intractable as he said. And I was proving to myself that I could keep myself safe in a way I hadn't in the past. Reminding Oded that I'd already been to Palestinian areas of the West Bank multiple times, that this was my third trip to Ramallah, and that I'd gone to Lebanon and Syria on my own and made it back in one piece, I grabbed my black backpack, keys, and coffee and reached for the door.

"Nu," Oded said, his voice softer. "*Mah iti*, Mya?" (What about me?)

"What about you?"

"If something happens to you, what will happen?"

"Then I'll be dead—*nothing* will happen."

"No. What will happen to *me*?"

"*You*?" I shrugged. "You'll be fine."

"*Ken*, ah?" (Yeah, right?) This was all Oded-speak for "I need you," words he couldn't say, words that didn't belong in our weird, noncommittal relationship that had continued far beyond its initial ten-month shelf life.

Oded lit a cigarette, took a drag, leaned it on the ashtray, and faced me. Fidgeting again with his beard, he tried another tack. "It's selfish of you to go," he said.

Name-calling. A sure way to rope me into an argument that would delay my departure. I didn't take the bait.

"OK, so I'm selfish," I said. "We can talk about this some more when I get back tonight."

"*If* you get back tonight."

I banged out the door and pounded down the stairs, irritated by the conversation, frustrated for locking myself into yet another relationship

I wasn't fully invested in and that kept me living in limbo. I saw my inability to meet Oded's small attempt at tenderness with compassion, and that shortcoming, too, upset me. I wanted to shed all this invisible armor I was wearing and be truly vulnerable and intimate with someone. I wanted to break through all these walls I'd built around myself to keep myself safe.

I hated how complicated and messy my life was; everything felt heavy, even the air, which, that day in September, was so thick with humidity that it felt like I was pushing my way up the street to the ATM. After getting cash to pay back Jacob for the bill he'd footed in Athens, I flagged down a sherut. As the driver sped toward the Central Bus Station, Oded's words echoed in my head: "You know, they lynch Jews in Ramallah."

However unwilling I was to admit it to Oded, I was scared to go to Ramallah. Though I'd been several times already, the fear still lingered around the edges of every visit. Reminding myself of what I'd told Oded just minutes before—"I need the byline"—I gripped my black backpack and looked out the window at Tel Aviv flipping past.

* * *

In Jerusalem, I disembarked at the Central Bus Station, made my way through the western Jewish part of the city to the Palestinian east, where I boarded a Palestinian bus to Ramallah.

After lumbering through East Jerusalem, we neared Qalandia, the road narrowed, and seemingly out of nowhere, the separation barrier popped up. In other parts of the West Bank, it was a chain-link fence topped with barbed wire—a fence Palestinians sometimes cut—but here, it was an impenetrable twenty-six-foot-tall mass of concrete. At the sight, my head felt thick; my eyelids, heavy. The wall did more than blot out the horizon—it was like a curtain had been dropped between me and my own mind. Every time I saw that mass of concrete, I felt exhausted, like the wall was a block inside of me, and I was filled with the urge to take to bed, to sleep, to never wake up.

It was a feeling, I realized, of absolute hopelessness.

The bus crawled its way through an opening in the wall, stuttered through a roundabout choked with traffic, and then inched toward the

Qalandia checkpoint, passing a large red sign that read, in Hebrew, Arabic, and English:

This Road Leads to Area "A"
Under the Palestinian Authority
The Entrance for Israeli
Citizens is Forbidden,
Dangerous to Your Lives
And Against the Israeli Law

I wondered why the sign included these words in Arabic. While some 20 percent of Israel's population are Palestinians, the state doesn't bother to put Arabic on many governmental forms and most street signs. So why here? Years later, one of my Palestinian students would tell me how deeply offensive the inclusion of Arabic on those Area A signs was to her—those words, she explained, were meant not for Israeli citizens but for her and other Palestinians in the West Bank. They were accusatory, she said, a way of saying, "You're all animals out here."

And then ahead, at the checkpoint, booths and armed soldiers awaited. Here, it was unlikely we would be stopped—this was a Palestinian-only checkpoint, and the heavy security existed to check people on their way *in* to Jerusalem, not those on their way out. But I found myself holding my breath anyway as the bus inched through the checkpoint. Passing under the corrugated tin roof, we were engulfed, for a moment, in darkness; I felt like I was on the bottom of the ocean. Then the bus made its way past the booths and soldiers, and we surfaced back into the sun, and I exhaled.

* * *

But when the bus came to its final stop, I tensed again. Now I would have to get off and make my way to Manara Square, where I would meet Jacob and his girlfriend, Rachel.

There was that voice inside my head again: "You know, they lynch Jews in Ramallah." But it was no longer Oded's. It was mine.

The horrible image of a Palestinian man flashing his bloody hands to a cheering crowd below flashed through my mind's eye, and I found myself frozen, stuck in my seat by the window, unable to get off the bus, watching as everyone else disembarked. When I was the last person left on the bus, the driver looked at me quizzically in the rearview mirror. Lifting his right hand in the air and—positioning it as though he was changing a lightbulb—he turned his wrist, a gesture meaning "What?"

Still, I didn't move.

Then he turned, looked at me, and motioned for me to get off the bus. Clutching my black backpack, I made my way through the aisle.

"*Al Quds*?" I asked, using the Arabic word for Jerusalem. I was trying to ask the driver if he was going back. If he was, I figured, I could just stay on the bus. Oded was right—I didn't need this byline.

But the driver clicked his tongue, meaning no, and I had to disembark.

I got down, exited the parking lot, and approached a taxi driver, asking if he would take me to Manara Square. He gave me a confused look and gestured down the street, telling me in Arabic to continue straight. "*Doogri*," he said, a word that Israelis also use as slang.

With no choice but to trust the man, I followed his directions and arrived at Manara, where I found Rachel, Jacob's girlfriend, waiting. Like Jacob and me, she was also an immigrant to Israel and held Israeli citizenship; unlike us, however, Rachel was South African.

With her olive skin and dark brown hair, Rachel blended in, save for the sunglasses and the striped scarf draped over her shoulders and chest that made her look like a tourist. I was surprised to find Rachel alone; she explained that Jacob was at home, working, and that she was going to guide me to the house. I hesitated, telling her that I had to get back to Tel Aviv by sundown. But because I wanted to give Jacob the money I owed him from Athens—and after all he'd done for me, I felt like I should give him the money in person—I followed her.

Once I was at the house, Jacob refused to take my money, and he began pushing me to spend the night. Just today the PA had called on Palestinians to go out into the streets tomorrow in celebration of the UN bid. There would be all kinds of fanfare, and Abu Mazen's speech would be broadcast outdoors on a big screen here in Ramallah. Wasn't that the whole reason I'd come out to the West Bank in the first place—to cover the bid? Shouldn't I go to the rally?

Jacob had a point. But still, I was reluctant. Jacob challenged me: "What—are you scared? Did your Zionist boyfriend or roommate or whatever he is say, 'They'll do you a lynch in Ramallah'?" he asked in English, aping an Israeli accent.

As much as Oded's words had grated on me, now that Jacob was making fun of him, I felt defensive.

Sensing the tension, Rachel jumped in. "You know, I was scared when we first moved out here," she admitted. Rachel and Jacob were two of the handful of Israelis who lived in Palestinian areas of the West Bank, among the Palestinians, for ideological reasons. "Then, one day, our landlord came to us and was like, 'Look, I know you two are Israeli.' Now he speaks Hebrew with us." Their landlord, as it turned out, had learned the language while he was in an Israeli prison—he was one of the hundreds of thousands of Palestinians who have been arrested since the occupation began in 1967. Many of these men, women, and children have been held without charge or trial in something called "administrative detention."

Rachel added that they kept quiet about their second passports—their Israeli passports—but that people who needed to know knew, and it was fine. "Jacob is like an honorary Palestinian," Rachel said. I guessed this was largely because of the work he'd done with the Palestinian Popular Struggle Coordination Committee before he'd become a journalist.

Is it really that simple? I wondered. Of course there were Palestinians who were citizens of Israel—they make up about 20 percent of the population inside the Green Line—so I knew that Palestinians could also be Israelis. But could the opposite be true: Could a Jewish Israeli become a Palestinian simply by virtue of taking a particular political stance and living among them? Or, if a Jewish Israeli couldn't become Palestinian, could they at least be fully accepted in Palestinian society? A bit naively, I wondered if the conflict had been needlessly complicated, if we could all live house to house, Israelis renting from Palestinians and Palestinians renting from Israelis, a checkerboard of Muslims and Jews who'd all thrown their lot in with one another and who understood that their fates were inextricably bound up together.

Whatever the answer, at that time I wasn't convinced that I could safely spend the night in Ramallah. Jacob and Rachel pushed some more, saying that they'd already made plans for us to go out that night with a big group of people—a group that would include Mohamed—to a bar called Beit Anisa. A bar? In Ramallah—a Muslim-majority city where I needed to cover my arms and legs so no one harassed me in the streets?

I was curious. Half the reason I'd gone to Beirut on my American passport three years before was to check out the nightlife.

So I relented. I would go out tonight with Jacob and Rachel and their friends, and then I would do my reporting tomorrow, when Palestinians hit the streets for the big PA rally.

Rachel showed me to the guestroom, where she'd already made up a bed for me. After dropping my backpack on the floor, I shot a text message to Oded saying that I was spending the night in Ramallah.

"*B'hatzlacha* [good luck]," he responded.

* * *

Situated in an old, stone Arab mansion in a residential neighborhood, Beit Anisa was tucked behind a wall topped with a wooden privacy fence and was invisible from the street. Having imagined Ramallah as a dangerous place that bred extremism, I was shocked when I followed Jacob and Rachel through a gate and discovered a garden, bathed in the warm, yellow glow of string lights. The tables were full of young Palestinians, mostly from the middle and upper class, largely nonreligious, many of them educated professionals. Some had gone to the local American or French schools; some had lived or studied abroad; some had a foreign parent; others were completely local. In the garden's privacy, the women wore clothes that they couldn't wear on the street—everything from tight jeans and heels to slinky dresses to tops that revealed collarbones and shoulders. Their makeup was flawless; their hair was perfectly coiffed. The men fell into two categories: Arab hipsters and those who looked like they'd just arrived from office jobs. The music was blasting; the place was packed and only getting more crowded by the minute. It reminded me of the bars I'd seen in Beirut.

I felt wildly out of place. Less because of the Israeli ID in my backpack and more because of my appearance. Though my outfit was fine for a Tel Aviv bar, here I looked dumpy and frumpy: my found-on-the-street black tank top, the thin black sweater that I'd bought for 10 shekels ($2.50), the clunky, almost orthopedic-looking black Mary Janes I wore because I'd anticipated spending my day on my feet, reporting, not going to a glam bar at night. I didn't have any makeup on and, earlier, I'd pulled my almost waist-length auburn hair into a messy pile on top of my head. Now the bun was sagging and it slumped down the back of my neck; frizzies had escaped and stood around my face.

As Rachel shrugged her way out of a black overcoat, revealing a short skirt underneath, I excused myself and dashed inside to the bathroom. Standing before the mirror, I took off my black sweater, balled it up, and stuffed it in my backpack. I yanked at the black tank top, pulling it down in a bid to make it a little more revealing. And then I took some clear lip gloss and rubbed it on my cheeks like blush and across my eyebrows in an attempt to add some definition to my face.

Now I looked frumpy *and* greasy.

Rachel had offered to loan me a dress for the evening, and I'd turned her down, thinking I had no one to impress, insisting on wearing what Jacob teasingly called my *schmatta*, Yiddish for "rags." Now I cursed my decision as I walked back toward the garden. I also regretted not showering that morning.

On my way back to the table, I grabbed a drink from the bar—arak with water—and then planted myself on the edge of our circle, which had grown while I was inside.

Shivering in my tank top, I tried to busy myself with my drink. But then it hit me: I wasn't prepared to cover this event tomorrow. I'd come planning to do my man-on-the-street interviews in English, but I realized that meant I would only get to talk to a very particular segment of the population. I wanted to do better as a journalist. I wanted to tell the story of how the Palestinian public—not the *English-speaking* Palestinian public—felt about the PA's move.

So I leaned toward Jacob and shouted over the music: "I need a translator!"

"What for? Everyone here speaks English!" he shouted back.

"No! For tomorrow!"

He looked around the group and then pointed. "That guy there, with Natasha," he said.

I knew Natasha already. I'd met her when I'd gone to cover a protest at Nabi Saleh, where Palestinians marched in hopes of reaching the spring that stood on the village's land. The small watering hole had been claimed, several years before, by Jewish settlers. Almost every Friday, the scene was the same—Palestinians tried to reach the contested spring, and the Israeli army turned them back with overwhelming violence. In December 2011, one protester would be killed when a soldier shot a tear gas canister directly into his face.

Looking at the guy next to Natasha, I realized I didn't know him.

"Who's that?" I asked.

"I think his name is Mohamed. He's a fixer," Jacob said, using the word for a local journalist who works with foreign media, setting up interviews, translating, and generally making sure that outsiders get the story somewhat straight.

Jacob led me around the circle to Natasha, who remembered me and greeted me by planting kisses on both of my cheeks. Jacob told her that I was looking for a translator, and she conferred with Mohamed. After he gave her a quick nod, she turned to me.

"Mya, this is Mohamed. Mohamed, Mya."

What I didn't know at the time—as he extended his palm and I placed my hand in his—was that Mohamed had already noticed me. When I'd entered the garden with Jacob and Rachel, he'd thought, "Who's *that*?" He'd begun to wonder immediately about this woman in black who hadn't bothered with makeup, whose hair was a mess. Mohamed didn't know that I was wearing black because I was mourning myself. To Mohamed, my *schmatta* and bare face had suggested confidence, open-mindedness, and rebelliousness—a don't-give-a-fuck attitude, a contrariness that he, a contrarian by nature, immediately found attractive.

As he'd looked at me, he'd tried to guess my ethnicity and nationality but couldn't quite pin it down. He noted a strong resemblance to his paternal aunts—Palestinian women with light hair and fair skin—but from my inappropriate clothes, messy hair, and lack of makeup, he figured I wasn't Arab. He knew I was a foreigner. But what kind? He guessed that I was Mediterranean—what kind of Mediterranean, he wasn't sure.

Though he'd found my appearance intriguing, Mohamed had decided against approaching me. For one, he was shy, and two, he figured I was just passing through. He'd recently been through a breakup with a Palestinian-Spanish woman who'd been born and raised in Europe, didn't have a Palestinian ID, and had entered the West Bank on a three-month visa; when she'd been unable to renew it, she'd left. She'd asked him to follow, to live with her in Spain, but Mohamed had decided he was never leaving Palestine, his homeland. He wasn't looking for another short-term relationship with a foreigner. Why sign up for heartache?

But now that this intriguing woman in black (me) was standing before him, Mohamed offered his hand, and I took it. His grip was tight but not overly so—it felt strong and confident. And, as we shook hands—palm to palm—I liked the feel of our skin pressed together.

When he let go of my hand, I stole a glance at his broad shoulders and his chest, which I could tell was defined even though he wore a gray sweater. Because the music was loud, I was standing close enough to Mohamed to smell his cologne, but what I really liked was the smell underneath the fragrance. Him. Rich and earthy and thick with spices: cumin and coriander and clove and cinnamon. The scent was warm and comforting, and it made me want to get closer, to rest my head on his chest.

And there was something familiar about Mohamed, like I knew him already. Only later would I realize that he bore a striking resemblance to my mother (yes, yes, the pull for both of us was Freudian); like my mother, Mohamed had dark hair, thick black eyebrows, almond-shaped eyes, full lips, and a strong chin. Later, after we married, we would visit his family's village, and some of his relatives would remark that, save for my coloring, Mohamed and I actually looked like each other.

But that was all in the future.

That night at Beit Anisa, Mohamed tipped his ear toward my mouth and listened intently as I told him about my work as a journalist and the places I'd published. When he tried to steer the conversation in a more personal direction, asking me where I was from, I told him that I was from Florida originally, and then I continued rehashing my resume. I didn't want to give him a chance to ask me too many questions for fear that I would let something about my Israeli identity slip. Finally, I told Mohamed about the story I was working on for the *Boston Review*. I just needed some help with the interviews. A couple of hours of work, maximum.

"What do you charge?" I asked.

"What is the *Boston Review* paying you?" he responded, taking a sip of his whiskey.

Not wanting to admit that I was doing the story for free, I said, "Never mind. What's your rate?"

"My rate depends on yours," he said, smirking, asking if the *Boston Review* was an academic journal. He already knew the answer.

"Yes," I admitted. "They don't pay. At least, they're not paying me."

"Well, if you work for free, I work for free," Mohamed said.

Something felt flirtatious about this haggling, and determined to keep things professional, I pushed back. "No," I said, "how much would you ordinarily charge per hour? I'll pay."

Mohamed insisted that I wouldn't, adding that, in his mind, I would be serving the Palestinian people by sharing their real feelings about the statehood bid—a view that probably looked very different than that of the politicians who were supposedly representing them. Most of the media would cover Abu Mazen's speech and would get the story wrong, he explained. Talking to the people meant I would get it right, and Mohamed wanted to help with that.

He told me to meet him on Manara Square at 10:00 a.m. and asked for my number in case we needed to get in touch.

I hesitated. I had an Israeli number, of course. And even though I'd met him through my network, fear started to creep in. *Who is this guy?* I wondered. *Is it safe for him to know that I live in Israel, for him to suspect that I might be Israeli?*

There was another thing: already, I liked him. I liked the intent way he listened. I liked how, when I'd tried to dodge his question about how much the *Boston Review* was paying me, he'd cut through my bullshit. And I thought he was really good-looking.

A little voice in my brain said, "A third man? You're crazy, Mya. You don't need to add any more complications to your life." I agreed, reminding myself that I already had an estranged husband in Florida who, after a four-year-long separation, was drawing up the divorce papers, and a faltering relationship in Tel Aviv that I wanted to get out of.

Besides, that little voice said, *even if you were completely single, he's Palestinian, and you are a citizen of the enemy state. Whatever spark you feel, the moment he knows about your ID, it's over. And do you really want to get involved with someone who lives on the other side of the separation barrier, in Ramallah, of all places?*

Telling myself that I needed to work with him for the story's sake, I gave Mohamed my number. Used to reciting it to Israelis, it spooled through my head in Hebrew, and I fought against the current of my mind, offering Mohamed the sequence slowly and deliberately in English instead.

Mohamed repeated the first three numbers: 052. "Cellcom?" he asked, referring to the Israeli carrier.

"Yes," I said. "I live in Tel Aviv."

He nodded but said nothing. He probably thinks I'm just some foreign journalist, I figured. Some live out here in Ramallah, but most are in Jerusalem and Tel Aviv.

Mohamed recited his number, which began with 059—Jawwal, the Palestinian carrier. We would be able to text each other for a fee, but calling would be astronomical; today, these carriers can't even call each other anymore.

Agreeing to meet tomorrow, we bade each other good night, and I returned to the other side of the group, taking up my post next to Jacob and Rachel, nursing my arak and water, shivering in the night wind.

* * *

Around 5:00 a.m., something—a loud sound—jolted me out of my sleep. It wasn't the buses lumbering up King George. I wasn't sure what the noise was, and I lay there in the room, trying to figure it out. Disoriented, I also wondered where I was. As my eyes adjusted to the predawn light, I saw a window and the familiar *trissim,* the rolling shutters common to windows throughout the Middle East, ambient light from the street leaking through pin-sized holes. For a moment, I was sure I was in Tel Aviv.

But this bed was too narrow, too small, and the window was on the wrong side of the room. And then came that sound again, beginning like a low buzzing, growing in strength and urgency and power, until it crested and echoed off the foothills: *allahu akbar, allahu akbar.*

It's the call to prayer, I realized. *I'm not in Tel Aviv. I'm in Ramallah.*

And I'm safe.

3

At 10:00 a.m., I stood on Manara Square in the same black outfit I'd worn the night before, my teeth unbrushed, recorder and notebook in hand. It was an overcast morning, and the sun struggled to push through the gray. Just as the limestone-faced buildings made the street seem brighter on sunny days, so did they make the surroundings seem dimmer and drearier on a day like this.

The streets were quiet, and I wondered why Mohamed had wanted to meet at 10:00 a.m. Later, Mohamed would confess to me that he'd suggested we meet early so he could have some time alone with me. But standing there alone that morning, I became suspicious. We were supposed to be doing man-on-the-street interviews, but there was no one around. With it being a Friday, the Muslim holy day, people wouldn't be out and about until later in the day, after the noon prayers. And Abu

Mazen's speech at the UN headquarters in New York City wouldn't take place until this afternoon local time.

Not knowing that his office overlooked Manara Square, I also wondered why Mohamed had asked to meet there. Because multiple roads converged at Manara, it seemed to me like the perfect place for a kidnapping—it would be easy for someone to come from any direction, grab me, and then peel out in another direction. I would have no idea where we were and where we were going.

I felt completely vulnerable.

Who was this guy? I wondered. Sure, he'd been part of the circle last night, but Jacob and Rachel didn't know him. Still, when I'd asked them this morning over coffee if they thought it would be safe for me to work with him, they'd assured me it was. But how did they know?

Yes, I decided, he wanted to get me here alone, early in the morning, so he could kidnap me. He'd seemed nice, but he must have figured out who I was, and he must have had some contacts in Hamas or another militant organization.

The air around me felt empty; the buildings, huge and menacing. I looked toward a corner, expecting a car to come skidding around it.

I felt a pounding in my temples. I had to get out of here. I looked around at the streets that led away from Manara, trying to remember which one led back to the bus station. I would board a bus back to Jerusalem. Even though the Qalandia checkpoint was legally off-limits to me, I would take my chances there. Better to get arrested leaving Ramallah than to die.

Certain I'd found the street that led to the outdoor bus station, I moved to leave the square, only to see Mohamed, in a bright blue sweater and jeans, striding toward me—his confident steps and that bright blue sweater of his slicing through all the bleakness. My concerns about being kidnapped dropped away, and a smile spread across my face.

"*Sabah alkhair* [Good morning]," Mohamed said, offering me his hand. We were close enough for me to smell him again—his cologne, his body, that spice that made me feel warm and at home—and once I took his hand, I didn't want to let go. Pressing our palms together just a second longer than was appropriate, I smiled, embarrassed, and he let go of my hand. As a boyish grin spread across his face, the last bits of my fear evaporated.

"Well," I said, "shall we?"

He gestured up the street, and we fell into step, walking side by side. As I looked down to switch on my recorder, I noticed that our footsteps were completely in time.

* * *

We spent several hours together that day. Later, when I transcribed the recordings, I realized we'd only spent about an hour interviewing other people; I'd spent most of the time interviewing him. I quickly got the basics: Mohamed was thirty-two, single, never married, no children. In addition to working, he was studying at a local university in hopes of finishing a degree in English education. Though his family was from a village near Hebron called Sa'ir, he'd grown up in Jordan. And though he told me a lot about himself that day, he talked even more about his family, offering me a detailed account of his family's history. Later I understood that, in a culture where family is tremendously important and a huge piece of one's identity, sharing details about one's family *is* a way of sharing things about oneself. Let me put it this way: in Arabic, fathers are referred to as Baba and they call their children the same; similarly, mothers, mamas, refer to their own children as "Mama." On a language level, the line between parent and child is blurred. Psychologically speaking, families follow suit.

But first, before we talked family, we did our reporting: we started by talking to a group of older Palestinian men who were sitting outside a cafe. One of the men said his family owned the land where Ben Gurion International Airport stands today, and he added that they had the paperwork to prove it. When we turned to the eldest of the men and asked his age, he said he was eighty-three.

"Older than the state of Israel," I said.

Mohamed laughed before translating for the man, who smiled.

"Where were you in 1948?" I asked, and the man recounted his story.

He'd been twenty when the *nakba* took place. Amid the war, after he and other villagers had fled their homes, he attempted to return to take care of the animals, only to be caught by Jewish soldiers who took him into a mosque to interrogate him. When they finished, they forced the man to strip to his underwear, and then, releasing him from the mosque, they told him to walk to Ramallah. And so he had made his way through the countryside like that—half naked.

I was moved by his story. Of course I'd read a lot about the *nakba*, and in Beirut, I'd seen testimonies on film. But I'd never spoken face-to-face with a Palestinian who had survived those events. Being forced to strip in a mosque, a holy place, and then walk through the land that had been taken from under his feet struck me as horrific. And as I listened to the man, I couldn't help but think of my grandfather, who was about the same age as this man.

My grandfather was sixteen in 1947 when the United Nations voted to partition the land into two states—one Jewish, the other Arab—and he'd listened to the vote on the radio. When it was clear that the majority had voted for partition, he'd whooped and raced out of their Williamsburg apartment and into the street, where he'd linked arms with other Jews, and they'd danced the hora.

When he'd returned home, my grandfather told his mother—who still hadn't learned English—that he was going to Israel to join the fight for a Jewish homeland. "Over my dead body," she answered in Yiddish, so he didn't go.

As Mohamed and I thanked the men and walked away, I wondered about Mohamed's family history and what had happened to them during the *nakba*. Were they refugees? Was Mohamed himself a refugee, too?

My recorder still running, I asked, "How do you feel when you hear the old people's stories? I mean, what about your family? Where was your family—"

I stopped there, unable to bring myself to finish the question with the words "in 1948?" in part because I didn't know what Mohamed's family had been through, and, therefore, I didn't know how sensitive the topic was to him. But also because, on some level, as I'd spoken to that nakba survivor, I'd begun to feel that the Israeli ID tucked in my backpack made me culpable.

"In '48?" Mohamed said, finishing the question, explaining that because his family was from the West Bank, they hadn't lost their homes or land in the war. But his family was "typical," he said, in that they'd suffered in other ways.

His father, Yasser, was in the Palestine Liberation Organization, classified by both the US and Israel as a terrorist group. Born and raised in the West Bank, Yasser became active with the PLO when he was studying for his undergraduate degree in Jordan, and he remained active when he was working on a master's degree in Egypt. In 1978, while Yasser was in the West Bank making preparations for his marriage to Mohamed's mother, Fatima—a match arranged by their fathers in hopes of staving off Yasser's arrest or deportation—Israeli soldiers detained Yasser without charge. While Yasser was in prison on administrative detention, Israeli soldiers interrogated and tortured him for forty days; after that, they held him for several additional weeks before deporting him to Jordan.

Just eighteen years old and fresh out of high school, the young Fatima was left with no decision but to follow this man—who was, for all intents and purposes, a stranger—to Amman. The Israelis, who controlled the border with Jordan (and still do today) rejected their families' requests to leave the West Bank and travel to Amman for Yasser's and Fatima's wedding. So the two were married there, alone, without their parents. Soon after, Fatima became pregnant with Mohamed.

In early 1979, heavy with child, Fatima returned alone to the West Bank so that Mohamed could be born in the same village, on the same land, as his father, both of his grandfathers, and all of their forefathers. It was more than an emotional decision: Mohamed's parents had decided he should be born in the West Bank for practical purposes, as well. For Palestinians, where one is registered and the type of identification card one has can literally be a life-and-death matter. Your Israeli-issued Palestinian ID impacts *everything*: freedom of movement, where you can live, whether you can inherit your family's ancestral land, what type of access you have to that land, what types of services you receive, if any. The list goes on and on. Without this ID, Mohamed wouldn't be able to inherit his land and he wouldn't be able to travel in and out of the West Bank without getting a visa.

So when Fatima was heavily pregnant, she returned alone to their village and gave birth to Mohamed in Yasser's family home. After she spent the customary forty days resting and recovering from the birth, and after Mohamed was registered with the Israelis as a West Bank resident, the two returned to Jordan, where they were united with Yasser.

And though their small family was together—and they would eventually add three more boys and a girl to that family, making Mohamed the eldest of five children—Yasser spent the next two decades enduring a difficult separation from his parents and his uncles and his brothers and sisters.

It wasn't enough that Israel had deported Yasser for being in the PLO; they also punished both him and his immediate family by denying his close relatives the exit permits they needed to leave the West Bank and enter Jordan. So Yasser's parents and most of his eight siblings had been unable to visit him in Amman. Yasser had tried to keep in touch with his family via phone. But because Israel and Jordan were enemy states until 1994, there was no direct line between the two; calls from Jordan were routed through Cyprus to Israel, making them prohibitively expensive, infrequent, and short.

Severed from his homeland and his family, Yasser had fallen into depression. The wage he earned from the PLO was low, and although the organization was rife with corruption, Yasser prided himself on being an honest man. So the family lived in poverty, something that ate at Yasser, who wanted to provide a better life for his family. He also struggled with the internal politics of the PLO, an organization that was far from united. Under the umbrella of that name "Palestine Liberation Organization," there were almost a dozen factions, all jockeying for power. One morning, as Yasser had left the family's home in Amman for work, he'd been attacked by a fellow Palestinian from a rival faction. His attacker had come at him with a knife, going for his throat but slashing his face instead. Yasser survived the attack, but it left him—and, by extension, his family—feeling embattled. So the family, Mohamed included, was under immense pressure, and it didn't just come from the Israelis. It came from other Palestinians; it came from Jordan. It came from poverty. It came from exile.

While the family's years in Amman were difficult in many ways, Mohamed also recalled his boyhood fondly. The family would often go on picnics in the foothills, where Yasser would help Mohamed see Palestine. It's a scene Mohamed would recount for me so many times over the years that I can easily see it in my head: Yasser would take his eldest son aside, bend so their eyes were at the same level, and then point toward the horizon. "*Shuf, shuf,* ya Baba [Look, look, Papa]," Yasser would say, calling his son by the very name his son called him, Baba, erasing the line between one generation and the next.

Mohamed's eyes would follow the invisible line extending from the tip of his father's finger, out toward the Mediterranean. "Do you see it, ya Baba?" his father would say. "There's our Palestine." And then his finger would move and Mohamed's eyes with it as Yasser pointed out the cities.

"There is Ramallah, and there is Bethlehem, and there is Khalil," he would say, working his way methodically from north to south. His arm would shift as he stretched it toward points farther on the horizon, naming the places on the coast.

"And at the top there is Akko, then Haifa, then Jaffa, our bride of the sea. There's Asqelon, and there's Gaza."

It was almost like how observant Muslims pray in line with the qibla, the direction to the Kaaba in Mecca's Sacred Mosque. Mohamed's father—who wasn't religious at the time, who drank whiskey back then and defined himself as a secular Muslim—kept himself and his eldest son aligned not with Mecca but with Palestine.

So there was this mental map that Mohamed both inhabited and carried inside of him—he always knew where he was in relation to Palestine. And, of course, like in every Palestinian home, their family also had a literal map of Palestine hanging in the living room. Unsurprisingly, Mohamed developed a love of maps, and when he was a boy, he would often ride his bike to the library in downtown Amman. A deeply curious child, Mohamed would spend hours there pouring over maps, not just of Palestine but of the world. He also grew to love tangible things from far-off lands and distant, unreachable pasts—coins and stamps. The latter he bought with the money that friends and his mother's family gave him when they visited from the

West Bank; Mohamed, using his mental map of Amman, took them around the city, a pint-sized tour guide whom they showered with smiles and tips.

This stamp collection Mohamed amassed would be one of the things he brought back with him when the family returned to the West Bank in 1996, the year after the second of the Oslo Accords was signed.

With the signing of the Oslo Accords, suddenly the PLO was no longer classified as a terrorist organization. Overnight, the same people who had been deemed enough of a threat to be deported were suddenly legit—so legit they could all come back and run a provisional government known as the Palestinian Authority, the PA. To some extent, this echoed Israeli history. Prior to 1948, the British considered Jewish paramilitary groups to be terrorist organizations. After the British withdrew and Zionist leaders declared independence, those same paramilitary groups became what is referred to today as the IDF, the Israel Defense Force. What is your terrorist group one day is a national army or internationally recognized government the next.

So Oslo took place, and the PLO submitted lists of their exiled members to the Israelis for approval to return. Finally, in 1996, after almost two decades of being stuck outside of the West Bank, Yasser got permission to come home. Mohamed was seventeen then and had just finished high school when they packed everything up and left for Ramallah, seat of the newly formed PA, the provisional body that would govern parts of the West Bank.

Not long after they returned to the West Bank, Mohamed got his first job in media. A new TV station was opening in Ramallah, and Mohamed had seen an advertisement that they were looking for employees. He applied to work in the commercial department—that is, behind the scenes—and got the job. But during the training, some higher-up heard Mohamed's smooth, deep baritone and thought, "Wow, whoever that is, is perfect for TV." (This, too, was a scene that Mohamed recounted for me more than once through the years.) This higher-up rushed into the room and was surprised to find an eighteen-year-old guy sitting there.

"Where's the man I just heard talking?" the higher-up asked.

"That was me," Mohamed said.

"Eh? You're a kid," the man said.

Mohamed was young, but he was very handsome, and he had that voice. That's how he ended up spending a couple of years on Palestinian TV (one of the many reasons that, over a decade later, when we were dating, we couldn't walk more than ten meters without someone stopping Mohamed to say hello).

While Mohamed enjoyed the work, the money wasn't great, and he was more of a behind-the-scenes kind of guy. So when his paternal uncle, who owned a car dealership in Khalil, called and said that business was good, Mohamed quit his job and went to Khalil to train with his uncle, the plan being that Mohamed would learn the business and then run a branch of his own in Ramallah.

But in the occupied Palestinian territories, politics permeate every aspect of life and disrupt even the best-laid plans. That's what happened to Mohamed. He moved to Khalil just before the Second Intifada hit and life in the West Bank ground to a halt. The economy tanked. People weren't buying cars. They weren't buying anything. Mohamed stayed at his uncle's house for a while, waiting for the situation to improve, so he could train and open that Ramallah branch. But the Second Intifada ground on for years; eventually, Mohamed gave up and returned to his parents' home in Ramallah.

His father offered to help him find work in the PA, but Mohamed declined. Like most Palestinian youth, he'd become cynical about the PA. It wasn't doing anything for the Palestinian people, he said. They were just collaborating with the Israelis.

His old job at the TV station no longer an option—the company having gone bankrupt—Mohamed tapped into his social network, which included a few foreign journalists. In the summer of 2006, Mohamed started working as a fixer and producer. He quickly built a client base, doing well enough to rent a large office that overlooked Manara Square; Mohamed had asked me to meet at Manara that morning because, five years on, he still had that office.

As was the case for me, Mohamed's work had slowed down when the Arab Spring hit. Although his overhead was low—he, like most unmarried Palestinians, still lived at home with his parents—he paid rent for the office and he didn't like an empty schedule. Mohamed liked to stay busy—he wanted to feel productive—and sitting idly at his desk was upsetting to him. So I wasn't a total charity case. He'd offered to spend the day working with me in part because he didn't have anything else lined up.

And also because he thought I was cute.

* * *

We stopped and interviewed a teenage boy who was working in a *dukkan*, a corner store, and who said he supported the UN bid. As we walked away, Mohamed shook his head. The youth today didn't know what the Palestinian revolution had been all about, he said. Today, they were willing to accept a state on a little portion of what had once been theirs. But the Palestinians hadn't been fighting for a state, Mohamed explained. They'd fought for the land—all of it.

Mohamed paused to point out the best falafel place in Ramallah. I hadn't had breakfast, so I got a falafel in pita, asking the man to go heavy on the tahini and even heavier on the *shatta*, the hot sauce. Mohamed, who didn't get anything to eat, continued to fill me in on his life story. And then we arrived at the square with the stage where a big screen was ready to display Abu Mazen's UN speech.

"Look," Mohamed said, pointing through the crowd, "Mustafa Barghouti."

"Oooo, let's interview him," I said.

Barghouti was a physician and a Palestinian Legislative Council member who had founded, along with the renowned Palestinian intellectual Edward Said, al Mubadara, the Palestinian National Initiative. Barghouti believed in one secular, democratic state for everyone; he believed in a model where no religious or ethnic group would take precedence over another, in a place where everyone's individual rights would be respected. In 2005, Barghouti had campaigned for president independently, conducting a humble grassroots campaign, walking the streets, chatting with people, shaking hands. And though he hadn't won—he couldn't compete with Mahmoud Abbas, who had been backed by the political might of Fatah—Barghouti had come in a respectable second, pulling in 20 percent of the votes. I'd heard Barghouti speak at a flotilla press conference in Athens that summer, and it was then that I'd begun to admire him and his views. The two-state solution was dead; one state seemed the only remaining answer. And, as long as no one oppressed anyone else, why shouldn't Jews and Palestinians alike be able to live everywhere?

As I moved toward Barghouti, Mohamed stopped me. "Finish your falafel first," he said.

"There's too many journalists here," I countered. If we didn't get Barghouti now, I'd never get a word with him. So I charged ahead, recorder in hand, Mohamed trailing behind.

As I began talking to Barghouti, he urged me to finish my sandwich. "Oh, that's okay," I said, hiding it behind my back, tahini and shatta dripping down my arm into my sleeve. While Barghouti explained that the bid for an upgrade would probably be unsuccessful and that, while it wouldn't change anything immediately for the Palestinians, it could call more attention to their plight, Mohamed disappeared. He returned moments later with a pile of napkins, which he gave me after taking the falafel and recorder from my hands. I cleaned up the mess on my arm and continued chatting with the politician. But as I was talking with Barghouti, I was thinking about how touched I was that Mohamed had brought me napkins, and I was thinking about the way he'd gently removed both the falafel and recorder from my hands. He was taking care of me.

Or at least trying to help me not humiliate myself.

Mohamed liked my unbridled enthusiasm and the way I didn't try to hide my excitement. He liked that I wore my heart on my sleeve. Mohamed had also found it endearing that I'd unknowingly interviewed Barghouti with a little red spot of shatta on my face.

At the end of the interview, my hand clean, I fished a business card out of my backpack. I was so excited to talk one-on-one with Barghouti that I hadn't thought about the fact that my name and profession were printed in both English and Hebrew. As I handed the card over, I felt Mohamed's eyes on it, and I suddenly became aware of the Hebrew. I'd told Mohamed very little about myself at this point, and I hadn't told him that I had an Israeli passport, of course. Part of me felt like I should tell him because he had a right to know who he was working with; the other part of me felt Mohamed didn't need to know anything beyond the fact that I was an American journalist. I was never going to see him again anyway.

There was another thing: while I was no longer worried that he posed some sort of security risk, I liked Mohamed and wanted him to like me, and Israeli citizenship wouldn't exactly be attractive to the son of a PLO guy, I figured. So, inwardly, I cringed when I realized Mohamed had seen the Hebrew on my business card. That was it, I thought. This guy was smart. Between the fact that I lived in Tel Aviv and the Hebrew on my card, he would put it all together. Whatever vibes we'd been feeling that day were done.

* * *

Figuring we had a good sense of how Palestinians felt about the UN bid, we headed back toward Manara. Along the way, Mohamed stopped and gestured toward a building.

"Look," he said.

I didn't see anything but a limestone wall and a closed store.

"What?" I said.

"That purple thing."

And then it jumped out at me. Embedded into an exterior wall was a lavender metal rectangle topped with some sort of open compartment, overflowing with cigarette butts. "Oh yeah! What is it? An ashtray?"

"No. A mailbox from the British Mandate," Mohamed said. "A piece of history."

We got closer, and I saw the emblem of a crown, flanked with the letters *G* and *R*. Pointing to them, Mohamed explained that they stood for "Georgious" and "Rex"—Latin for "King George," who'd ruled Great Britain during the British occupation of Palestine.

"My apartment in Tel Aviv," I told Mohamed, "is on the corner of Sheinken and King George."

A King George here, a King George there. The nakba, the Green Line, and the wall all seemed to drop away for a moment, and we stood there together, imagining a land that hadn't yet been divided.

I imagined a place where everyone was free, and I felt, in that moment, I'd found a kindred spirit.

* * *

Mohamed guessed that Palestinians would take to the Qalandia checkpoint to protest the occupation. The demonstrations would be a good way to show the futility of the UN bid—even if the UN recognized Palestine as a member state, Palestinians on the ground would still have to deal with the massive infrastructure of the occupation. So we boarded a servees to head toward the checkpoint. As I made my way to a seat, the servees jerked to life; lurching forward, I grabbed Mohamed's knee to steady myself. Aware of how inappropriate it was—in Palestinian culture, not even *married* men and women would touch each other like this in public, never mind acquaintances, like us—I apologized and quickly pulled my hand away. But the feel of his knee, sturdy and solid, lingered in my palm, and I considered the body underneath that bright blue sweater and jeans.

On the back bench, we sat a little closer than we should have, the edges of our thighs almost touching and then colliding momentarily, like the briefest of kisses, as the servees bounced over speed bumps and potholes. And there was that scent again. I wanted to bury my nose into Mohamed's neck and inhale him fully. I didn't *want* to like this guy, but I did. I'd liked the way he approached our interviewees; I'd liked the way he'd politely pause them to translate for me; I'd liked the way he'd answered my endless questions, openly sharing his family's story with me and the little details of his childhood—his love of maps and coins and stamps and his bike rides to the library. And when I'd been thrilled to come across the Palestinian politician Mustafa Barghouti, I'd liked the slight smile that had come across Mohamed's face, the look of gentle amusement as he'd reminded me to finish my falafel. I thought it sweet that Mohamed had rushed to find napkins to clean up the mess flowing down my arm into my torn black sweater—a gesture that left me feeling like he not only understood my aspirations but would support them.

While so many people here on both sides of the Green Line saw the conflict and the world in black and white, Mohamed struck me as someone who saw shades of gray, and he seemed to understand that I did, too. He seemed thoughtful. Kind, patient, and tolerant. And that moment gazing at the mailbox together—imagining a Palestine that hadn't been divided—made me think that, maybe, if he were to discover that I held an Israeli passport, he might be able to think of me as more than just a citizen of the state that oppressed his people.

* * *

When we arrived at Qalandia and got off the servees, we found a cluster of journalists, including Jacob. One by one, young Palestinian men emerged from the adjacent refugee camp, some with T-shirts tied over their faces, masking everything but their eyes, and they began to accumulate in front of the checkpoint. Then came a sound—*ping!*—a stone bouncing off of one of the enormous steel towers, charred black from having been set on fire in the past.

Ping!

One soldier emerged from the checkpoint and then another.

"Oh, God," I said to Mohamed, "I'm scared. I was at the protest here on Nakba Day."

He nodded and said he had been, too. I could tell from the look on Mohamed's face that he was nervous, and I assumed that, like me, he had also run from the gunfire on Nakba Day. Only later, when we were dating, would he tell me what had happened to him at Qalandia years before. It was here that an Israeli soldier had held a rifle to his head and threatened to kill him.

Now soldiers were trickling out of the checkpoint.

"Get ready to move," Mohamed said, gesturing up the street, back toward Ramallah.

And then came the first round of tear gas, announced with that sound I knew from scores of other demonstrations: the *thunk* as the canister was fired, the hiss as it streamed through the air, leaving streaks in the sky that, in another context, could feel festive.

Thunk. Hissssss.

Thunk. Hissssss.

The tear gas flew into the air, long white fingers tearing through the fabric of the sky, and everyone started to run. Mohamed went in the direction he'd pointed, toward Ramallah. But in this moment of imminent danger, I reacted instinctively, without thinking, and found my legs carrying me not away from the checkpoint and the soldiers but *toward* them. Not because I felt they would protect me but, rather, because I wanted to get past them, so I could reach the place on the other side of the checkpoint, the place I felt safe—Israel.

This didn't even register with me at the time. Tear gas stinging my eyes and nose, I ducked into a small corner store where I'd taken refuge alongside protesters and other journalists during past demonstrations. I walked to the back of the store and grabbed a water out of the cooler. As I headed to the cash register, I was overcome with a vision of my apartment in Tel Aviv: my yellow living room, the many windows, the bright green kitchen, the blue bedroom with the art deco stencil I'd painted onto the wall in place of a headboard. That same heaviness I'd felt when I'd seen the wall the day before hit me now. I just wanted to crawl in my bed and lie there, staring up at the soaring ceiling, smelling the salt air and the basil plants on the windowsill, listening to the passing buses, thinking about the people inside. I didn't care about the kitchen that electrocuted me and the tree growing up the drain that made showering impossible. I didn't care if Mohamed had noticed that we'd run in opposite directions.

I just wanted to get home.

* * *

Because Mohamed and I had parted ways without saying goodbye, I texted him after I'd returned to Tel Aviv and thanked him for his help. Sitting at my desk, I transcribed the interviews we'd done in Ramallah. Though I could have fast-forwarded through the segments of Mohamed and I chatting, instead I listened, enjoying the sound of his deep voice. The pauses in our conversation felt pregnant, the air gathering and tightening around us until I broke the tension with another question.

He liked me, I realized. I could hear it in his voice.

I liked him, too, in a way that I hadn't liked anyone since before July 4. It was like every bit of my body was alive. This feeling—so strong, so overwhelming, at once familiar and completely unfamiliar—frightened me. I was relieved he was so far away.

When the *Boston Review* posted the story several days later, I emailed the link to Mohamed, who promptly replied, "Nice work. Let's get together next time you're in Ramallah."

A thrill shot through my body. But I was determined not to respond to Mohamed's email. My life was complicated enough already. Not only did I want to get out of my relationship with Oded; I was certain that I was incapable of receiving and giving love. I'd hurt enough people. I didn't want to hurt anyone else, and I didn't want to get hurt.

Something about the force of my feelings for Mohamed frightened me. Getting involved with a Palestinian would be complicated. And I wanted to avoid the vulnerability that came along with love.

So I slammed my laptop shut and ran into my electrified kitchen, determined not to see Mohamed again.

4

Just when I was out of money again and had resumed spending my Friday afternoons picking through the produce piles at the shuk, I got a job with a small, radical left-wing nonprofit, the Alternative Information Center (AIC). The first joint grassroots Israeli-Palestinian organization that advocated for Palestinian rights and an end to the occupation, the place was legendary. When I told Oded's parents that I was starting there, they'd been impressed even if they didn't agree with the organization's politics. Being affiliated with the AIC also gave me instant street cred with both the Israeli Left and Palestinians.

But like the Israeli Left itself, the AIC was in a death spiral. The short explanation: During the Second Intifada, Israeli politics had shifted further to the right, and by 2011, nongovernmental organizations that received foreign funding were under scrutiny in Israel—so much that international donors were getting spooked and were increasingly reluctant to contribute. As the occupation ground on, ties between Israelis and Palestinians, even those who were politically aligned, were becoming increasingly fraught, making it hard for joint initiatives to survive. There was also the matter of physical separation. The AIC had two offices: one in Jerusalem and the other in the West Bank, in the Christian Palestinian village of Beit Sahour, which was next to Bethlehem and partially in Area A. Increasing movement restrictions meant that our Palestinian colleagues in Beit Sahour usually couldn't come to Jerusalem; when the Israeli employees of the AIC went out to our Beit Sahour office, we were risking arrest by going to Area A.

But I hadn't known that the organization was on its last financial legs when I'd applied and interviewed with them. They'd just told me that their website traffic was down, and they were looking for someone to single-handedly revive it. My name had preceded me. The folks at the AIC knew my work already and expressed excitement about bringing me on board. While I felt that the job would conflict with my journalism in some ways, in others, it would help: the AIC had Palestinian contacts in the farthest corners of the West Bank; working there would deepen my knowledge of the conflict and broaden my network. We also agreed that I could cross post whatever I wrote for the AIC on a website called +972 Magazine, which was published by a collective of independent Israeli and Palestinian journalists that I'd recently been invited to join. At that time, +972 didn't pay, but the AIC would, and that meant I would be able to stay in Israel a little while longer and continue my work.

I was thrilled to get the job and excited about the prospect of moving to Jerusalem, a city I loved. The move also seemed like it would present a natural break in my relationship with Oded, who wanted to stay at our apartment in Tel Aviv, despite the fact that he couldn't afford the rent on his own.

* * *

On my first day in the Jerusalem office, I wondered what I'd gotten myself into. The office was half empty and littered with piles of old, abandoned office supplies. I'd imagined the place as a hub of activity where the political issues were alive, and I would find a community of like-minded people. But the nights of impassioned readings and debates were long gone; the central room that had once hosted vibrant gatherings went mostly unused. Among my Israeli coworkers, morale was low. The week I started, the woman who had hired me and who was supposed to be my manager disappeared for a three-month leave. She claimed to be sick, but one day, en route to Haifa, she bopped into the office, a backpack slung over her shoulder. My other boss often drank beer at his desk as he browsed Facebook.

And no one in the Jerusalem office of our joint Israeli-Palestinian organization actually spoke Arabic. It seemed obvious to me that, if we were going to be a collaborative organization, and if we were going to throw our weight behind the Palestinian cause, we needed to know the language. So I signed up for Arabic classes at Al Quds University, and I threw myself into the language and the job.

On a November afternoon, two months after I'd met Mohamed, I headed out from the Jerusalem office to report on a unique protest in the West Bank. Palestinian activists had organized a demonstration they called a "Freedom Ride," an intentional nod to the American civil rights movement of the 1960s. They would board an Israeli bus in the West Bank and try to ride it into Jerusalem, knowing they would be stopped and unable to pass through the checkpoint, despite the fact that it stood outside the Green Line and on occupied Palestinian territory. The action was supposed to call attention to the fact that settlers—who live in the occupied Palestinian territories on Palestinian land and who use roads built on the land, as well—had freedom of movement and could exit and enter the West Bank at will while Palestinians, on the other hand, were subject to a regime of IDs and permits and checkpoints.

The Palestinian activists were already surrounded by a throng of journalists when I caught up with them at a bus stop outside the Israeli settlement of Psagot. Seeing the crowd, several bus drivers slowed but refused to stop. When one finally pulled to a halt, the activists began to board, and the journalists surged forward to accompany them; I was one of about a dozen journalists who made it inside.

The six Freedom Riders included Huwaida Arraf, one of the flotilla organizers; the Palestinian scientist and author Mazin Qumsiyeh, who would be nominated for a Nobel Peace Prize in 2025; Badia Dweik, a prominent Palestinian activist from Hebron; and Basel al-Araj. Basel was a popular youth activist and up-and-coming intellectual who would be assassinated by the Israelis in 2017 at the age of thirty-three; he and Mohamed were friends.

After boarding, Basel and the others took seats on the bus. They remained quiet, holding signs that read "Resist Injustice" and "We Shall Overcome" and "Boycott Apartheid." Eventually, the bus began to move. But when it arrived at the Hizma checkpoint, the Israeli police and army were waiting. After directing the driver into a dirt lot, they informed us that no one—not even journalists—was allowed off the bus. So we all waited for the police and army to get on.

At some point, I looked up and saw Mohamed in the aisle.

Not knowing he was friends with Basel, I was surprised to see him—so surprised that I forgot that I'd forbidden myself from responding to his email and that I'd been determined not to like him and those hazel eyes and his smell and his smile. I forgot that I'd tamped down on my own heart.

"Hey!" I shouted down the aisle. "What are you doing here?"

"I'm going to Jerusalem," Mohamed said, flashing me that boyish grin he'd given me when we'd met at Manara Square.

I put my black backpack on and made my way toward him.

"If they let us through, let's grab a drink," I said, shocked to hear my own words. For one, of course the police and the army weren't going to let us through. And two: had I just asked Mohamed out on a date?

"Let's," he answered. "Where should we go?"

Before the Second Intifada, it had been relatively easy for Palestinians to travel between the West Bank and Jerusalem, and Mohamed had often come into the city despite the fact that he refused to apply for an Israeli-issued permit. Mohamed, as a Palestinian from the occupied territories who held a Palestinian ID, wasn't supposed to enter Jerusalem or Israel without Israeli permission, but he refused to comply on principle. In Mohamed's mind, this was Palestine. All of it. Not only had a map of

Palestine hung in his living room his entire life but the Israeli government had confiscated some of his family's land in the West Bank—tracts that Mohamed would have eventually inherited himself—and had used part of that land to build a road for the Jewish settlers. Why should he have to turn around and ask the same people who had stolen his land from his family to move freely through that stolen land?

He wouldn't.

So from time to time, Mohamed had risked arrest by making his way into Jerusalem without a permit, and he knew the city well. We chatted about the places we both loved in Jerusalem, indulging in the fantasy that we would be able to enter together and move about freely. But it was just that—a fantasy.

As an Israeli citizen, I was free to move about everywhere, except for Area A and the checkpoints that were off-limits to me. Mohamed and I embodied exactly the disparity that the Freedom Riders were trying to highlight. Still, we planned an itinerary as though this discriminatory system didn't exist, as though our arrival to the city was imminent. All we had to do was ride this bus into Jerusalem, which lay on the other side of the checkpoint just a few meters away from us.

But the bus didn't move.

Instead, the police and army boarded and began to check IDs, removing the activists one by one, carrying them off. The activists didn't resist, but they didn't help either, making their bodies limp, forcing the policemen and soldiers to struggle with their weight.

Mohamed and I followed the activists off the bus and then stood outside by the rear exit, watching Israeli forces drag the demonstrators through the dusty parking lot. The protest over, journalists milled about, trying to get comments from the Israeli spokesman.

And then three policemen approached Mohamed, surrounding him, asking for his ID. He showed them his PA-issued press pass and told them he was a journalist. They repeated their request, and after he produced his green Palestinian ID, they grabbed his arms and led him toward a police car. Anger surged through my chest. What right did they have to detain him? There couldn't possibly be a charge of any kind—Mohamed hadn't entered Israel without a permit. Maybe they had declared the area a "closed military zone" and that was their justification?

Or maybe they had no justification at all.

Things like this happened all the time in the territories, where the Palestinians were subject to Israeli military law while the Israeli settlers who, according to international law, lived there illegally were subject to Israeli civilian law.

Whatever was happening, it was unjust, so I followed the police, shouting at them in Hebrew, "He's a journalist! We have freedom of speech in Israel!"

They ignored me, stuffed him into the back of the car, and drove away.

* * *

That night at my new place, which lacked furniture, I sat on the cold terrazzo floor, typing up my article about the Freedom Ride, scrambling to file it for both +972 and the AIC. My phone rang, an unfamiliar number flashing on the screen. I answered, and it was an Associated Press reporter.

"What happened to your boyfriend?" she asked.

"My boyfriend?" I repeated, puzzled, wondering if she was referring to Oded. He hadn't been at the Freedom Ride.

"Yeah, you know, the Palestinian guy," the reporter said, impatient.

"Oh, Mohamed? He's not my boyfriend," I said, adding that I'd texted him a little while ago to see if he was OK but still hadn't heard back.

As I spoke with the reporter, I wondered what had made her think that Mohamed and I were a couple. Was it the way we smiled at each other? The way we stayed close together? The way we talked? How I'd yelled at the policeman?

I wanted to ask her but didn't want to seem like a teenager with a crush on some cute guy.

The reporter's phone call made me realize how strong the chemistry between Mohamed and me was; her question made my feelings for Mohamed even harder to deny.

But feelings were the last thing I wanted.

So after Mohamed texted me to let me know that he was fine—the police had questioned him, and once they understood he wasn't an activist, they'd let him go—I swore to myself that I wouldn't contact him again. Sitting there in head-to-toe black, I turned my focus back to my work, the only thing in my life it seemed I could keep a handle on.

* * *

A month later, Oded showed up on my doorstep with our cat and a moving truck behind him. Unable to pay the rent alone at our old place in Tel Aviv, he'd run out of money. Though I wanted this relationship to be over, I hadn't yet worked up the nerve to break up with him.

"Guess you're stuck with me," Oded said and shrugged.

I was annoyed with both him and myself. His parents lived just a couple of miles away from me. He could have—*should* have—moved in with them. Why wasn't I putting my foot down? I wasn't scared of being alone, per se: As an only child, I was used to being alone. Leaving the confines of this relationship frightened me because doing so would leave me emotionally vulnerable. If I was tucked safely away inside a dysfunctional relationship, I wouldn't be available or open to the possibility of real intimacy and real love.

Then the manager whose work I'd been doing while she was out on a three-month leave returned and let me go two days later; I fell headlong into a depression even deeper than the one that took hold of me after Miguel and I had agreed to file for divorce. Wearing black wasn't enough anymore. When Oded returned from work or school in Tel Aviv every day, he found me on the couch, curled up in front of a space heater, the apartment otherwise dark. I ignored the text messages from friends who were increasingly worried about me. When I did answer, I would agree to meet up only to end up canceling because I couldn't bear the thought of getting dressed or walking to the light rail.

The sink overflowed with dishes; the place was filthy. I couldn't keep up with anything. And I resented Oded for not noticing and not helping.

The only things I kept up with in that time were the Arabic courses I'd already registered and paid for—if the money was spent already, I didn't want to waste it. My Arabic classes were in the Old City, and on the way there, while I was riding the light rail, when the train went onto the bridge that went over the road below, I imagined my body falling from the side. I thought about the Mediterranean Sea and wondered what would happen if I got in and just started swimming until my arms and legs gave out.

But never did I consider reaching out to Miguel and asking for help or to go back to him; nor did I ask anything of my parents. Their house wasn't my home. However fraught my relationship was with this place, I wasn't leaving.

5

Every day, I felt like there was an enormous boulder in my chest, pushing on my ribcage, robbing me of breath. But I had to make the best of things. I pitched and pitched, and freelance work began to pick up once again. Though I was getting by, I decided to downsize to a tiny studio apartment because lower overhead meant more freedom to pursue the journalism and creative writing projects I cared about. I think, on a subconscious level, I was also trying to push Oded out without actually having that difficult conversation with him. He didn't get the message though; he moved with me.

As the days grew longer and the weather warmed, I began to find the energy to reach out to all the people I'd ghosted in the winter. I went through my phone, systematically responding to text messages

I'd received months before but hadn't answered, including one from an old friend, an American Israeli writer, David.

"I was just thinking about you," he answered. "We need someone to teach English composition this fall. Send me your CV. Xoxo."

David worked at Al Quds University, a Palestinian university in East Jerusalem. Al Quds is in a village called Abu Dis, which stands outside the separation barrier which, in that area, is a concrete wall; however, technically speaking, most of Abu Dis is inside the Jerusalem municipality, which is under Israeli control. David taught literature in a program there known as Al Quds Bard, AQB for short, named as such because it was offered in collaboration with Bard, an American liberal arts college in upstate New York.

I sent a short cover letter and my CV to David, who passed it along to the higher-ups. I got the job. Even though it was legal according to Israeli law for me to be in Abu Dis as it was part of East Jerusalem, my superiors advised me to keep my Jewish Israeli identity under wraps because it might upset our students, all of whom were Palestinian. When I was on campus, they warned, I was an American and only an American. And, oh, Abu Dis was a conservative village, so I'd better cover up. I wouldn't have to wear the hijab or anything, but I should dress modestly. Knees and elbows covered. Nothing too tight.

* * *

A month later, I was on a Palestinian bus, donning long sleeves, making my way to my 8:00 a.m. class. The bus hurtled up a hill, and suddenly, the wall seemed to pop up out of nowhere, blocking the view of the valley below. To our right, a smaller, lower wall—the edge of the university. The bus stopped alongside campus, and I got off, stepping onto the dry, dusty shoulder of the road, passing empty soda bottles and battered snack bags and other bits of litter as I made my way to the main gate.

"I'm a professor," I told the security guard at the entrance, hoping he wouldn't ask any questions.

He nodded for me to pass.

I made my way through the front hall with its sheet glass windows—which, about a year later, would be shattered by Israeli soldiers during a campus raid—and came to the building that housed our program. After finding my classroom on the ground floor, I entered. And then I waited. And waited.

Was something wrong? Was I in the right room? My class had been capped at fourteen students, so I wasn't expecting a huge group. But there was *no one*.

And then a young woman with the palest, whitest face I'd ever seen, framed by a navy-blue hijab, came in. She wore a matching floor-length abaya in the form of a long coat with a wide collar and large buttons.

"Where is everyone?" I asked.

"Drop add," she said in English, with an unmistakable Arabic accent. "No one goes to class." She shrugged.

No one, that was, except for her.

The young woman, who introduced herself as Neda, came from a refugee camp next to Hebron called Al Arroub. Her family originally hailed from "forty-eight," she said, using the term many Palestinians use to refer to the lands inside the Green Line, so they don't have to say the word "Israel."

"Whereabouts?" I asked, expecting to hear the name of one of the hundreds of Palestinian villages that had been depopulated during the war.

"Kiryat Gat," Neda said.

"Kiryat Gat?" I asked, surprised, heat blooming up my chest and throat as I remembered its proximity to the kibbutz where I'd spent six weeks digging up sweet potatoes and struggling to learn Hebrew when I'd first arrived in Israel, before I'd moved to Tel Aviv. Kiryat Gat was where we went to do our shopping, and I had a clear vision of riding into town with Stav, the volunteer coordinator, listening to one of Israel's most beloved singers, Arik Einstein, golden fields undulating alongside the road. I saw us in Kiryat Gat's grocery store, talking about the trouble I was having in *ulpan*, "Hebrew class," and I remembered reading the carton of milk: *halav*. I remembered waking up in my shared room on the kibbutz to the sound of the rustling of the breeze blowing through the eucalyptus trees and the doves cooing.

I remembered spending my evenings running on the security road that followed the barbed wire fence circling the kibbutz. I'd tried to pretend that the fence between me and the rest of the world wasn't there; I'd tried to pretend I didn't hear the helicopters buzzing to and from the nearby army base. I'd tried to pretend that my feet weren't moving in time to the thudding propellers.

"But isn't Kiryat Gat a Jewish city?" I asked.

"Yes," Neda said. She explained that her family came from Iraq al-Manshiyya one of the Palestinian villages that had stood in the area. "The Jews," she said, had expelled her grandparents, along with all the other Palestinian residents, from the land in 1949. Several years later, the young state of Israel built the new town of Kiryat Gat in its place.

Like talking to the old man that day I'd worked with Mohamed, this wasn't anything I didn't know about intellectually. But to stand before a young woman who had grown up in a refugee camp because her family had been dispossessed by my people, to stand before a young woman who, this morning, had to go through military checkpoints manned by my countrymen to reach this classroom—which was just feet from the separation wall—shook me to the core. I felt enormous guilt. And there was rage, too, at the overwhelming sense of injustice.

It took me a moment to gather my thoughts and to shift back into teacher mode.

I hesitated to start class, thinking that some more students might drift in. I looked down at my lesson plans and the class roster I'd printed out. The roster was full of young women. Of a class of fourteen, only four of my students were men. Although Palestinian women are unlikely to work, young Palestinian women are more likely to get some higher education than their male counterparts.

After a few more young women showed up, I did an abbreviated version of our lesson and then dismissed them for the day, telling them I'd see them Wednesday.

"Inshallah [God willing]," Neda said, with a quick nod and a smile.

I had expected my students at Al Quds to be somehow different from the ones I had taught when I was in graduate school in Florida.

But here they were, only the most diligent few showing up during drop add.

Of course, there was one crucial difference—my students in the West Bank had crossed military checkpoints to get here.

They left their houses in the morning without knowing, for certain, if they'd make it to campus or if they'd make it home at the end of the day. In the United States, my students had a feeling, however illusory, of control. In the occupied Palestinian territories, there was none of that. The prevailing sense was that someone else was the master of your destiny, and it was a mood that hung over everything constantly and colored everything people do. Though the word *inshallah* is ubiquitous throughout the Arab world, living under the uncertainty wrought by dispossession and military occupation and statelessness made the meaning of the phrase even sharper.

* * *

To get students acquainted immediately with the process of writing and revising, I was to respond to their final papers from a three-week crash course, called Language and Thinking, that preceded the start of the semester. One of my students, Ibtisam, turned in a paper in which she'd discussed the inhumanity of the occupation, taking the argumentative tack of saying that while the state of Israel had been created after the Holocaust, the genocide was a myth. If it had happened, she conceded, it was only three million Jews who had died. Maximum.

My stomach turned when I read the paper. In our first classes, Ibtisam had quickly distinguished herself as one of my brightest students—she was engaged, her bright green eyes following me from beneath her black hijab as I wrote on the white board. As I paced the room during discussions, her hand always shot up in the air so she could contribute. She wasn't shy about sharing her opinions, and she was diligent in her studies. She'd also grown up in the States. So I was surprised when she turned in that essay.

Not knowing what to do, I'd set Ibtisam's paper aside and consulted another professor on the bus back from Abu Dis one afternoon. I confessed that the student's Holocaust denial had rattled me, and I didn't know how to respond. The professor advised me to put my feelings aside and address it from the perspective of argument and counterargument.

So I did. Advising Ibtisam to do more research, I suggested that addressing the counterargument was more powerful than denying it. Ibtisam's revision was beautiful. The Holocaust had happened, she wrote, and it was a tragedy that had robbed six million Jews of their lives. But it didn't justify what was happening in Palestine today.

* * *

My daily commute to and from the university gave me a taste, however small, of both the uncertainty that my students grappled with and the lengths they went to to get to campus.

Even though I lived in Jerusalem and our campus was also technically in Jerusalem, segregation and checkpoints made my commute from one side of the city to the other as arduous as going from Tel Aviv to Ramallah had been. I had to make my way to East Jerusalem, where I boarded a Palestinian bus, only to sit and wait. Because Israeli buses are heavily subsidized, they leave on schedule whether or not they're full; Palestinian public transportation, on the other hand, can't afford to do this. So drivers wait until there are enough occupants to cover the cost of the journey, meaning that you never know for sure when you're going to set out. While waking up at 5:00 a.m. and leaving my apartment at 6:00 sometimes put me on campus at 7:15, giving me enough time to make a Nescafé and start class feeling centered and focused, on other days, leaving at 6:00 meant I'd be rushing through the door at 8:01, harried, Neda already there in her seat at the front of the seminar table, waiting.

At the end of the day, there was the ride back to Jerusalem, which was even worse. Again I boarded the bus without knowing what time it would set out. After waiting anywhere from five minutes to an hour, it would start down the road, kicking up dust as it passed small stone houses, stray dogs, litter, and the wall. And then we'd hurtle down the mountain, take a sharp right turn, and merge with the traffic headed toward Jerusalem.

And then came the checkpoint.

The A-Za'im checkpoint stands between the Palestinian neighborhoods of Abu Dis and Azzariya—both of which are part of the Jerusalem municipality and under Israeli control—cutting them off from the rest of East Jerusalem. While Israeli settlers breezed through the checkpoint unmolested, every day, our Palestinian-only bus was pulled over into an empty lot next to the checkpoint, where we got off, leaving our stuff behind. As soldiers got on and searched the bus—presumably checking it for explosives or weapons or just to remind riders that the occupation reached into every last corner of their lives—we lined up in what can only be described as a cattle chute, similar to the one I'd walked through at Qalandia: metal fencing formed a narrow aisle with an opening at the back, where we entered, and an opening at the front, where a soldier stood between us and the bus we needed to reboard to get to Jerusalem.

As Jewish Israeli drivers zoomed through the checkpoint just meters away, we stood—in the blistering heat and sun of late summer in the Middle East—and went through the cattle chute one by one, presenting our ID cards to the soldier: opening them up and holding them next to our face before the soldier gave a slight nod or just looked at the next person and we were free to return to the bus.

Because East Jerusalemites have Israeli residency and blue ID cards, like Israeli citizens, I blended in with the crowd, experiencing this trip as a Palestinian would. Until one day, I didn't.

When my turn came and I held up my blue ID, the soldier—a heavyset young woman with long, dark hair pulled back into a sleek ponytail—did a double take. I knew why. Palestinian residents of Jerusalem's IDs specify that they are Jerusalem residents; this specification distinguishes them from citizens. But even among Israeli citizens, IDs are slightly different depending on whether one is Jewish or Arab. The IDs of Palestinian citizens of Israel lists their grandfather's name, which isn't listed on the IDs of Jewish citizens. In that manner, the state can specify whether the ID holder is a Jewish or Palestinian citizen of Israel without expressly stating it. And soldiers, of course, know this.

After the soldier did a double take, she took the ID from me and held it, studying it in disbelief. My stomach hurtled upward, toward my mouth, and I tried not to vomit.

"Are you a Jew?" she asked.

I nodded.

"What are you doing here?" she asked.

I patiently explained to the soldier that I work in Abu Dis and that, yes, it is legal for me to be in that village because it is part of the Jerusalem municipality.

"What do you do *there*?" she asked.

"I teach at the university."

She looked at me doubtfully. After waving another soldier over to deal with the people in the line behind me, she pulled me aside.

"Are you OK?" she asked.

Clearly, I was fine. But her question revealed much about the moment. At the time, there were a number of right-wing anti-miscegenation Jewish organizations promoting the idea that Jewish women were being kidnapped by Arab partners and forced to live in Arab villages, where they were being abused. A Knesset committee had held a hearing about mixed marriages between Jewish women and Muslim men that included discussion about how to prevent such relationships; another Knesset committee held an emergency meeting on the topic of "the abduction of new female immigrants by minorities." I realized this soldier thought I was one of those women. She thought she had the opportunity to rescue me from some horrible situation.

"I'm fine," I answered. "I'm a teacher. At the university. I'm fine. Thank you."

She handed me the ID back.

I boarded the bus, and then the girl who'd been behind me in line boarded, too. And then another student. And another. They'd all seen and heard this interaction go down. They'd heard the soldier ask me if I'm Jewish, they'd heard me speaking Hebrew, I realized, meaning that my cover of being just an American was blown. Word would spread, I knew, and it would spread quickly. Would I be fired? Would I be in physical danger? I wasn't sure. But I knew my bosses had asked me to keep my identity quiet for a reason.

6

The first few weeks, the excitement of a new job had carried me up and out of bed. But as the four-hour round-trip commute began to exhaust me—and the tension that came from going through the checkpoint every day seeped into my bones—it became increasingly difficult to muster the energy to get up at 5:00 a.m. to embark on the journey. I loved teaching, and I was happy when I was in the classroom. It was just the trip there and back that was fraying my nerves. Every morning, my alarm would go off, and I'd lie there, regretting every decision I'd made in my life. Getting married. Going to Israel. Staying as long as I had. Taking up with Oded. Getting divorced. Everything. My whole life was a fucking mistake.

Then a face would float to the surface of my mind's eye: Neda.

I saw her on that first day, when almost no one else showed up, in her navy-blue hijab and her abaya. In the early morning darkness, I saw her—her face round and white like the moon—and I rose from bed.

If for nothing else, I was making this trip for her.

As I dressed in the dark and made my Nescafé, other students would come to mind, too. Ibtisam. She'd turned in a beautiful, nuanced revision of her first paper, and I could tell she'd learned a lot—not just about the Holocaust but, just as importantly, about counterargument and about researching even things she was dubious about.

Though I was exhausted and full of trepidation about the commute, I was buoyed by Neda and Ibtisam and all the young women who were attempting—in the most difficult of circumstances—to exert some control over their lives. Getting up and going to campus every morning was not just an act of faith for these girls, I realized. It was an action that showed faith in themselves. It was their attempt to have some self-determination in a place that stripped them of all agency.

I set my jaw and gritted my teeth as I walked from the light rail toward the Palestinian bus station, picturing my students on their way, too. I didn't care about their nationality or their religion or their politics. They were my girls, and I was with them.

* * *

Now that I had a steady income, I didn't need to use my free time hunting for jobs; I was free to return to the type of social-justice-oriented journalism I loved. And because my daily life was rooted outside the Green Line and commuting to campus helped me shed the last of my fears about traveling in the West Bank, my focus, as a journalist, continued to drift away from marginalized groups inside of Israel and became almost entirely about the conflict. When Al Jazeera green-lit a story about Palestinian families that had been separated between the West Bank and Gaza—a heartrending story that showed how the occupation made the most basic, most quintessential parts of life impossible—I knew that not only would I have to report it from the West Bank, but that I would also need a translator.

Yes, I'd been studying Arabic for several semesters now, and while my Arabic was rapidly improving and I understood a lot, I wasn't yet proficient enough to interview.

Mohamed.

There was his email in my inbox, and there was his number saved in my phone. We hadn't spoken in almost a year, since that night the police had hauled him off from the parking lot outside of Hizma checkpoint. Remembering the phone call from the AP reporter who thought we were a couple, my stomach lurched at the thought of seeing him again.

But I called anyway.

"*Ahlan*, hello, ya Mya," he answered, his voice warm and deep. I couldn't help but smile.

I told Mohamed about the story and asked if he was available to work in the coming weeks. "This one's for Al Jazeera, by the way," I added, "so this time I *will* be paying you, whether you want me to or not."

He laughed and agreed to work together. He would set up all our interviews for next week, and after teaching my Monday morning class, I would travel from Abu Dis to meet him at his office in Ramallah.

Ahead of our meeting, I googled him to see what he'd been up to workwise, and I saw numerous reports from NGOs and small media outlets that, in the summer of 2012, Mohamed had been beaten by PA policemen. He'd been covering a Palestinian protest against the PA, photographing plainclothes policemen as they arrested a demonstrator. When the police had noticed Mohamed, they'd grabbed him and had tried to pull the camera from his neck; when they'd found him unwilling to let go, they'd begun to hit him. The attack had only escalated from there, and the policemen had dragged him to the station, where the beating had continued to the point that Mohamed had needed hospitalization.

* * *

The day I was supposed to meet Mohamed to work on the Al Jazeera story, I woke up at 5:00 a.m., got dressed in the dark, and slipped out the door, my digital recorder tucked in my black backpack. After the two-hour commute to Abu Dis, my morning class, and meetings with students, I headed toward the parking lot where I would find a servees to Ramallah. And then I stood outside the yellow minivan, watching other passengers board, finding myself unable to get on.

I couldn't see Mohamed; I couldn't spend the day reporting with him. My feelings were so strong for him already; I was sure that, if I did spend the day working with him, I would fall in love with him. That would be a disaster. I didn't want to fall in love with anyone, let alone someone who lived on the other side of a wall.

And I was certain Mohamed wouldn't love me back. I was a citizen of the enemy state. I was a citizen of the state that had detained, interrogated, and tortured his father and then deported him to Jordan. I was a citizen of the state that had confiscated land from Mohamed's family and that occupied the place Mohamed thought of as his own.

Terrified of my feelings, I watched the servees fill up and pull away. It was like that moment in my old apartment in Tel Aviv when, after I'd received an email from Mohamed, I'd slammed the laptop shut and dashed into the kitchen. But this time was different—now I had a deadline.

I left the parking lot and crossed to the other side of the road, where I boarded the Jerusalem-bound bus. After taking a seat, I texted Mohamed: *I'm sorry, I'm not feeling well. Need to reschedule. How about next week?*

Salamtik, feel better, he responded. *Sure.*

But the following week, it was the same thing all over again. I walked to the servees but couldn't board. We rescheduled again. The third time I canceled, I didn't even bother walking to the servees. I sat at my desk in the shared office, so gripped by fear I was unable to get up and leave the building. Feeling embarrassed and guilty—how selfish and inconsiderate of me to schedule and cancel again and again!—I shot Mohamed a text message. This time, I didn't even bother with a lame excuse. I simply told him that I was sorry I couldn't make it. While Mohamed took it in stride, he warned me that the interviewees would lose patience with my endless canceling. So if we rescheduled a fourth time, well, I'd better stick to it.

A stack of student papers before me, I sat there at my desk, clutching my cell phone, thinking: *If I don't get this story done, I'm going to blow my relationship with Al Jazeera.* I thought about finding another fixer. But I didn't want to. I wanted Mohamed.

* * *

Another morning, another 5:00 a.m. alarm. As I lay there, hating myself and trying to muster the energy to get out of bed and begin my two-hour commute, I realized that I had it all wrong. For so long I'd told myself that I couldn't love other people. And I'd also believed that my inability to love others made me, in turn, unlovable. The story I'd been telling myself was that I'd died on July 4, on that night in the woods, and that all that had remained was a hollow, heartless shell.

But as I forced myself out of bed, I realized that story was wrong. I realized what I did every morning was about so much more than earning a salary. I was devoted to my students. No, it wasn't romantic love but I realized I was capable of great love—I proved this every time I held Neda's face in my mind's eye so I could get out of bed. I remembered, too, the way I'd doggedly pursued stories about foreign workers and their children and the asylum seekers from Africa—how intent I'd been on advocating for these people, how passionate I'd been about telling their stories—and I realized I could be devoted to other people.

It was cool that day, and when I got dressed that morning, I put on something other than black. I added a short gray jacket to my outfit and red ballet flats. It was the first time in over a year that I didn't look like I was going to a funeral, and as I walked to the light rail, the dome of the sky felt higher, the morning full of possibilities.

Yes, I'd marooned myself here, in this troubled land. But I had a job I loved and could pursue stories I cared about. I had a life ahead of me.

Later that day, I reached out to Mohamed to reschedule our interviews. Tolerant and patient, he didn't ask whether I was actually going to keep the appointment; I offered him some reassurance anyway. "I swear I'm going to show up this time," I said. "I'm on deadline."

7

When I arrived at Manara Square, I found Mohamed there, waiting, wearing a pair of mirrored sunglasses and a broad smile. He offered his hand, and as I took it, I felt a surge of energy shoot up my arm.

"*Hala hala* [welcome welcome], ya Mya," he said, his smile broadening into a grin.

But then the handshake was over, and Mohamed was all business, hustling me toward a taxi as he explained that we needed to get a move on if we wanted to make our first appointment, which was at Birzeit University. That was where Ali, our first interviewee of the day, worked.

I'd gotten Ali's name, contact information, and details of his case from an Israeli NGO, Gisha (Hebrew for "access"), an organization that advocates for freedom of movement for Palestinians in the Gaza Strip. I knew the broad outlines of Ali's story already: He was from the

West Bank, from a small, beautiful village named Battir. Right next to the Green Line, Battir is known for its olive terraces, which had been named a UNESCO world heritage site, and its legendary eggplants. But Ali's wife wasn't from the West Bank; she was from Gaza. Although she'd attended university in the West Bank, when she'd gone back to visit her family, the Israelis had forbidden her from exiting Gaza again, so she'd gotten stuck there, and the couple had endured years apart. Knowing all of this, I'd assumed Ali to be an older man.

But when we met Ali at the media center on campus, I was struck immediately by his youth. He was thirty-one and with his Che Guevara cap, scruffy red beard, and Converse sneakers, he looked even younger.

In perfect English, Ali explained to Mohamed and me that he'd met his wife, Rihab, in class at university. It was during a lecture about mythology that he'd first noticed her.

"She started to talk," he said, resting his hand in his chin, his eyes staring at the surface of the table as though it was a screen and the moment was playing before him again. "And I was like, 'Oh, my God, there is a beautiful girl, and she is talking about serious things in an intelligent way.'"

For Ali, Rihab was the package deal—gorgeous, outspoken, brazen, expressive. He fell hard.

After just a month, he confessed his love to her. And then he got to work wooing her. He smiled as he recalled doing "crazy things" to get her attention and win her favor. After scaling the side of her dorm, he climbed onto her balcony. He spray-painted love poetry on the sidewalk outside the building. The feelings were mutual, and the two quickly became a couple.

As many Palestinians had been decades before, the two were communists. As such, they opposed the traditional, cultural mores that they believed stemmed from Christianity and Islam. Defying strongly held Palestinian norms, they moved in together before they were married, something virtually unheard of in any Palestinian city or village, whether in Israel or in the occupied territories.

But at some point, Rihab needed to go back to Gaza to visit her family. It had been years since she'd visited and she'd delayed the trip because she feared that she would get stuck there and would be unable to finish her degree. So she went after graduation. Once she was there, the couple's greatest fear came true—the Israelis wouldn't let Rihab exit and return to the West Bank, where Ali was waiting for her.

My eyes filled with tears, which I tried to hide by staring at my recorder. I didn't want my reaction to upset Ali. Out of the corner of my eye, I glanced at Mohamed. He wasn't crying, but he grimaced, and I knew he was moved, too, by their story. Mohamed's sensitivity and empathy touched me.

Just as Ali had unrelentingly pursued Rihab, he was equally determined to get her out of Gaza. When Rafah, the crossing with Egypt, opened, she left Gaza, and the two reunited in the United Arab Emirates, where they defied their communist mores and got married. Love mattered more to them than ideology.

After spending a year and a half together in the Emirates, the two tried to return to the West Bank as husband and wife, only for the Israelis to turn Rihab away. So they went to Egypt, where her family was living at the time. And from there, Ali began to attempt to navigate the very political system he detested in hopes of getting his beloved to the West Bank.

Israel controls the population registry for the West Bank and Gaza, despite the pretense of having withdrawn from the latter in 2005. However, Israel doesn't take the paperwork directly from Palestinians. Palestinians hand over their documents to the Palestinian Authority, only for the PA to pass it along to the Israelis. It wasn't just the Israelis Ali didn't want to deal with. It was the PA, too. Many Palestinians consider the PA the ultimate collaborators, an arm of the Israelis.

But Ali had no choice but to play the bureaucratic game. So he filled out and submitted the necessary forms and documentation to the PA, only for the Israelis to claim they didn't receive the paperwork. "I don't know where the PA put the papers," he told me. "Maybe in the garbage."

So Ali filled out and submitted the same paperwork again. And again. He also tried appealing to numerous high-ranking PA officials. Nothing helped.

In the meantime, Rihab, on the advice of PA officials who said the couple's case for reunification would be stronger if she was in Gaza, had returned to Gaza alone. Not only were there the Israeli military operations to contend with, living in the superconservative, largely religious Gaza Strip was difficult for Rihab, who didn't wear a hijab.

By the time Mohamed and I interviewed Ali in the fall of 2012, the couple hadn't seen each other for over three years, and he was considering a move to Gaza, a place that even Palestinians considered hell, he said, a place where he might not find work, where the two would struggle to survive, just so they could be together. "For her, I will go to hell," he told us.

My throat caught again, and I felt tears welling up in my eyes.

His friends and family were telling him to give up. He should accept reality, move on, and find someone else, they said, advice that left Ali, already cynical about the PA and the Israelis and the Egyptians, even more jaded. He hoped that getting his story out into the world would help. Maybe someone who could help would read it and intervene. But he had doubts about that, too.

Upset by the story, Mohamed and I thanked Ali and left the campus. We stood on the shoulder of the road, waiting for a servees. It was late afternoon, and a hill—green from winter rains—was behind Mohamed. The sun was starting to ease itself down in the sky, like a woman using a ladder to lower herself into a pool, the light dipping just the edge of its toes in the Mediterranean, and it was that particular shade of gold that foretold the end of the day. It shined on Mohamed from the side, illuminating those bright hazel eyes, rendering his olive-toned skin caramel. That was the moment I fell in love with him.

As we waited for the servees, we talked about Ali and Rehab's situation. Could it be resolved? Mohamed wasn't optimistic. And to him, the fact that the PA couldn't do anything pointed to just how powerless the Palestinian government was—it was a dummy regime, a puppet of the Israelis that did nothing for the Palestinian people, Mohamed said.

We talked about politics and human rights and how international law protects the right to family; I told Mohamed about the ways, inside the Green Line, Israel also violated migrant workers' right to family. We talked about how unjust Ali and Rihab's situation was, and I understood that, as we'd sat around that table and listened to Ali's words, our mutual indignation and our opposition to Israeli policy had bonded us together, solidifying the feeling we had that, until that moment, was based on little more than chemistry, on pheromones.

We returned to Ramallah and went to Mohamed's office on the top floor of one of the buildings overlooking Manara Square. The sounds of life flowed in through the open balcony doors, bouncing off the high ceilings, the space around us amplifying the vendors' cries and the hum of conversation. He showed me the view from the balcony, which looked down on the lions that represented the city's founding families, who were Christian Palestinians. Today, Ramallah has a Muslim majority, in part due to the way the nakba had rearranged the population, in part due to the fact that Muslims have a higher birth rate.

Mohamed made coffee for himself and tea for me. Then we called our other interviewees, including Nisreen, a woman in the Gaza Strip who had spent most of her life in the West Bank but whose identity card pegged her as a Gaza resident. Despite the fact that she'd married a Palestinian with a West Bank ID, despite the fact that Nisreen's children had been born in the West Bank, in 2007 some Israeli soldiers at a checkpoint had seen her ID and deported Nisreen to the Gaza Strip straightaway—without even allowing her a chance to see her ten-year-old daughter and her son, who was a toddler at the time. No goodbye, no nothing. They'd taken her directly from the West Bank to Gaza, where she had spent the last five years without her family. Despite the fact that her address had been updated in the population registry—she was officially registered as a resident of the West Bank now—she had been unable to get the exit permit she needed to leave Gaza.

And so Nisreen was stuck there, her relationship with her children limited to tortured phone calls.

Before she'd been deported from the West Bank, Nisreen recalled, every night, as she put her children to bed, she'd measured their warm bodies with her bare hands, saying, "Let's see how much you grew today."

It was this detail that undid me. Because Nisreen couldn't see me, I wept openly—silently but openly—as she spoke, the tears streaming down my face. I managed to contain my crying long enough to ask a question, and then, as she spoke and Mohamed translated, the tears took over again, and I sat on this chair like that, sobbing, the air around me feeling so empty, so cold. And just as his reaction to Ali's troubles had endeared him to me, my reaction to the mother's stories touched Mohamed. Never had a journalist cried in front of him and certainly not the way I had.

When we finished the last phone call, we sat silently. It was already dark outside, and Mohamed began to roll a cigarette.

"Do you smoke?" he asked me.

"Not tobacco," I said.

He nodded, opened a drawer in his large, heavy wooden desk, and pulled out a cigar box. He flipped it open and produced a sliver of hash.

"This?"

I nodded.

"OK," he said, a slight smile on his lips. He lit an edge of the hash, crumbled a tiny corner into some tobacco and mixed the two. The crinkling sound of the rolling paper filled the air.

"I saw what happened to you this summer at the protest," I said. "I was so sorry to see it."

"Thank you," Mohamed answered, not looking at me, concentrating instead on the joint.

He lit it, put his lips to it, and pulled, the tip glowing red. He passed it to me. The air grew sweet with the smell of hash and thick with tension. I could feel that something was happening between us. I knew I needed to tell him the truth about who I was.

"I have an Israeli passport," I blurted out.

Mohamed nodded.

"I know. I googled you," he said, smiling, adding that he'd guessed it the night we'd met, in part because I was friends with Jacob. There'd been another clue—the business card I'd handed to Mustafa Barghouti. He'd spotted the Hebrew on it and guessed that I wasn't just a foreign journalist.

"Did you serve in the army?" he asked. I understood then that while my citizenship was, on some level, acceptable, having served in the army would be a red line, an absolute nonstarter to a romance.

"No, no," I said, passing the joint back to him, explaining that I hadn't been subject to the mandatory draft because of the simple fact that, when I'd become a citizen, I'd technically still been married.

I gave him the short version then: that Miguel and I had separated before I came to Israel to volunteer, that I'd intended to volunteer in Jaffa, but I'd seen these black-market kindergartens in south Tel Aviv that had broken my heart. That I started writing about migrants and, feeling that my presence in Israel would do more good than harm, that I'd decided to take citizenship, so I could continue to use my journalism to advocate for marginalized communities.

I told Mohamed how, when I'd become a citizen, I had to go to the Ministry of Interior to pick up my Israeli ID. I'd entered an office where a heavyset woman with short, spiky, bright-red hair sat at a large, imposing wooden desk. Behind her was an Israeli flag; on the wall, there was a framed photo of then-president Shimon Peres.

She held a blue Israeli ID in her hand. Israeli IDs come in a little plastic folder, and under the flag and the watchful eyes of Peres, the clerk had opened the ID, looked at the photo inside, and then turned her attention to me.

"So, Mya, you want to make *aliyah*?" she asked me in English, with a heavy Hebrew accent.

Aliyah means "ascension," and it's the term Israelis use for immigration. Only Jews can immigrate legally to the country, and new immigrants to the country are called *oleh hadashim*, literally "the newly risen."

But from everything I'd seen already, I wasn't rising up to something lofty, to some ideal, to some perfect place. No, the state of Israel was a mess. And I was taking citizenship in hopes that I could play a role, however small, in fixing things.

I told Mohamed how I'd tried to explain some of this to the clerk.

"No," I said, "*aliyah* is a political term I don't agree with. I'm becoming a citizen."

She did not look happy.

I stuck out my hand to receive the ID card, which she did not give me.

"Let's try this again," she said, tapping the ID card on the desk. "So, Mya, you want to make aliyah?"

"Yes," I said meekly. And then she handed the ID over, and I rushed out of the room.

Mohamed laughed.

I told him then how, ironically, getting Israeli citizenship had pushed my politics even further to the left. Before I had citizenship, I hadn't felt the need to take a stand on the conflict. But once I had that ID, once I was a part of this state, I felt a need to know as much as I could. I'd learned that Israel was depriving Palestinians of their human rights. And that wasn't good for any of us.

Mohamed passed me the joint, and we left it at that. Ali and Rihab's story hovered over both of us. The unrelenting machine of Israeli bureaucracy had made their relationship impossible. But alone in Mohamed's office overlooking Manara Square—suspended in the air—it was like nothing else existed, and we marveled at how brazenly Ali and Rihab had defied so many mores and taboos. Their bravery made us both feel like anything—even our crazy love—was possible.

* * *

By the time we finished the joint and chatted a bit, it was dark. The sound of vendors slamming their shutters, their padlocks clicking, echoed up from Manara Square. With the roads and sidewalks empty and quiet, I heard the streetlights buzzing. When the sound registered, my body jolted with the realization of how late it was. There's no Palestinian public transportation at night; if I waited any longer, I wouldn't be able to get back to Jerusalem.

"Oh no, I have to go," I said, gesturing outside, toward the dark. "The servees!"

Mohamed turned to look. "It's late. You'd better hurry," he said. "I'll walk you down."

We rushed down the stairs and stepped out onto Manara. The square was empty, so we passed that British mandate mailbox, rendered gray in the yellow lights, and walked up the street until Mohamed found a taxi and tucked me in, telling the driver to take me to Qalandia, tapping the roof after he'd closed the door.

But once we got to the checkpoint, there was no bus, no servees, no nothing. The place was totally quiet. I had no choice but to cross, even though it was technically illegal for me to do so here. As I walked toward the metal teeth of the turnstile, I braced myself by recalling that I'd crossed without problem the day Mohamed and I reported the *Boston Review* story. I remembered holding my ID up to the glass, the soldier glancing at it before waving me through, ignorant, perhaps, of the law. Or maybe he'd just taken me for one of the Palestinians from East Jerusalem, a group that is allowed to use Qalandia.

This is going to be OK, I told myself.

I plunked my stuff down on the x-ray machine's conveyor belt, walked toward the booth, and pressed my ID to the glass. The soldier looked up and did that double take—a look I'd seen at the A-Za'im checkpoint one afternoon just before a soldier pulled me aside for a quick interrogation. I knew immediately that I was in trouble.

He asked me where I was coming from.

Ramallah was off-limits, and I could have—should have—said I was coming from somewhere else, anywhere that was technically part of the Jerusalem municipality. I could have said I was coming from Kufar Aqab or even Qalandia camp. But if I was pressed for detail—a street, a contact—I wouldn't be able to come up with anything. And getting caught in a lie would only make things worse.

"Ramallah," I admitted.

"Ramallah?" the soldier repeated back to me. "What were you doing there?" he asked in Hebrew.

"I'm a journalist," I explained. "I was working on an article."

"A journalist, huh? Then show me your press pass," the soldier shot back.

"I don't have one," I said. "I'm a freelancer."

"Freelancers can get press passes, too," he responded.

In other moments, at other checkpoints, I'd found myself explaining the laws to soldiers who often don't know them. I'd found myself saying things like, "Yes, you've caught me here at this checkpoint, but I'm exiting Area B, which is, technically legal for me to be in," or "Yes, I'm leaving a Palestinian area, but it's in Area C, all of which is under Israeli control." But with this one, I sensed that there was no point in arguing and trying to explain that it was next to impossible for a freelancer to get a press pass and that it was extremely rare for me to actually need to show anyone a press pass. So I stood there, saying nothing, my hand and ID still pressed to the glass.

He popped a little drawer out like at the bank and asked me to put my *teudat zehut* in. I obliged, and it disappeared under the glass. And then a door opened, and a different soldier summoned me into a tiny room.

The joint hadn't worn off, and now, sitting between these two doors, my head spun. Which door had I entered through? The one on my right? Or the one on my left? Somewhere on the other side of the thin wall that stood between me and an unknown number of soldiers I couldn't see, I heard my ID number being repeated. But I could only hear one voice. Was the soldier making a phone call? Was he reporting my number? Or inquiring about it?

I heard my identity number being repeated again, now the numbers coming at me in disembodied Hebrew.

What was going to happen to me? Was I going to jail? And what would come after that? If I was stuck in jail, I might lose my job. I wasn't sure if they would arrest me, but at the very least, there could be fines to pay.

I sat there, high and increasingly disoriented as the seconds, minutes—hours?—ticked by. And then one of the two doors opened—was it the one that I came through? I didn't think so, but I wasn't sure. A hand, attached to an arm, the olive-green sleeve rolled up to the elbow, tossed my ID card in, onto the floor.

Not a word.

I picked it up and stood, not knowing what to do.

"You can go," a voice from nowhere said. I tried the door. It was locked.

"The second one," the voice said.

I tried it, and it opened. I gathered my things and exited the checkpoint, stepping into the dark.

I couldn't go through this a second time.

I promised myself that I wouldn't call Mohamed again.

8

But I couldn't stop thinking about him. I thought about the late afternoon light falling across his face when we stood outside of Birzeit, waiting for a servees, his hazel eyes looking magically backlit, glowing golden green. I thought about his reactions to our interviewees, how the emotion and empathy was plain on his face. I thought about those full lips and his smell.

I knew I'd fallen in love with him that day while we were interviewing, but I was conflicted. Part of me wanted to run to him; the other part of me was certain that I would be setting myself up for heartbreak.

But the human desire to love and be loved is strong, and that's why, a few months after we'd done that Al Jazeera story together, I found myself picking up the phone again, texting Mohamed, despite myself. Using journalism as a cover, I wrote that I had some ideas I wanted to kick around with him, which, technically, was true. I was working on some pitches for some new stories. But I could have finished them up on my own. When Mohamed invited me to come out to the office in Ramallah to bounce some ideas around together, I wondered if this was an excuse for him to see me, too.

So I made the trip out there. We spent the afternoon talking about the media. Mohamed was burned out on journalism, he said. He'd started to tire of it all even before the Arab Spring because he found journalism overwhelmingly negative and one-dimensional, with the media depicting Palestinians as either heroes or villains. "What if the media just depicted Palestinians as they are?" he asked. What if the media depicted Palestinians as ordinary people—complicated people, like all humans, but ordinary nonetheless—attempting to live ordinary lives in extraordinary circumstances? Mohamed wanted to start a good news media outlet, he said. But we both knew that would never fly in a profession where, "if it bleeds, it leads."

We talked politics, too, an issue that we were more or less aligned on, albeit for different reasons. We both believed that the only way to make real, lasting peace was by sharing the land. I'd arrived at this conclusion for pragmatic reasons. Oslo had been a failure, and the window for a two-state solution had closed. Today, there were half a million Israeli settlers in the West Bank, and they weren't going anywhere. And UN Resolution 194 guaranteed the Palestinian refugees' right to return. What else was there to do but to make a shared Israeli-Palestinian state that spanned the river to sea? Mohamed believed in one state because all the land was Palestine, he said. It couldn't be divided. But he'd also learned enough about the Holocaust to be sympathetic to the Jews, and he understood that the millions of Israelis who already lived here weren't going to just up and leave.

When I asked him about this thing that I'd heard—that the Palestinians want to push us into the sea—he clicked his tongue and shook his head. That was propaganda, he said. It wasn't the Palestinians who said that. It was the Egyptians. Regardless, a shared democratic state where everyone had equal rights was the only solution, he said.

Besides, Mohamed said with a smile, unshackling the land also meant liberating the Jews from a version of Zionism that oppressed not only others but the Jewish people themselves. This was a conclusion I'd come to on my own. It was something I thought about every time I crossed a checkpoint: in the process of enforcing the occupation—that is, in the process of dehumanizing an Other—young soldiers were losing their own humanity. And that was the great irony of the place. In this land that was supposed to set us free, we'd found something to chain ourselves to, curtailing our freedom.

Mohamed and I stepped out from the office to take a hummus lunch in a nearby restaurant. The hours flew by, and at the end, we hadn't settled conclusively on a story for me to pitch.

"I could come back out next Thursday?"

"That's a good idea," Mohamed said.

* * *

We started meeting almost every Thursday under the guise of journalism. And even though I dressed up and wore makeup for these meetings like they were dates, and even though the air crackled with sexual tension during our time together, we kept it strictly professional. After all, I still had a boyfriend in Israel. Not only had I gotten to know Mohamed well enough to know he wasn't down with cheating, I, too, didn't want to cheat on Oded. I didn't want my life to be any more complicated than it already was. And if Mohamed and I were going to enter a relationship, I wanted it to start on the right foot. I wanted everything to be aboveboard, virtuous, free of sin.

So we talked about history, politics, psychology, philosophy. We learned so much from each other; Mohamed broadened my perspective about the conflict. Not only was the PA not legitimate, he said, but that wasn't just because Abu Mazen had stayed on long past his term. The PLO had been started by the Arab nations and not even Palestinians themselves, he pointed out. "We have no real national movement," he told me, "and the national movement that we do have came from the outside. That's why the Jews are winning." I was intrigued. I loved his mind, the way he interrogated everything, just like me. I loved that Mohamed was willing to call into question even the holiest of the holies—the PLO.

Our conversations were exuberant, full of excited nodding and finishing each other's sentences. We got along so well; we started to believe that everyone else could, too. While the connection we were building with each other was very real, I wondered if it was something that could exist only in this little two-person bubble we were also creating. As long as we were alone together on the top floor of that building overlooking Manara Square—enveloped at once in the silence of Mohamed's office and the sounds of the street below, able to hear the world but detached from it—this one state of ours felt realistic. But we were suspending ourselves inside of a dream.

On one of those Thursdays, reality seeped back in when I lingered a little too long and, next thing I knew, it was dark outside.

How was I going to get back to Jerusalem? The buses had shut down hours ago. The servees, too. I wasn't going to chance getting caught at Qalandia again. The first time the soldiers had probably been teaching me a lesson by sticking me in that tiny room; surely there was some sort of record of me being there. I was certain the second time they caught me at Qalandia, I would be arrested. A taxi would be the only way out. It could circumvent the checkpoints that were for Palestinians only and could whisk me out through a settler checkpoint. It would be expensive, but Mohamed knew someone who would do this kind of thing.

He called, and after a year and a half of studying Arabic, I understood. "I've got a cousin here," he said on the phone, winking at me. "She needs to return to Jerusalem, but she needs to go out through Hizma."

"A cousin?" I asked, in English, when he hung up.

"That's what we call you guys, the Jews, sometimes," he said. "You come from Isaac; we come from Ishmael. You're our cousins."

A few minutes later, he walked me downstairs, put me in the taxi, reminding the driver again that this "cousin" couldn't go through Qalandia, telling him, *"Dir balak aleiha,"* take care of her.

As the car pulled away, I began to cry. I loved this guy.

My feelings were simple and uncomplicated. If only the circumstances were.

I knew that, while I had more privilege than the average Palestinian, it would be impossible for us to build a life together. I couldn't live legally in Ramallah. The odds were slim to none that Mohamed would be able to live with me in Israel, if he even wanted to. And there was no way I was going back to the United States. This tortured land was my home.

"*Shoo malik, ya amar* [What's wrong, moon]?" the driver asked, using the sort of term of endearment that a father would use with a child or a husband with a wife.

When I began to explain in my rough Arabic, he interrupted and said he spoke Hebrew. I switched languages and said, through my tears, that I was in love with Mohamed but that it would be impossible for us to ever be together.

The driver laughed. I wasn't the first Israeli girl he drove in and out of the territories to see her Palestinian boyfriend. He even ferried Israeli women—*married* to Palestinian men—in and out of the West Bank.

"*Metookah* [Sweetie]," he said, in Hebrew. "With love, everything is possible."

* * *

But I couldn't bring myself to break up with Oded—even though that studio was way too small for the two of us—so Mohamed and I found ourselves in a holding pattern. I kept up our Thursday meetings, even though they meant more time on the road. Getting on a bus or servees was the last thing I wanted to do. Between the commute to Ramallah and the commute to Abu Dis—and all the tension that came with going in and out of the West Bank, using some checkpoints legally, sneaking through others, worrying about soldiers all the while—I was exhausted.

I would take a room, I decided, in Abu Dis, where I would spend the workweek.

The university had a faculty dorm, and it would cost me next to nothing to live there. I would spend the weekends at home, in Jerusalem. Oded thought I was crazy; he offered to buy me pepper spray, so I could protect myself if someone figured out who I was and attacked me.

As usual, I bristled and called him a racist. But, to Oded's point, Adnan, the Palestinian administrator on campus who did the paperwork for the dorm and who procured my key, also thought my move was totally nuts. Legal, yes—technically speaking, there was no law forbidding me from living in Abu Dis—but, as an Israeli, it was crazy for me to move to a Palestinian village.

When I visited Adnan in his office, the door was open, and of course, as he was a man and I was a woman, it remained open as we both filled out the appropriate forms. And then he asked me for my ID. I hesitated.

I was a Bard employee, and before that point, all the paperwork I'd done had been on the American side. I hadn't filled out anything here at the Palestinian university. Knowing my American passport lacked a visa and that Adnan would probably ask for one, I realized there was only one thing for me to do. I put my blue teudat zehut on the desk, and Adnan gasped, looked around the room to make sure none of his officemates saw anything, and slid it under a sheet of paper. Too worried about attracting attention to shush me, Adnan put a finger to his lips and held that finger—an exclamation point—against his mouth, his eyebrows raised for emphasis.

When he finished the paperwork, he glanced around to make sure no one was looking at us and slid my ID back to me. I slipped it into my purse and followed him out to the parking lot to his car. He had a master key for my room but didn't have a spare to give me. We would have to go into the village to get one made.

Once we were in the car, with the doors closed and windows up, Adnan had so many questions. I gave him the short version—explaining how I'd come to Israel and taken citizenship so I could stay in the country, work as a journalist, and tell the stories of those who don't usually appear in the media. I told him about the left-wing Israeli-Palestinian organization I'd worked for. Adnan knew the NGO well, and he nodded enthusiastically.

I told Adnan about starting at the university and the commute from West Jerusalem and how, at the checkpoint, a female soldier had pulled me aside, concerned I'd been kidnapped. I told him about how physically and mentally exhausting it was to go back and forth from West Jerusalem to the West Bank every day.

"You are most welcome here," Adnan told me, adding that he personally was opposed to the idea of Jews and Palestinians living separately in separate states. He believed in one state and that we could live together in peace.

"In the early days, I was DFLP," he told me, referring to the Democratic Front for the Liberation of Palestine. "But now, I'm a Fatah man, because I have a family and I need a job." Everything out here in the West Bank was connected somehow to Fatah, the ruling party that filled the ranks of the PA. And, of course, it was the PA that paid the wages of the university employees. So if Adnan didn't support the party—or at least pretend to—he could find himself unemployed.

As we bumped along over a road, Adnan gestured toward some yellow Fatah flags hanging from a building and muttered a particularly colorful curse—*coos emek,* Arabic for "your mother's vagina."

"We say that one in Hebrew, too," I told Adnan.

"I know," he said, laughing, and I joined in.

* * *

The faculty dorm was one floor in a building known as al burj, the tower, because it was relatively new and, standing at fourteen stories, it was one of the highest structures—if not *the* highest structure—in Abu Dis. Al burj stood on the edge of the village; there was something forlorn about the place. While the lower floors housed a few offices, the tower was barely inhabited. Much of the building was unfinished, a concrete shell waiting for someone to come tile the floors and paint the walls and put in cabinets and lights and all the things that made a place usable.

Reaching the faculty dorm meant taking an elevator up past all these empty spaces to the thirteenth floor, which was finished, but barebones. The floors were tiled, the walls were painted, but that was about it. The kitchen, which lacked cabinets, was equipped with a sink, a stove that didn't work properly (the range was fine, but the oven wouldn't heat up), and a plastic table and chairs. The living room consisted of a few scratchy, overstuffed brown sofas, and an ancient TV that got just a few stations. My room was cavernous and held a desk made out of particle board, a twin bed, another uncomfortable, overstuffed brown sofa—a reject from the living room, I suppose—and a very basic manufactured wooden cabinet for my clothes. There was no fan or AC, only a space heater and a window that offered a view of the edge of the village and the foothills beyond. I kept the window open for fresh air and, at night I often couldn't sleep because of the chorus of barking dogs and howling jackals, their voices echoing through the Judean mountains.

Spending half the week in Abu Dis was at once less and more confusing than commuting between Jewish West Jerusalem and the West Bank. When I was in the village, I was completely immersed: My students were Palestinian. My colleagues were, by and large, Palestinian. The children I passed on the street on my way to and from campus every day? Palestinian. The stand where I stopped to buy vegetables? Obviously the vendor there was Palestinian, too. The owner and employees of the grocery store where I picked up staples like coffee and milk—they were Palestinian. The guy I bought my pita from was Palestinian.

Dressed appropriately for the village—covered from my collarbone to my ankles not because I hoped to pass but out of respect for the locals' norms—I moved through the streets undisturbed. The people I interacted with tolerated and even complimented my Arabic. On some level, I felt like part of this place.

So, one afternoon, when an Israeli army jeep came tearing down the street in the middle of the village and everyone around me bent over to pick up a stone to throw at the vehicle, I found myself moving in time with the bodies around me. And then I caught myself, and I gasped as I considered the boys inside that jeep: fellow Jews who celebrated the same holidays as I did. Out of their mouths came the language that I'd resurrected myself in, Hebrew. I thought about the chai I'd worn as a child and the silver necklace I'd gotten in Tel Aviv that bore my name, מאיה.

I stood, my hands empty, and watched the jeep skid around the corner as local boys pelted it with stones.

And then I went back to Jerusalem for the weekend, where I was completely surrounded by Israelis and immersed, once again, in Hebrew. It felt like I was living a double life. My hope had been that the room in Abu Dis would ease this conflict that I felt between my Israeliness and my increasing identification with the Palestinians. But that room in Abu Dis, and the sense of belonging I felt in the West Bank, only left me feeling more confused.

My politics, which Oded had already found extreme, seemed even wilder to him now that they went beyond teaching at a Palestinian university and studying Arabic and writing stories about the occupation. I was *living* there, in the West Bank. Intent on improving my Arabic, I often listened to Arabic music at home; when Oded would return from work, he would enter and give me a weary look. And when, ahead of a Halloween party, I'd dyed my graying auburn hair a few shades darker to complete my Amy Winehouse costume, Oded had announced, "You look like an Arab." When I'd maintained the color because it complimented my skin tone and covered my grays, Oded had gotten louder with his objections, just as he criticized me for getting a tan every summer. "Don't get too dark," he always said.

I don't want to elide complexity here. Oded had actually come a long way, politically speaking. All those times he'd sat next to me, helping me translate interviews from Hebrew to English, had made him aware of issues he hadn't known about. Curious, he'd started reading and learning on his own; he'd discovered the writing of an Israeli dissident, Yossi Gurvitz, and had become a big fan. I'd dragged Oded to protests inside of Israel, mostly demonstrations against the deportation of migrant workers' children. I'd even managed to drag him to a protest in the West Bank in a Palestinian village called Susiya, which was threatened with demolition, so he could see with his own eyes what was happening here. He'd been shocked and upset and he'd disavowed nationalism of any kind.

So his politics had changed quite a bit since we'd started dating, but still, my decision to live in Abu Dis was taking it all to another level in Oded's mind. And I think Oded correctly sensed that this other place, Palestine, was pulling me away from him, from us, from the place we lived and the people we lived among. He could never admit these feelings to me as it would point toward the nationalism he'd sworn off.

One Friday morning, when I was back in West Jerusalem, we went to the market as we had so many times. In Israel, the weekend starts

Thursday night, and it's almost like a national ritual: shopping and *sponja*, "mopping the floor," on *yom shishi*, Friday, ahead of Shabbat. We forgot our little grocery buggy but stocked up on food, anyway. On the light rail, on our way back out to our tiny studio in Kiryat Yovel, Oded complained endlessly about helping me carry the bags. He hammed it up as we stepped off the train. Slumping his shoulders, his head sagging forward, he held the bags low to the ground, as though they were too heavy, as though they were a great burden.

In that moment, I understood how much this relationship was a burden to both of us.

We wanted different things: He never wanted to get married; I knew, at some point in the future, I wanted to try marriage out again. Oded was determined not to have children, and I wanted five. I loved Oded dearly but like a brother. This wasn't a match. What had started out as a ten-month language-exchange, friends-with-benefits kind of thing had stretched into five years.

As I took the groceries from Oded's hands and shimmied my arms through the plastic handles—"I'll take them," I told him in Hebrew—I thought about all the times fear had rendered me passive, trapping me in relationships that prevented me from being vulnerable and taking emotional risks.

Since leaving the US, I had faced so many fears. But most of them revolved around my physical safety. I'd traveled to Lebanon and Syria. I'd gone to protests in the West Bank. I'd run from live ammunition. I'd shed the last of my doubts about my ability to keep my body safe. Now I had to face my fear of being alone.

When we were inside the studio, I finally broke up with Oded.

We agreed to use the studio like a timeshare, with him going to his parents' house when I came back. But on Sunday, I took a big suitcase with me to Abu Dis. I wouldn't just stay here, in *al burj*, during the week. I would pass *yom shishi* and Shabbat here, too. However isolated, however alone.

9

Despite the fact that I was single now, my relationship with Mohamed still wasn't romantic. I sensed that Mohamed liked me, but concerned he would reject me because I was technically an Israeli, I didn't make a move. And I knew enough about his family to guess that they wouldn't be thrilled if their eldest son brought home an Israeli girlfriend; I figured that Mohamed's concerns about his family were holding him back. So we kept up the facade of being colleagues.

One afternoon, as I traveled from Abu Dis to Ramallah, where Mohamed and I were working on a story, I noticed a mushrooming of new buildings in a Palestinian village called Kufr Aqab. It seemed like every time I passed, there was a new tower going up. What was going on here? Why was this place booming?

I did some research and learned that this once idyllic village—now densely populated and full of towers built without permits—revealed much about the pressures Israeli policies put on the Palestinian residents of East Jerusalem. Palestinians were moving out here to this area beyond the wall but, technically, inside the municipality of Jerusalem because it was more affordable and they believed it was a way to hold on to their Jerusalem residency. Even though this area was under Israeli control, the Israeli authorities neglected Kufr Aqab; the infrastructure was stretched to the breaking point. I successfully pitched the piece to Al Jazeera and began reporting the story of Kufr Aqab, half a decade before a mainstream media outlet or two would notice what was happening out here and follow suit.

Mohamed helped set up an interview with a local neighborhood committee that was attempting to address the village's growing problems. When we went out there to interview the head of the committee, the man made small talk, asking me numerous questions about myself and what brought me to the topic of Kufr Aqab. That's how he pieced my story together: an American Israeli who *lived* in Abu Dis and taught at a Palestinian university. What a curiosity! He picked up his phone and called another one of the men on the committee, urging him to come meet me. Feeling safe here with Mohamed and these men, I didn't worry about people knowing who I was.

And I wasn't the sort of journalist who plowed through questions and refused to answer any from her interviewees. Building relationships in these communities would help me do a better job covering them. Not only was I curious about how the second man would react to me and my life story, I was also happy to serve as an example for this man: I was living proof that there were Jews who didn't want to set themselves apart from the Palestinians but who believed that we could live together, house-to-house, door-to-door.

The second man showed up. A Palestinian East Jerusalemite who spoke Hebrew, as many Palestinians who work inside of Israel do, he dove into a conversation with me. What was supposed to be a relatively quick visit to discuss Kufr Aqab's problems and the committee's proposed solutions turned into a couple of hours of sitting with these two men, one of whom was trying to convert me to Islam. I nodded and smiled all the while.

Mohamed, deeply secular and tired of the whole thing, leaned in close and whispered, "Don't you know how to redirect an interview?"

"This guy is my elder," I said, referring to the man who was hosting us. "I'm showing him respect."

Mohamed raised his palms to me. "OK. As you wish." He smiled to himself, leaned back in his chair, rolled a cigarette, and puffed away. I found his remark condescending, but whatever irritation I felt quickly fell away. If he was feeling impatient, that was his problem, not mine. I didn't feel any pressure to make him happy by hurrying things along.

Though I wasn't going to convert to Islam, just listening to this man's case was a way of showing him I respected him. And it was a way of proving to myself—and Mohamed—that we could all live together. The lesson wasn't lost on Mohamed. While he was annoyed with the visit on a professional level, later he would tell me that day was a turning point for him emotionally. That I was patient, open-minded, and tolerant with the men signaled to Mohamed that maybe I would be able to deal with life in the West Bank; maybe, Mohamed thought, our love was possible.

It was then that Mohamed decided he was going to put his feelings—he was going to put himself—on the line.

* * *

After I finally got my questions in and we'd been served baklava and coffee—the latter being the sign that our host was ready for us to leave—we bid the men goodbye and stepped into the dusk outside. It was too late for me to get back to Abu Dis, and we stood on the shoulder of the main road, Qalandia camp and checkpoint to our right, at the bottom of the hill, cars lurching over the speed bump, kicking up sand and dust as they sped toward Ramallah. When a break in the traffic came, we darted across the street to a clump of buildings that included a pizza joint.

Inside, we followed the waiter up a narrow staircase, where he offered us a table facing the window. I took a seat and was surprised when Mohamed sat down next to me. He was wearing that blue sweater again—the same one he'd worn the first time we'd reported together—and I sensed the warmth of his body. I looked down at his knee, covered by his jeans, and I remembered grabbing his leg when the servees lurched forward that day. I remembered the electricity that had shot up my arm when I'd held onto his knee to steady myself and how I'd snatched my hand away. Now here was his knee again. So close to mine. I wanted to grab it, but I couldn't, of course.

Heat rose from my chest to my face, and I turned my head so Mohamed couldn't see me blushing. The tension of wanting to touch him but knowing I couldn't was unbearable, the quiet between us so loaded, that I was relieved to hear the waiter's footsteps on the stairs.

The waiter appeared, breaking our uncomfortable silence with a menu. I read the Arabic, we quickly ordered, and night fell as we looked out the window, chatting about Kufr Aqab and the men's attempts to convert me to Islam. I explained to Mohamed that I didn't find any conflict between my identity and living among Muslims. I could listen and learn from conversion attempts, but at the end of the day, I could stay Jewish. "You know," Mohamed said, nodding, "one of the prophet Muhammad's neighbors was a Jew."

We also discussed Al Andalus, Muslim Spain, the cultural center during Islam's golden age; at the university, our spring semester curriculum included a unit about Al Andalus, which I was teaching at the time. Muslim Spain had been a place of peaceful coexistence and cultural exchange: Jews had thrived there, and that fertile environment of cross-pollination had left fingerprints on everything from Hebrew poetry to Jewish religious philosophy. We talked, too, about the fact that, historically speaking, the Jewish people had fared better in the Muslim and Arab world than they had among the Christians. No, things hadn't been perfect. But we'd been safer with the Arabs than we'd been in Europe. There we were, again, drifting out of the harsh reality of our present, slipping into the fantasy of another time, another place, another life without conflict, without occupation.

I relaxed into my chair. Stretching my feet forward, I crossed them at the ankle and looked out the window, watching the headlights flash skyward as cars jerked over the speed bump. I felt optimistic. I was at ease next to Mohamed and comfortable in this new life. I loved my job, I loved my students, I liked the air in Abu Dis, I liked walking to campus every morning through the village, and I liked being called "Professora."

I liked the vegetable stand and the grocery store and chatting with the man who worked there who'd grown up in Michigan but had *chosen* to come back here—to the West Bank, however troubled—where the air was sweet and the views were sweeping, where, if you looked the right way, you could see beyond the borders all the way to Jordan.

* * *

With Palestinian public transportation closed, I called Sarah, an American woman and my boss at the university. I knew she was out in Ramallah that day, finishing research for her dissertation about former Palestinian political prisoners who'd done time in Israeli jails. She was wrapping up, and though she couldn't take me to Abu Dis, I could ride with her to Jerusalem.

With time to kill before Sarah picked me up, Mohamed suggested we go to Café La Vie, a Ramallah spot popular with young, liberal Palestinians and foreigners. We took a servees into the city and walked along a tree-lined street to La Vie, where we grabbed a table in a corner and ordered drinks: wine for me, beer for Mohamed.

The waiter plunked a bowl of peanuts down on the table. Here we were, sitting side by side again. Lost in my own desire, I found myself at a loss for words.

"Look, the reason we keep having these awkward pauses is because we like each other," Mohamed said.

"I don't know what you're talking about," I said, plucking a peanut from the bowl, rubbing the red skin off, and snapping it into impossibly small pieces. His comment frightened me because it opened the door to so many feelings; I busied myself with the peanuts, stripping them, pulling the two halves apart, breaking the sides into successively tinier pieces until they were as small as I could get them. I dropped the pieces and started again.

Mohamed watched me destroying the peanuts for a moment before continuing. "We can give dating a try," he said. "But I can't make you any promises. I don't know if it's going to work, and I'm not optimistic, you know, because of our ID situation." Some families might accept a Jewish Israeli woman, he said, if her politics were right. But his family, he explained, would be totally opposed to the match.

I felt tears forming in the corners of my eyes, and my lip began to quiver. Oh God, I can't cry here.

I *liked* this guy. And this was different from my relationships with Miguel and Oded—I'd simply gone with the flow and fallen into those relationships because they were easy and they had allowed me to hide out from the world, from life, rather than facing it head-on. But with Mohamed, I had to make a conscious decision about whether to pursue this relationship that would be a fight upstream, a fight against so much, against circumstances completely beyond our control. That would demand that I cross checkpoints where I might be apprehended by the military—my own army—just to reach him. That demanded that I risk detention and arrest just for a date. If Miguel and Oded had been the default because both relationships had been easy and offered safety, this was the exact opposite. If true love meant taking risks and making oneself vulnerable, well, then, this was it.

Flooded with emotion, not wanting to cry in public, I excused myself and went to the bathroom, where I pulled myself together.

Returning to the table, I sat down and stuck my fingers back in the pile of peanuts. "OK," I said, nodding. "OK. Let's try."

That was the moment that Sarah showed up.

"Whoa," she said loudly as she strode toward our table, a camel-colored coat draped over her arm, her straight, dark hair framing her face. Her eyes drifted toward my fingers, the ground-up peanuts. "Looks intense. What's going on here? Are you two getting married or something?" she asked, laughing at her own joke.

"Not yet," we said in unison.

Surprised, we looked at each other and smiled.

"Awwww, you two are *such* lovebirds," Sarah said, still standing, her coat still hanging from her arm. She rolled her eyes. "I hate to break up the party, but I have to get back to Jerusalem, Mya. You coming?"

I stood and said goodbye to Mohamed. He stood, too. It was awkward. We had just decided to date, and yet because we were in public, we couldn't show each other any sort of affection. So, in lieu of a kiss, I offered him my hand—just as I had that first night we met at Beit Anisa in 2011. He looked down at my waiting palm, grinned, and squeezed my hand tight.

"*What* was going on there?" Sarah asked me as soon as we were outside La Vie.

I told her everything as I followed her to the car: about our day reporting, about getting stuck at the interviewee's house in Kufar Aqab, about eating pizza and sitting on the same side of the table and what he said about the awkward silences and how we'd decided to date despite our IDs.

"I know you like him, Mya. But you're getting yourself into a mess," Sarah said as we left Ramallah and the car lurched downhill toward Kufr Aqab. Sarah herself had been married to an Egyptian man she'd met in Cairo; the two had just filed for divorce. Mentioning the cultural differences that she and her husband had struggled with, she added that it would be much harder for Mohamed and me to have a relationship because of the occupation. "Think this through a bit. If it works—and it probably won't, these things never do—but if it *does* work, where would you guys even live?"

She had a point. According to Israeli law, I couldn't enter, much less live in, Area A. And Israeli policy would make it difficult—if not impossible—for us to live inside together.

"Who's talking about living together? I'm just trying to get the guy into bed," I joked.

Sarah laughed. "Seriously?"

"Sarah," I said, "I *like* him. I really like him."

Sarah knew about Miguel. She knew how I'd stayed with him for all the wrong reasons. Without me telling her, Sarah understood the importance of me actively pursuing a relationship, even one that came with risks, because it was a relationship that I actually wanted, a relationship that hadn't fallen into my lap, that wasn't transactional, that was about one thing and one thing only: love.

"OK, but I don't want to see you get hurt."

Eager to change the subject, I pointed toward Qalandia, looming on the horizon, growing larger as we drew closer. "Remember, I can't go out that way," I said. "Make sure you take Hizma."

10

One Friday, after spending the night in Jerusalem, I headed out to Ramallah so I could see Mohamed before continuing to Abu Dis, where I would spend the weekend. With the Jewish holiday of Purim near, I picked up some *oznei Haman*—the cookies we eat for the occasion—and a bottle of screw-top wine to take with me. Mohamed and I had agreed to have a picnic to celebrate the holiday, unhooked from the political meaning it had taken on in Israel.

After I met him at the office, we took a taxi out to the edge of Ramallah, and then Mohamed led me into an olive grove. From his backpack, he produced a blanket; from mine, I took out the cookies, wine, and plastic cups. I explained Purim to Mohamed in broad brushstrokes—telling him the story of Esther, an undercover Jew who saved her people from destruction—including the idea that you're supposed to drink until you can't tell an enemy from a friend. We toasted to that.

As we sipped wine and looked out over the olive trees, Mohamed pointed down the hill, toward a spot on the horizon that I couldn't see. "There's a settlement over there," he said, adding that, sometimes, settlers came into this orchard and burned trees. He stood, helping me up, and as we walked through the grove together, he pointed out damaged trees. For a moment, an image flitted through my head: settlers, men, emerging from the trees and finding me, a Jewish woman, with a Palestinian man. Inside Israel, Jewish vigilante groups beat Arabs for dating "our girls"; as a journalist, I had covered a rally that was organized specifically to protest mixed relationships. For a second, I realized that even here, in this peaceful olive grove, we could both be in danger.

But the brightness of the day made it easy for me to push such dark thoughts away. It was the end of February, and there wasn't a cloud in the sky. Above me, I saw that particular blue that only comes in winter, the color that looks like God has thrown his arms back to let the sky soar. A breeze tickled the olive leaves—gray on one side, silver on the other—rendering them a shimmering sea. The sound of the leaves flipping reminded me of rain, and as I stopped to listen, I turned my face toward the sun, closing my eyes for a moment. When I opened them, Mohamed was leaning against a boulder, rolling a cigarette. Joining him, I stood close, feeling the warmth of his body next to mine.

And then, from Ramallah, the call to prayer sounded, rippling down the hill, bouncing off the stones, reverberating through my body. This moment, this place, the context, the settlements—none of it mattered. The call to prayer reminded me of something bigger that existed outside of all that, and I felt that we, too, existed separately from this world. Mohamed tipped his head toward mine, as though he was listening to me, and nuzzled my cheek with his chin. Realizing he was too shy to just go for it, I turned my mouth toward his. He pulled me close then, our stomachs touching, as our lips met, and we kissed for the first time.

* * *

Two days after our first kiss, Mohamed's cousin Arafat died in an Israeli jail cell.

Arafat, who was only thirty years old, had been arrested on suspicion of throwing stones at Israeli soldiers. He had been taken to prison, where the Israelis tortured him during his interrogation. And then he died, leaving a pregnant wife and two young children behind.

When I saw the news, I picked up my phone to text Mohamed. But what do you say to your Palestinian boyfriend when your countrymen have just killed his cousin?

I saw the news. I'm so fucking sorry.

Thank you, he responded. *There will be a funeral in the village. I will go.*

I monitored the news even more obsessively than usual. The funeral was covered by major outlets; when I saw the photos of the thousands of people surrounding Arafat's body, the corpse wrapped in a Palestinian flag aloft on the crowd as they ferried it to its final resting place, I searched for Mohamed's face.

Holding an Israeli ID made me a symbol—or even a part of—the state that had taken his cousin's life away. I didn't want to intrude while he was grieving, but I wanted to let him know I was there for him. Not knowing what to do, I messaged him: *How are you?*

I'm okay, he answered. *I went to the funeral today. It was very sad.*

I told him again that I was sorry and let him know I was here for him if he wanted to talk. Mohamed didn't respond. Yeah, if I was him, I wouldn't want to speak to me right now, either, I thought. And if he did text or call, what could I possibly say? What comfort could I offer him? What did it matter what my politics were or where I lived or worked? No beliefs could resurrect his cousin; no ideology could change the fact that Mohamed's kin had died in an Israeli prison and that I was a citizen of the state.

I checked my phone again. Nothing. That's it, I thought, my heart sinking in my chest; we're through.

11

So I was surprised when, a few days after Arafat's funeral, I stepped out of the university's gates to find Mohamed waiting for me, wearing an olive-green jacket and aviator sunglasses. Here, in public, in this conservative village, he didn't even offer me his hand. Instead, he grinned, and though he didn't say it, in his smile, I sensed that seeing me didn't upset him. Rather, it was a relief for Mohamed, not a reminder of the occupation but an escape from it.

Resisting the urge to take him in my arms, I offered a chaste hello, and we began to walk, Mohamed holding his hands behind his back—a posture, I would later learn, he'd picked up from his father.

There wasn't much to do in the village other than have lunch at a place my colleagues at AQB jokingly called Hamas Hummus—nicknamed thus because the men who worked there had posted the four-fingered sign

Egyptian protesters used to signal their support for the Muslim Brotherhood—so we headed there. After having hummus and *chai ma nana*, "tea with mint," we took a long, looping walk together through the village. Not daring to touch or hold hands, Mohamed keeping his hands behind his back the whole while.

Abu Dis wasn't the most scenic place. Yes, many of the buildings were made of the same limestone that made Jerusalem shine white in the sun. But out here, beyond the wall, without any green spaces, with the houses and businesses smooshed right up to the dusty road, the buildings didn't glimmer as they reflected the sunlight. They reflected, rather, the grayness of the street and the litter and the dirt, lending the village a tired, sooty look.

But, then, suddenly, between two buildings, I glimpsed a slice of a rolling green valley. The contrast between the village, which seemed swathed in gray, made this verdant sliver all the more striking.

"Look, look!" I exclaimed, pointing.

In my excitement, I grabbed Mohamed's arm. It was strong and firm—Mohamed was so real, so present, so close to me—and yet, remembering that I wasn't supposed to touch him, I yanked my hand away. And so we stood, side by side, on the shoulder of a dusty road, marveling at that little slip of green. Suddenly, our date felt magical, like we could at once delight in Abu Dis and transcend it if only we looked in the right spots.

* * *

This is how the early days of our courtship unfolded.

We fell into a rhythm of Mohamed coming to Abu Dis once a week and me going to Ramallah once a week. But between Hamas Hummus, another restaurant, and walking through the village, we quickly exhausted our Abu Dis date options. So I started taking Mohamed to *al burj*, "the tower," where we could sip tea on the roof and look out over the Judean Hills toward Jordan, Mohamed reminiscing about his childhood there, about his school friends—his best friends had been a set of twins—and the stupid pranks they played and the trouble they got into. He told me about going to the PLO offices with his father and how proud he'd felt to accompany his dad to work and how the secretaries had doted on him. He told me how there had been this constant parade of visitors to the family home and how his parents had followed to the letter all the strict cultural mores around receiving visitors. They'd served meat to all these people even though they couldn't really afford it—sometimes Mohamed's father had borrowed money so he could buy meat for their guests—and his mom had spent hours upon hours cooking for their visitors. Carrying out the huge, heavy trays of food had damaged her back, Mohamed said, adding that he'd also felt neglected while his parents did all this entertaining. That was part of what had turned him off from the culture at a young age. All the obligation, all the sacrifice. All the preordained roles and rules. Mohamed believed in freedom.

Mohamed told me that, because he'd been very bright, his family had tightened their already tight belt so he could go to private school. But there, he'd felt weird because all his classmates were wealthy. And though he'd had friends at school, he always knew he was different. I could commiserate. Though I'd gone to a public high school, many of its students came from the wealthiest areas of Gainesville; a lot of my friends were rich kids, and there was always this invisible, unarticulated divide between us.

We'd both been outsiders. And though moving to the West Bank was a return home for Mohamed, of course—and he'd spent many summers in Sa'ir with his mom and his brothers—he'd continued to feel like something of an outsider here, too. Because his accent was a little funny from growing up in Jordan, sometimes other Palestinians would ask him where he was from, an exchange I witnessed on numerous occasions.

"*Min hon* [From here]," he would answer, bristling.

"But you have a white accent," would be the response, the phrase referring to a sort of plain, generic, nonregional accent—an oddity in a place where accents and vocabulary could vary greatly from one village to the next. By one's accent and word choice, Palestinians could start to read each other from the moment they met, immediately pegging the person in front of them to a place and, sometimes, by extension, to a family.

"You have a white accent" was a comment that chafed Mohamed's nerves. It was ironic, right? He had a nonspecific accent because he'd had the quintessential Palestinian experience: exile. He'd grown up in Jordan, because his father had made the ultimate sacrifice for the Palestinian people—he'd joined the PLO and gotten deported. And then people had the nerve to ask Mohamed where he was from.

We also talked a lot about history—the real goals of the old-school Palestinian revolution was one of Mohamed's favorite topics. And though we both called ourselves secular, we talked about religion. I'd read the Quran twice, which was exactly double the amount of times that Mohamed had read it, and we talked a lot about Islam, which Mohamed felt had been corrupted by the Saudis. We talked about the parallels between Islam and Judaism—both of us agreeing that us Jews and Muslims ultimately had more in common with each other than we did with the Christians—and we talked about the future of this land and what we imagined the place could be.

What language would we all speak? we mused.

English, Hebrew, and Arabic. All of them, we decided.

Our conversations were one big language exchange as we shared Hebrew and Arabic words with each other, remarking on the similarities and differences.

And I told him what I wanted from life, my four Rs. I wanted to read, write, run, and raise a bunch of kids. Five.

"You don't want five kids," he said, smiling, shaking his head. He was the eldest of five. His parents hadn't had any time for any of them.

What I wanted from life was relatively simple, and Mohamed liked that; he, too, wanted a simple life. He felt that I was earnest and joyful and saw that I had a knack for carving out joy everywhere I went. Though he wasn't crazy about Abu Dis, he liked that we managed to have lovely dates there, despite the fact that they often took place on the scratchy brown couches that were crowded into the dismal living room of a half-completed building.

Sometimes we took to the communal kitchen. As I cooked lunch for us, Mohamed told me more about his family, which made me uncomfortable because already I had the sense that I was never going to actually meet them.

But his stories about his family also endeared him to me and helped me understand him better. Mohamed's little sister was his parents' fifth child, and she'd been born when Mohamed was eighteen. He'd picked her name and helped his mom take care of her when she was a baby. He was gentle and calm, and it was easy for me to imagine him with his little sister; it was easy for me to imagine him being a warm, caring father someday.

But now his sister wasn't a baby anymore. Already the parents of young men who hoped to marry his sister had shown up at his family's door. Mohamed's father had turned all these potential matches away. The family agreed that Mohamed's sister would finish her education first, and then she would do as she pleased. I understood that Mohamed wasn't some traditional, patriarchal, conservative guy. Women could and should stand on their own, he said; men shouldn't tell them what to do. For Mohamed, it wasn't just about gender roles. It was about freedom. Having lived under the three occupations—the Israelis, the PA, and the conservative, Palestinian culture—Mohamed believed everyone needed to have control over their own lives. Everyone had to be masters of their own destinies.

And that was one of the reasons he was dating me—Mohamed wouldn't let society or politics or his family or anything else dictate to him whom he could date, whom he could fall in love with. He was keenly aware that, on the one hand, many Palestinians called for liberation while maintaining an oppressive culture. Liberation, he believed, had to be absolute and for everyone. Women included.

Though we believed in liberation and freedom and making our own choices, and though we badly wanted to go to bed together, we were still up against the reality of the fact that we were in the middle of a conservative Arab village. So we didn't dare to get physical on these dates, even when we were alone on the roof of the building. And I was too scared to sneak Mohamed into my room because Adnan had a habit of popping by al burj to say hello.

On one occasion, my colleague who also lived in the dorm—a young Mexican American poet I affectionately called Professor Tomas—and I decided to cook lunch for Mohamed. Adnan happened to show up as we were sitting down to eat. Professor Tomas quickly claimed Mohamed as his guest, and Mohamed looked down at his lap, studying his hands, avoiding eye contact with Adnan as he paced through the kitchen—back and forth, back and forth—the heels of his dress shoes clicking on the linoleum floor.

But I found it even more uncomfortable when Adnan showed up when Mohamed *wasn't* there. Many Palestinians, men in particular, view *ajnabiyaat*, "foreign women," as fast and loose, easy to bed and free of the commitments and complications that come with local ladies. Was Adnan popping in to keep a protective eye on me? Or did he have his eye on something else? He'd dropped hints, mentioning that his wife lived with his children in another part of East Jerusalem that was inside the wall and that he spent the week out here in Abu Dis alone. And so Adnan's presence, which I'd initially found comforting, became something that caused me a lot of anxiety. What if he popped into the building when I was completely alone, when all of my colleagues were gone?

Like Adnan, the whole village was always watching everything. One afternoon, a Palestinian colleague I'd become friends with, Reema, had me over for lunch; the next time I'd visited, Reema told me her neighbor had showed up shortly after I'd left, asking about the *ajnabiyah*, "the foreign woman." Reema confessed that she wasn't a fan of the monitoring and gossip and that it impacted her life in real ways—for example, she longed to go out for a run or walk but couldn't do so because the neighbors would talk.

"Even if you cover?" I asked. Like many Palestinian women, Reema wore the hijab.

"Yes," she said. Covered or not, the movement of running or even taking a brisk walk—with all that jiggling and shaking—would be considered provocative. Even before Reema articulated all this to me, I'd sensed that running through the village was a no-no, and I hadn't dared to exercise. Instead, I marched up and down the concrete stairwell of the burj, which was eerie as the middle half of the building was unfinished. And though I felt free in Abu Dis in ways I hadn't in Jerusalem—mainly because Mohamed could reach me here and I didn't feel conflicted because I wasn't going through the checkpoint every day—in other ways, I began to feel confined.

* * *

There were other things I was self-conscious about, like taking phone calls from Oded. He called one day, just before Passover, as I was walking alone from campus back to the burj.

When I answered, Oded asked me, in Hebrew, if I had plans for the holiday.

Conscious of the fact that I was walking through a Palestinian village, I answered him in English, telling him I didn't.

"Do you want to come for the holiday?" Oded asked, adding that his mother had told him to invite me.

"Does she know we broke up?" I asked.

"*Barur* [Of course]," he answered. "But she wants me to tell you that she still considers you a daughter of the house. You're part of us."

I walked in silence for a moment, not knowing what to say. Part of me desperately wanted to go. As a child, we hadn't done anything for Passover beyond putting some matzah on the table. Since I'd arrived in Israel, I'd spent every Passover with Oded and his family. It was there, in their home in Beit HaKerem—at a long table, full of food and family, including Oded's uncle, who was a rabbi—that I learned all the rhythms and rituals of Pesach. And with the holiday upon us, I longed for my people.

But I also felt conflicted. Every year, the Israeli army shut down the West Bank for Passover, curtailing Palestinians' already restricted freedom of movement. Part of me felt that it would be hypocritical to live and work in the West Bank—to throw in my lot with these people in so many ways—only to zip back into Israel and enjoy the holiday while they were all out here under closure. How to explain all of this to Oded? And as I was walking through the village?

"Mya," Oded said. "*At sham*?" (Are you there?)

"*Ken*," I said, forgetting where I was for a moment, accidentally letting the Hebrew word slip. "Yes," I said, correcting myself.

"So do you want to come?"

"I can't," I said.

"Why not?"

"I just can't."

"*At betucha*, Mya?" (Are you sure?)

I told him I was.

* * *

But I couldn't just let the holiday pass; I decided to celebrate it in Abu Dis instead, in the burj. Because the Jewish day begins at sundown, Passover—like all the holidays—starts at nightfall, and the seder, the ritual meal, is held in the evening. I invited Mohamed, but he wouldn't be able to make it because he would have no way to get back to Ramallah at night. So there, in the communal kitchen, Professor Tomas and I had a small Passover seder, complete with wine and matzah. We read a short version of the Haggadah, and we marked the ten plagues the Jewish people had survived by using our pinkies to put ten drops of wine on the edge of our plates.

The next day, as I walked through the village on the way to campus, I braced myself, sure that someone would come up to me and confront me about the holiday, about my Jewishness. But no one did.

Emboldened, I invited Mohamed to spend the night with me in the tower. We'd been dating for several months now, and we hadn't gone beyond kissing; we both wanted to make love. We would have to do it on a Thursday because that was when Adnan went back to Jerusalem every week. And so we planned.

The week after Passover, Mohamed arrived shortly after nightfall, donning jeans, a polo shirt, and a backpack. There was something sweet and earnest about it—like he hadn't headed out to make love to his Jewish girlfriend for the first time but, rather, to go camping. Maybe that's what he'd told his parents, who still didn't know I existed.

We took the elevator up to the thirteenth floor, passing all the empty levels, and emerged into the hallway. But we didn't go straight to my room. We went, first, to the communal kitchen where we would have dinner with Professor Tomas, who made tortillas from scratch. I cooked the chorizo that Professor Tomas had brought back with him from the States, and the three of us shared a bottle of honey-pepper vodka. We lingered around the table, which was covered in a plastic tablecloth—me tracing the patterns with my fingers—until we were certain it was too late for Adnan to show up, until we were certain he would definitely be back in Jerusalem, with his family. And then Mohamed and I finally made our way to my room. He set his backpack down, and we climbed into my twin bed, where we made love for the first time.

In the morning, we snuck out of the building early before anyone was out on the street and walked through the village to the servees stand, where we boarded a Bethlehem-bound minivan. There, we would have lunch with an American journalist named Beth—the first friend, other than Professor Tomas, that I introduced Mohamed to. We got a rotisserie chicken from a place near her apartment and sat on the floor of her living room, eating it together with *shrek*, a super thin flat bread, and *tomeh*, whipped garlic.

When Mohamed went onto Beth's roof to smoke a cigarette, leaving us alone, she gave me her verdict: "He's sweet."

Tucking her straight, dirty blonde hair behind her hair and tipping her chin down, she looked at me with her big turquoise eyes and smiled. "I like him," she said.

Though Mohamed and I hadn't talked about it since that conversation at La Vie, I started to feel then like we were a couple. We'd made love. He'd met one of my closest friends. Maybe we weren't living in a fantasy. Maybe this was real.

12

After that first night together, now, when Mohamed visited me in Abu Dis, we skipped Hamas Hummus. We skipped the leisurely strolls and the glimpses of green. We didn't bother with tea anymore or the rooftop either. Doing our best not to rush through the village—doing our best not to look like the two young lovers rushing to bed that we were—we walked to al burj and took the elevator up to the thirteenth floor. Alone, finally, we hurried to my room, where we stripped down and delighted in each other's warmth, in each other's bodies—Adnan and his master key to my room be damned. Sometimes we didn't even make it to my bed, and we would make love, instead, on the overstuffed brown couch that took up one side of my room. We did this without talking about his family or our future or where the relationship was or wasn't going. I took it for granted that we were together and that we would be forever.

Now when I visited Mohamed at his office in Ramallah, we shut the balcony doors and closed the blinds and stripped down and made love on the chairs. Sometimes the chairs just seemed to get in the way, and we ended up on the hard, cold terrazzo floor, and—in those early days of our blooming romance—my knees ended up perpetually bruised and sore as did the base of my spine. Mohamed covered my throat and neck with bites and hickeys, which I hid with a bright red scarf. When we were apart, I would finger the scarf, feeling the bruises underneath, and I would smile, recalling our latest meeting and looking forward to the next.

But we would have to take a week off from our frantic lovemaking because, in May, Mohamed was going to Gaza.

He would accompany a French TV station that was doing a segment about the blockade's impact on Gaza's fishermen. Mohamed had never been to Gaza before and was excited about the trip. He recalled visiting the West Bank one summer as a child and wanting to accompany his grandfather, a farmer who had a bumper crop of grapes that he intended to drive over and sell in Gaza. But his grandfather laughed at the idea because, even back then, in the 1980s, Mohamed would need a permit to enter Gaza and this was *before* Israel revoked Palestinians' general permits in 1991. Movement restrictions, of course, had only gotten tighter since then.

To get to Gaza, which was about an hour's car ride, Mohamed would have to make a two-day trip. The combination of his West Bank ID and the blockade meant that he couldn't just travel through Israel, which would have been the shortest way. He would have to exit the West Bank via Allenby Bridge, enter Jordan, travel to Egypt, cross via land there, and then head to Cairo to find a way to Gaza. From Cairo, he would take a car to Rafah, the Egyptian-controlled crossing.

* * *

We kept in touch as best we could throughout his trip. He called me from Gaza one evening while I was in Jaffa visiting friends, incidentally, another mixed Jewish Israeli-Palestinian couple. But our phone call was short because it was absurdly expensive for Mohamed to call an Israeli number.

So Mohamed texted from Gaza. One morning, he wrote to let me know that he was about to go out on a fishing boat with the television crew. I knew that the Israeli navy often shot at these fishing boats, and I spent the day unable to concentrate. I went through the motions of teaching, but otherwise, I couldn't think. I stared at the phone, waiting for word that Mohamed was OK.

Finally, around nightfall, the message came. While the Israeli navy had warned them that they were getting too close, the trip had gone well. They'd finished their reporting, and he would be leaving Gaza soon.

But then it was five days of silence.

I wanted to give Mohamed space. I didn't want to be the clingy, needy girlfriend. I was independent and self-sufficient and fine on my own. But I was rattled. Was he OK? Had something happened en route back to Ramallah? If something had happened, I would have heard about it. So my fear became that the trip to Gaza and seeing how awful the conditions were there under the Israeli blockade had made him reassess his relationship with me—something I wouldn't have blamed him for. Or maybe I'd been naive in thinking that we were together. Maybe his trip to Gaza had felt like a natural breaking point for Mohamed, an easy way to disconnect and blow me off.

Nervous, I called. "Are you back in the West Bank?" I asked.

"Yes," he said, "I got back yesterday."

"Yesterday? Why didn't you call me?"

He didn't respond. I pressed the phone to my ear, tighter, as though I would be able to hear his thoughts if only I listened hard enough. I'd already learned that this was how Mohamed dealt with things he would rather not deal with—by simply not responding. This is the wall he'd thrown up already when I'd tried to gently probe him to figure out what, if anything, his parents knew about me. And I knew that once Mohamed was in not responding mode, there was no forcing him to answer anything.

So I didn't bother to repeat the question. I asked another one instead: "When will I see you?"

"Tomorrow," he said.

I wasn't sure he would show up. And, yet, there he was the next day at the university gate wearing a blue-and-green plaid short-sleeve button-down shirt and jeans, a backpack slung over one shoulder. He had a horrible sunburn. I could see from his face that he was burned to a crisp. As we walked to al burj, Mohamed confessed that he'd been embarrassed to see me looking like this and that he'd been waiting for his skin to heal before he came to Abu Dis again. But I didn't quite buy the excuse. I sensed that there was something else going on. I just didn't know what.

It was hot, and inside my dorm room, Mohamed took off his shirt, draped it over a chair, and plopped down on my couch in his jeans and white tank top. *Why didn't he get into my bed?* I thought, wondering if it was a sign that he was done with me, that he'd only come here to break up with me. He pulled his phone from his pocket and implored me to sit down next to him—he wanted to show me all the pictures from Gaza and tell me everything about his trip.

But it was hard for me to keep my hands off him. I was surprised when he pulled away.

"Don't you want to see Gaza, Mya?" he asked.

"Of course," I said. I'd reported on the place and the Israeli blockade; I'd always wanted to go and see it with my own eyes.

He showed me photos of the first leg of his journey and told me how, when he'd entered Gaza via the Rafah crossing, he'd been interrogated first by the Egyptians and then, finally, Hamas. Ironically, it was the Palestinians that had the most questions for him. Why was he coming to Gaza? What would he be doing there? Did he have a wife and children? No? He didn't? How, in the world, was it possible that he, at thirty-three, was still unmarried?

Mohamed laughed and shook his head, repeating then what he'd told me many times already: he felt like he was living under three occupations—that of the Israelis, the Palestinian Authority, and the conservative, traditional Palestinian culture.

"So what did you tell them?" I asked.

"That I just hadn't met the right one in the past. But that I was working on it." He winked at me. But the gesture annoyed me because something still felt off.

Eventually, the Hamas men had let him enter. In Gaza, Mohamed found the people suffering. But he also found them resilient, creative, dealing with their circumstances as best they could.

At some point, I broached the topic of five days without a phone call.

"I didn't call my *parents* the whole time I was gone," he scoffed.

"OK. I'm not your parents. I'm your girlfriend. Right?" Yes, I'd assumed we were together, but we'd never discussed our status. We'd never agreed to be exclusive, and five days of silence had left me wondering what I was to Mohamed. A foreigner he enjoyed fucking in Abu Dis? A potential partner? Where were we going?

"Right," he said. "But—"

"But what?"

"To tell you the truth, Mya, it was hard for me to call you because of what I saw in Gaza. Because of your ID." That was code for "Because you're Israeli."

"You know I'm against what's happening in Gaza—you know I'm against the blockade." I'd written a number of articles about the blockade, including one about the psychological impact on Gaza's population. Though I understood Israel's security concerns, the blockade seemed counterproductive to me, something that would only lead to an escalation of violence.

"I know. And I don't hold you responsible for anything," he said. But other people—his family—wouldn't see things the same way. He didn't want to keep our relationship a secret forever, but he was concerned about how the world around us would perceive me and us. I understood how conflicted he was.

He sighed deeply and grabbed me, pulling me on top of him. "*Ach minik* [Oh, how I suffer because of you], ya Mya," he said, as he began to kiss me, flipping me over, putting his weight on me.

When we'd finished, he told me he'd brought me gifts from Gaza. From his backpack, he produced a jar of sand, taken from Gaza's shore, and one half of an enormous bivalve shell—"I have the other half," he said—and a black satin stole, emblazoned in yellow with the words "Islamic Jihad."

"I thought this would look good on you," he joked, draping it over my neck. Whether I was reading it correctly or not, it felt like a message—convert or we're through. As I took the sash off, dropping it on the couch, Mohamed presented me with one final gift—a white T-shirt adorned with the Palestinian flag and the words "Free Gaza."

* * *

The following week, Mohamed met me at the university gate one afternoon, and we made our way towards al burj with the express intent of going up to my room. It had been hot the week before, but now, as May drew to a close, it was even hotter. We rushed through town, eager to seek the shade of my room, eager to peel off each other's clothes.

When we were just meters away from the building, we neared a clump of taxis and servees. Usually the drivers milled about, chatting. But today, they surrounded us, forming a tight ring. And then came the questions, in Arabic, of course, and addressed to Mohamed.

"Who are you?"

"What is your family name?"

"Where are you from?"

"What are you doing here?"

"How do you know the professora?"

"Why are you walking through the village with the professora?"

"Where are you two going?"

"To the burj? What are you going there for?"

"And what will you *do* inside the building?"

While I knew that a Palestinian *woman* could get into a tremendous amount of trouble for fooling around with someone outside of wedlock—honor killings in Palestinian society, though rare, *do* happen—it had never occurred to me that even Palestinian men could be in harm's way. Men, I thought, operated with impunity, more or less. Apparently, I was wrong.

I was terrified. My stomach quaked, and under the long-sleeve shirt and pants I wore, sweat rolled down my neck and back, pooling in the bottom of my shirt—not because I had some image in my mind of what might happen but because the opposite was true. I literally had no idea what came next. Would they beat Mohamed and rape me? Would they restrain me and set upon him? I thought we'd been flying under the radar all this time; I'd felt invisible and had thought no one had noticed our little dates in the village. Clearly, I was wrong. People had taken notice, and now they were intervening.

Later, Mohamed would explain to me that the idea of honor transcended individuals and families. It also had to do with place. And these men of this place wanted to make sure that we weren't defiling their village. This wasn't about my Israeli ID. The issue was that we were breaking *all* the rules, violating cultural norms, and that, too, put us in danger.

I listened as Mohamed answered all their questions, giving his family name and his parents' home village, explaining that we were both journalists who worked together and that we were headed inside to collaborate on a story. The men accepted Mohamed's explanation and dispersed. Relief flooded my body as we walked to the burj. But even once we were inside the building, my hands shook with fear. Abu Dis, I realized, was no place for us to conduct a courtship. With both the semester and my lease ending, it was time for me to move.

13

My friend Beth was headed to Gaza to do some reporting, and she offered me her place in Bethlehem for the month of June. Though Bethlehem and Ramallah were farther apart than Abu Dis and Ramallah—and reaching each other meant that we would have to pass through the dreaded checkpoint known as the Container—Mohamed and I figured this was a better option than me being in Jerusalem, where there was a wall between us. Even though, according to Israeli law, Bethlehem was legally off-limits to me, we agreed that it was far safer for me to be out in a Palestinian area of the West Bank than it was for Mohamed to enter Israel illegally on a regular basis.

Although Bethlehem is, today, a Muslim majority city, the remaining Christians have a strong presence and this historically Christian area is more liberal than the surrounding Muslim villages. So Bethlehem also seemed like a better place than Abu Dis for us to continue our courtship. I accepted Beth's offer, and she let her Christian Palestinian landlord know that a friend would be in her apartment while she was gone.

Though Mohamed and I promised to spend as much time together as we could, he was busy working on a short documentary about the failure of the Oslo Accords, as told through the plight of Bedouin families who lived in an area of the West Bank referred to as E1. The project also offered Mohamed the unique experience of living in the Bedouin camp while they were shooting. So, for most of the month, I was alone in Beth's apartment, tucked behind an unassuming door in the Old City, on Bethlehem's limestone-faced Star Street—which is believed to mark the same path Jacob and Mary took to the manger where Jesus was born.

The studio apartment felt at once tiny and expansive. It had just enough room for a bed, a couch, an armoire, and a kitchenette; the bathroom was little more than a wash closet—there was a shower head that stuck directly out of the wall by the toilet. But this was an old place, likely built during the Ottoman era or even earlier, and it had those vaulted ceilings that gave the apartment a feeling of enormity. And because all of the Old City is built on the side of a mountain, peeking out of Beth's little window offered me a sweeping view of the city, a patchwork quilt unfurling itself on the hillside. Her window faced the west, and I could sit and watch the sun drop, casting an orange glow upon Bethlehem that faded to pink and then to lavender before the city settled into a deep navy blue for the night.

With Mohamed gone, I focused on my writing. Taking a break one day from my work, I emailed my mom, telling her about Mohamed. My parents are quite liberal and, in theory, had no problem with me dating a Palestinian. Still, my mother expressed concerns about the relationship, about our ability to navigate the cultural and political divides. It wasn't outright disapproval, but it wasn't the support I'd been hoping for. I was disappointed but unsurprised.

When I wasn't writing, I was with Lena—a Christian Palestinian woman who was close with Beth and our other friends—either sitting at the Casa Nova, our favorite spot, or out running together in Bethlehem and the neighboring area of Beit Sahour. Bethlehem was different than Abu Dis. Even though Christians were now the minority and

Muslims were the majority, in this historically Christian area, not only could Lena and I go out and run; we could wear T-shirts and shorts when we did so. With a little more freedom and a group of friends here in Bethlehem, this month felt less like it was about me and Mohamed and more about me being on my own. Yes, I'd taken the sublease so it would be easier for Mohamed to reach me. But with Mohamed gone, I began to think I could build my own life here whether we were together or not.

* * *

On break from shooting the documentary, Mohamed came to visit. Ahead of his arrival, I went to the outdoor market and got everything I needed for his favorite dish, stuffed eggplant. Back at Beth's I scraped out the insides of small, egg-sized eggplants, filling them with the meat and tomato mixture I'd made from scratch, and set the pot to simmer on the stove.

Night fell. The food was ready. But where was Mohamed? Was he OK? I texted him, but he didn't respond. Maybe he's out of minutes, I told myself.

Or maybe something happened on the road.

Anxious, knowing there was nothing I could do, I decided to walk to the servees stand, which was down the hill, on the other side of the bus station. Surely, as I did so, I'd run into Mohamed along the way. Everything would be fine, and we'd walk back up to the apartment together. But then, dressed, I stopped at the door. What if I left as he was arriving and we didn't pass each other on the way? He would get here, and I would be gone. I didn't want to leave him standing there in the street.

So I sat down on the futon, which I'd been using as a bed, and tried to busy myself with a book.

Finally, a knock. I opened it, and there he was, in a white linen shirt, the street dark behind him.

"We got stopped at the Container," he said. "And the soldiers took me off the servees."

"Jesus. Are you OK?" I asked as he stepped inside and I closed the door.

He pulled me into his arms, and I smelled him, his sweat familiar and comforting.

"Do you want to talk about it?" I asked.

"Not now," he said, slipping a hand into my blouse.

Unbuttoning his shirt, I said, "You should have told them you were on your way to fuck your Jewish girlfriend."

* * *

Later, as we lay together on the futon—our limbs tangled, a white sheet across us—Mohamed told me what happened at the Container: When they'd entered the checkpoint, Mohamed explained, a soldier had pulled the minivan over. After opening the door and peering in, he pointed at Mohamed. "You," he said, signaling for him to get out. Frightened, Mohamed complied. The soldier led Mohamed behind the booth, where he searched him. Finding nothing, he told him to return to the minivan.

Mohamed was unharmed, physically, but he'd been frightened by the randomness of it all. When the soldier had opened the servees and looked at the occupants, why had he singled out Mohamed, of all people? I puzzled over it myself and envisioned him, sitting there, in the minivan, trying to figure out what the soldier saw: a young guy of average height—five feet nine inches—lean, freshly bathed, clean shaven, and well-dressed in a white button-down linen shirt, a backpack at his feet. I couldn't imagine what in the world was menacing in this soldier's eyes. The simple fact that this man was Palestinian?

And though Mohamed didn't articulate this as we lay there in bed together, I understood that being hauled off a servees and searched had felt like a violation of his physical self. The moment had been a reminder that he didn't even have control over something as basic as his own body.

It had also triggered a memory of another confrontation with a soldier, which Mohamed shared with me: During the Second Intifada, he was attempting to make his way back to Ramallah from Sa'ir, where he was living and working with his uncle. There was a section, close to what is today Qalandia checkpoint, which looked very different back then and which left Israeli soldiers out in the open, where the Israelis had forbidden Palestinian vehicles. So Mohamed, like everyone else, had gotten out of the servees and was walking toward Ramallah, past Qalandia. It was winter, *shitta* in the Palestinian dialect, which also means "rain." True to the word, it was cold and wet; Mohamed had been trudging through mud when, suddenly, he found himself tackled by two soldiers and pinned to the ground.

Mohamed didn't speak Hebrew, so he hadn't gotten everything they'd shouted at him. But he'd understood a snippet, and the words had stuck with him. He repeated them to me: *"Kadoor b'rosh shelcha!"*

A bullet in your head.

Upon hearing those words—my beloved language used in such an ugly way—I felt like a noose was tightening around my heart while the muscle kept fighting to expand. I put my hand on my chest, and my breath caught in my throat.

Mohamed continued. After he'd spent some time lying in the mud, a soldier kneeling on his back, another standing guard, they'd let him go, and he'd continued that way, to Ramallah, his clothes sullied, his spirit split.

I told him then that I remembered that first day we'd spent reporting together and how tense he'd seemed at Qalandia. I'd figured it was about the protest that had taken place on Nakba Day, the live ammo. That had been the most intense and most frightening demo I'd been to. But that wasn't what was on his mind when he was at Qalandia—it was that moment a soldier kneeled on his back, put a gun to his head, and said, "Kadoor b'rosh."

That, I realized, was one of the terrors of the occupation—the randomness, the total lack of control, the feeling that anything could happen at any time.

* * *

Having spent a couple of weeks apart, and it being June and oppressively hot, we whiled away most of the weekend in the apartment, those high ceilings pulling the heat up and away. We left briefly—once to get me a Palestinian phone so Mohamed and I could text and call each other like normal human beings—and then again to have dinner at a local Mexican restaurant.

As we walked up Star Street, away from Manger Square and the Church of the Nativity, Mohamed got a text message. His uncle's house had been raided by the Israeli army. No one had been arrested, and everyone was physically fine. But the soldiers had trashed the place—dumping the contents of drawers on the floor, flipping mattresses over. For no good reason, Mohamed said, *al faddi*, "all for nothing."

I remembered then one time I'd gone to Jerusalem for a few days to do some reporting. Oded's brother, Amit, had picked me up at the bus station. Amit was younger, and he'd recently finished his mandatory army service with a combat unit in the West Bank. As he drove, we'd started talking politics, and he'd told me about doing night raids like that for no other reason than to remind the Palestinians that the army was there. "Just to keep a boot on their neck," Amit had said, in a matter-of-fact, run-of-the-mill way, with neither approval or remorse.

Amit's words ran through my ears then. And I was also struck by the fact that even here, as Mohamed and I attempted to spend a nice, quiet weekend in this little nest of an apartment tucked on a hillside in this stone cradle of a city, we couldn't escape the occupation. Not even for a day.

A solemn mood descended on both of us. Only after we started to eat did Mohamed break the silence and tell me, "You know, this isn't the first time the Israelis were at my uncle's house."

"Did they search it before?" I asked. "In the past?"

He shook his head. "No. They demolished it."

"What?"

"The house he lives in now—he just finished building that one. Before that, he lived in a different house, the one in front of him, until the army came and tore it down."

"Why?" I asked, regretting the question right away because of the look Mohamed gave me.

"Eh?" he said. "What do you mean 'why'? You know how it is. For no reason at all. The house had been built *before* 1967, before the occupation began. My uncle added on to it; the army came and said he hadn't gotten a permit to build. They tore it down."

"The addition?"

"No. The whole house."

As a journalist, I knew this was true. I'd covered the issue of building permits and home demolitions, and I knew that the Israelis almost never granted Palestinians permits to build or add on to homes and that forced Palestinians to build "illegally" to keep up with natural growth. I also knew that, occasionally, the army showed up and flattened houses that Palestinians couldn't have possibly gotten Israeli permits to build because they'd gone up *before* Israel took control of the territory. It was a catch-22, of course. And though I'd heard about it, as an Israeli, there was part of me that still didn't want to believe it.

"Really?" I said.

"What, you don't believe me? I saw it with my own eyes," he said, putting his fork down and pointing to the corner of his right eye. "I was living there *when they did it*. We were visiting for the summer; I was nine. We woke up one morning, and there was the army at the door. There was the bulldozer. We walked outside and watched them tear the house down."

I put my fork down, too. "What did your uncle do?"

"What did my uncle do? He was in administrative detention then."

"Why?" I knew administrative detention was detainment without charge but, still, a part of me wanted to believe that there was a claim of some kind. That Mohamed's uncle had been accused of something.

Mohamed was visibly annoyed by my question. "Shoo 'why'? What why? No reason. It was 1988. They were taking all the men to administrative detention back then. They would take one, hold him three months, six months, whatever, let him out, take someone else. It was my uncle's turn. He was in jail; when he got out, his home was gone. This is what he came back to: rubble."

There were no questions left for me to ask, nothing for me to say. I couldn't eat and Mohamed couldn't either. And so we sat like that, our dinner growing cold.

* * *

Sunday morning, we were in bed, wrapped in those white sheets—talking about the five love languages and using my laptop to take a cheesy quiz to figure out what our love languages were—when we heard a key in the lock and the deadbolt clicking.

Who could possibly be coming in? Beth had told her landlord that I would have the apartment while she was gone.

Alarmed, Mohamed and I both scrambled out of bed, grabbing our clothes off the terrazzo floor—Mohamed stepping into his green pants and putting on that white linen shirt and buttoning it hastily, me pulling a dress over my head—managing to finish just as the door swung open. We stood in the center of the room, freshly dressed but disheveled, our eyes wide, as a young Palestinian man—short, thick, with auburn hair—held the door open and looked down, gesturing toward the three steps that descended into the apartment. He hadn't noticed us yet. "*Tfadli* [Please]," he said, in Arabic, to the older woman, dressed in slacks and a short-sleeved top, her hair coiffed, who carefully entered and made her way down the stairs, only to look up and gasp when she noticed us.

The young man noticed us then and shouted, in Arabic, "Who are you? What are you doing here?"

"I'm Beth's friend! Who are *you*? What are *you* doing here?"

"This is *my house*!" he cried. Later, I would find out he was the landlord's son. "And who are you?" he gestured to Mohamed then.

"I'm her husband."

"No, you're not. You're not married!" the man answered. Because, if we were, why would we be at Beth's place? He moved forward now, toward us, aggressively. "I want to see your papers. Show me your papers. *Prove* that you're married."

The woman stood by the open door, aghast.

Mohamed stepped back, unintentionally drawing attention toward the messy futon, those tangled white sheets.

The young man looked from it and us and shouted that this was his family's home. His father—whom Beth rented from—had been born here and his grandmother before that, and we were bringing shame to them. "*Eib aleikum* [Shame on all of you]!" he boomed, furious, taking a step toward Mohamed, who backed up.

It wasn't just the immediate danger of a fistfight, of injury, of the police arriving. We'd besmirched his family's honor by having out-of-wedlock sex in their home. In Palestine, this was the sort of thing that could start a clan war, engulfing both families in violence.

So Mohamed tried to defuse the situation. Trying to placate the man, Mohamed raised his hands, palms up, explaining, from what I could make out, that we'd only recently married and that he hadn't yet filed the necessary paperwork with the PA. Beth had loaned us the apartment, so we could have some sort of small honeymoon in this sweet city that we both loved. We were sorry.

Buying the explanation, the man stepped back, smoothed his hair, stood up straight, and offered us an apology, too, explaining that the apartment had great sentimental value, and he was bringing his aunt to see it.

And just like that it was over. Only then did I realize I'd been shaking.

We were supposed to be relatively free in Bethlehem. Yes, it was illegal for me to be there. But cordoned off in Area A, we wouldn't see Israeli soldiers, and as long as I wasn't going in or out of the area, it was unlikely I would be arrested. Though we'd both known that Christian Palestinians were conservative, we'd thought that Bethlehem—a Christian town—would be slightly less conservative than Muslim cities and villages. But even here things weren't so different than they'd been in Abu Dis. Our ability to court would be limited; our days together were numbered. Acknowledging this, we agreed we would have to make a decision about our future. We wouldn't be able to be boyfriend and girlfriend forever. If we were going to stay together, we were going to have to get married.

14

Upon Beth's return, I went back to my tiny studio in Jerusalem, where I was still paying rent. The lease wasn't up until August, and Oded decamped to his parents' place—which was just a few miles away—so I could have the place to myself before a short trip to the United States. Bard was flying me to New York, so I could attend a pedagogy workshop on campus; I would return to Jerusalem just as Ramadan was ending, and Mohamed promised to come visit me for Eid al-Fitr, the three-day holiday that marks the end of the holy month.

"But how?" I asked.

Mohamed assured me that he would find a way in. I knew, of course, that thousands of Palestinian workers managed to get into Israel every day without permits and without going through the checkpoints. The wall wasn't impermeable because it wasn't complete—some parts were still a fence. And in some sections, that fence had holes, made by Palestinians with wire cutters.

Still, I was doubtful that Mohamed would be able to get in. And so I was surprised when, as I deplaned at Ben Gurion International Airport and turned on my phone, I got a message from him.

I'm in Jerusalem. Waiting to see you.

I moved through the airport as fast as I could. At passport control, I felt a fluttering in my chest as the clerk stamped my passport and welcomed me home, in Hebrew, just like any other Israeli. And then I immediately felt ashamed. My boyfriend lived on the other side of a wall.

Bag in tow, I rushed out of the airport and boarded a *sherut* headed to Jerusalem. Not only did I want to see him; I was worried about him walking through the streets alone. While he understood a bit of Hebrew, he didn't speak it. What if he ran into some right-wingers? Just a year before, in August 2012, a mob of Jewish Israelis had attacked a group of Palestinian teenagers. One of the boys had been beaten so badly he had nearly died. "Only a miracle saved him from death," an Israeli policeman told the local newspaper *Haaretz*. Much of the international media called the incident a lynching.

So it felt urgent to me to be with Mohamed as he walked the streets of Jewish West Jerusalem. I felt responsible for him and his safety. I told myself that I could protect him because I spoke Hebrew. Or, because I knew the language and the culture and the cues, I would be able to read a situation faster than Mohamed, and I would be able to tell if he was in danger, something he couldn't do on his own.

But walking through the streets with me could also be dangerous. Less than a year before, six Jewish Israeli teenagers had beaten a Palestinian man as he'd walked through West Jerusalem with a Jewish Israeli woman. Inside of Israel, going out in public together came with risks, more for him than for me.

* * *

Looking out the light rail window, I gasped—I thought I saw Mohamed, striding up the hill that led to Kiryat Yovel.

I called to ask. "Did I just see you from the train?"

"Yes, I'm almost to your neighborhood."

Arriving at the stop, I got off and walked away from my apartment, toward Mohamed, who was wearing that white linen shirt again. We embraced on the sidewalk; he took my suitcase and followed me home. As I unlocked the gate to the courtyard that I shared with my neighbor, I eyed the stairs that led to the owners' house. I loved Mohamed's dark olive skin, and I loved the way the white shirt contrasted with his tone, bringing out his color, making him look even darker, but I imagined the owners' reaction if they were to come down the stairs and find us here in the courtyard.

The owners, a lawyer and an architect, leaned left, I knew. When the wife, Kinneret, had first shown the apartment to me, I'd told her about the Israeli-Palestinian organization I was moving to Jerusalem to work for. And she'd taken care to mention to me that among the previous occupants had been a young, unmarried Palestinian couple from East Jerusalem who wanted to live together, which would have been impossible in East Jerusalem. So I knew that my landlords' politics were fine. But it was a whole other thing, I realized, to have a Palestinian from the territories staying illegally in the apartment for the night.

I imagined Kinneret standing there. She had these habits of cocking her head to the side, of folding her arms just below her bosom, resting them on the tiny hint of a belly she had—just a hint, Kinneret had five kids but was quite thin—and she spoke quickly, her words like fluttering wings. I could see her like that, questions flapping around us. Once she figured out Mohamed lived in Ramallah, what would she do? Would she ask him if he had a permit? Certainly, as a lawyer, she knew that all the permits Palestinians got came with the stipulation that they were not to spend the night inside.

And then I thought of my neighbor, who I shared the courtyard with, a young guy who still went to reserve duty, who, when he returned, left his army boots outside the door. I remembered that one winter, they were muddy; another time, during the dry season, the boots were dusty, leading me to guess that he must do his reserve duty in the West Bank. Oh, God. All we needed now was someone who served in the West Bank getting a glimpse of Mohamed. He would be able to size Mohamed up in a second. Would he turn Mohamed in? Would Mohamed be arrested? Harmed? Would I get into trouble, too?

And how would *Mohamed* feel if he saw my neighbor's dirty boots lying in the courtyard?

Looking toward his doorway, I prayed the boots wouldn't be there. They weren't. And if they had been, Mohamed would have been oblivious—he was busy admiring the courtyard, which was enclosed by a fence covered with passion fruit vines.

I hurried Mohamed into my studio and closed the door behind him.

As I watched Mohamed look around my apartment, I realized how surreal this must be for him. This was Palestine—the place he'd always seen on the map that hung in his parent's home. And on the map, it looked empty. And yet here were all these homes full of Jewish people. Of course, this wasn't his first trip in. He'd been to Tel Aviv, and he'd been to the center of Jerusalem many times. But this quiet corner of southwest Jerusalem was something new to him. He'd never been out here. I wondered if he realized there were neighborhoods like this everywhere, all across the country. He still called the place Palestine or, sometimes, forty-eight. But didn't he know there were millions and millions of people here and that they weren't going anywhere? That many of them had nowhere to go? I tried to imagine Mohamed living here, with me, and it seemed impossible.

And how had he gotten in anyway? I asked him then, pointing out that, despite the wall, he'd made better time to Jerusalem from Ramallah than I had from Tel Aviv.

Mohamed laughed, pulled me onto the couch, took his phone out of pocket, and showed me a photo. There was that familiar West Bank sand, a chain-link fence cut, the edges of the hole rolled back, and a woman in a hijab on the other side, making her way through a ditch, with a man's help. It took me a moment to understand what I was looking at.

"A hole in the fence, right by Qalandia," Mohamed explained.

"Noooooo," I said, shocked.

"Yes! A soldier saw the crowd, and he came and warned us not to cross," Mohamed said, laughing. "Then he went away, and we crossed anyway."

He flipped through the pictures, showing me the crowd and images of people making their way through the hole and over a ditch.

I couldn't believe it. "And then what? Once you were on the other side?"

"We took a bus the rest of the way to Jerusalem—the same bus as the people who had gone through the checkpoint."

It blew my mind. Separation was real, and yes, it made a very serious impact on people's lives. And still, there were holes. Like the land itself, we refused to be divided.

* * *

I'd brought lots of Latino goods back with me from the United States, basics like refried beans and chorizo. Mohamed had never had a burrito, so we had them for dinner, watched a little TV, and then tried to go to sleep. But the jet lag was brutal, and around midnight, we went out for a walk, taking to the quiet, narrow alley that led eventually to a small park.

The alley was one of my favorite parts of the neighborhood, winding between the houses that were tucked behind walls, winding between hanging laundry and balconies and the sounds of Friday evening dinners taken outdoors and leisurely Saturday breakfasts and the smells of cooking and the snippets of conversation. Sundry plants peeked out over the walls that divided the courtyards from the alley, trellises covered with squash plants, the vegetables ripe in the late summer and enormous, hanging from the vine. A lemon tree here, olive trees there; tiny, tart oranges hung off branches; camellias, passionfruit. The moon was full that night, shining down on the alley, on us, lending it all a silvery glow.

Mohamed stopped in front of a honeysuckle vine and plucked off one of the tiny trumpeted flowers.

"Open your mouth," he said.

I did, and he gently tipped my head back, dropping the dew from the honeysuckle onto my tongue. I'd never known you could actually do that. I'd never tasted nectar before, and it was even sweeter than I'd imagined.

"Mmmmm," I said.

Mohamed smiled.

We walked, marveling at the moon and the few stars we could see despite the streetlights, admiring the plants, all these tendrils hanging over the wall, reaching for us, beckoning, like we both belonged to this secret garden.

We emerged into the small park and sat down on a bench. As much as a life together inside of Israel had seemed impossible in the daylight as I'd stood there thinking about Kinneret and my neighbor and his army boots, now, in the dark, it felt real and possible; it felt tangible, like those drops of honeysuckle Mohamed put on my tongue. I wanted to stay here, with him, forever.

* * *

In the morning, we went hiking in the Jerusalem Forest, a short walk from my apartment. I'd spent many Saturdays picnicking there; I'd also spent many afternoons running alone in the woods.

The Jerusalem Forest connected Yad VaShem, the Holocaust Museum, with Ein Karem, a Palestinian village that had been depopulated in 1948, during the nakba. Unlike many other Palestinian villages that were emptied in 1948 and demolished, Ein Karem had remained intact, and today, those beautiful old Arab houses were full of Jews; occasionally a descendant of a Palestinian family who'd owned the home showed up and knocked on the door. It was a story I knew well—not because of journalism, not because I read it in a book, but because I had family, however distant, who lived there in Ein Karem and because it had happened to them.

One day, some years ago, Uncle Aviram—technically a cousin related to my mom through marriage—heard a knock on the door. Aviram answered it to find a Palestinian man standing there. The man—whose name was never a part of this story—announced to my uncle that his parents had lived in this house prior to the war. This house belonged to his family. Opening the door wide, Aviram stepped back and invited the man in.

Aviram walked him through the house, showing him the second floor he'd added to the original one-story structure, the kitchen he'd renovated, the living room he'd decorated. Then he offered the man coffee. Steaming cups before them, the two sat: a Christian Palestinian refugee who lived now in Bethlehem; Aviram, an American Jew who'd immigrated to Israel in 1963 and married a native-born Israeli woman, with whom he'd had three children, raised here in Ein Karem, in this very house. When their cups were empty, Aviram tucked a lock of his curly gray hair behind his ear, stood, and tried to show the Palestinian man to the door. It was then that the two began to argue.

That was where the story, recounted to me by one of my American aunts, ended. How had the argument ended? What happened to the man? No one had any answers about the Palestinian man's fate.

I didn't share any of this with Mohamed as we set out on the path; all I told him was that this would take us to Ein Karem. I was ashamed to admit that I had family—however distant—living in Palestinian houses. And as we set out, I had other concerns. Aviram had died a couple of years ago, but what if I ran into my cousin? She leaned left, I knew, and wouldn't care if I was dating a Palestinian, but the thought of running into her made me aware of the fact that it was a Saturday, a popular time to visit Ein Karem. It wouldn't be just us there. What if someone realized Mohamed was from the West Bank and called the police? Or what if the police just happened to be there and they stopped Mohamed and asked for his ID and permit? What if he was arrested?

Out here, in the forest, though, we were free of all that. As we walked the trail, Mohamed strayed off the path to show me wild zaatar, spicier than the domesticated one I was familiar with. He plucked leaves off the plants, and as he handed them to me to chew, he told me how his father had done the same with him when the family had gone on picnics in Jordan.

As we walked, Mohamed pointed out other plants and talked about some that were out of season, like *khubeza*. Arabic for "bread," the round-leaf plant resembled pita; Palestinian refugees had foraged and lived off khubeza after the war began in 1947, Mohamed added.

The path split, and I led Mohamed uphill, past a row of fig trees. The fruit was round and full but still green. We touched them anyway, squeezing them slightly to see if they were ripe enough to eat, but they were still hard. For a moment, I imagined this place prior to 1948; I wondered if these fig trees had belonged to someone. I wondered, too, about the almond trees—from which I'd collected green almonds in the spring, bringing them back with me to Abu Dis to share with Mohamed and Professor Tomas in the tower. I ran my fingers through the wild fennel and smelled my hands, wondering if once, many years ago, there had been a Palestinian woman who'd walked here with a lover, wondering if she'd done the same thing with her hands.

When we emerged into Ein Kerem as it stands today, I was beset by conflicting feelings. I'd made this hike many times, and I was glad to see the familiar stone street and the wall and that particular turn in the road that I knew so well. *But how does all this look to Mohamed?* I wondered, this Palestinian village that was empty of Palestinians.

And it was sad that *I* was the one who knew the way around this place. Mohamed knew the plants in the Jerusalem Forest in an intimate way. But I was the only one who could get us through the woods, who could negotiate the streets and alleys, who could show him the shortcut, the staircases that led back up the mountain, depositing us on the sidewalk across from Kiryat Yovel.

* * *

After trekking up the stairs, we stopped by a *makolet*, a "corner store," bought a couple of beers and plopped down on a park bench, hot and tired from our hike. I stretched out, resting my legs in his lap. Mohamed wrapped his hands around my calves; I liked feeling his fingers on my bare skin. We sat in silence, looking out over the Jerusalem Forest together.

"If we get married, where will we live?" Mohamed asked.

I sat up then and looked at him, those hazel eyes of his glowing like they were backlit. I searched them now trying to figure out if he meant it.

"Seriously?" I asked, knowing the answer. Mohamed was a serious guy. His words were always measured and careful. He wouldn't have said it if he hadn't meant it.

"Yes. Seriously, ya Mya. *Bahibbik.*" (I love you.)

That was the first time he'd said those words to me. And for the first time, we talked seriously about marriage. There would be legal obstacles.

Because we had different IDs, living inside of Israel together would be next to impossible. At that time, Israel had a ban on family unification—that is, a 2003 law prohibited Israeli citizens from extending residency or citizenship to residents of the occupied Palestinian territories or the enemy states of Iran, Iraq, Lebanon, or Syria. So if we married, and we wanted to live inside of Israel, Mohamed would have to get a permit, which we would have to renew once a year. And though the permit would allow him to live with me inside of Israel, it would not allow him to work legally. Renewing once a year would also mean that we would live under constant threat of not being approved, of being separated. And living in Israel illegally would be too difficult and too dangerous.

What about America? No. Mohamed wasn't leaving Palestine, he said.

If we were going to get married and live together, it would have to be the West Bank. That's when Mohamed told me that his father was building a house for the family. It would be a typical Palestinian compound, an apartment building. On the bottom floor, the first apartment would be for Mohamed's parents and his younger sister, who was still in high school. Each son would get a floor and an apartment in which they would be able to live with their own family. This was a cultural thing. The groom or his family provides the house, which is referred to as "opening a home."

So when the building was finished, Mohamed would be expected to marry. We both agreed that marriage was a big step and that we needed to spend more time together, so we could decide properly whether we wanted to move forward. But we couldn't spend a lot of time together if I lived in Jerusalem. So we discussed the idea of me moving out to a Palestinian area of the West Bank, even though all of those areas were off-limits to me, legally, as an Israeli.

Since Mohamed lived in Ramallah, we talked about me moving there. But that meant a long commute—it could take an hour or more to get from Ramallah to Abu Dis. And while there was only one checkpoint on the way, and I'd noticed that that checkpoint was unmanned 95 percent of the time, the threat of flying checkpoints, spontaneous checkpoints that soldiers set up using an army jeep or two in the road, loomed large.

A move to Ramallah posed another problem for me: Aware of my tendency to flee into the safety of relationships, I didn't want to be too close to Mohamed. I wanted to stand on my own two feet. But I was also aware that I had this tendency to distance myself from people, as well, and if I stayed inside the wall, in Jerusalem, I knew I would be cutting myself off from him. I wanted to open myself to love. So I would move outside the wall. But where?

Not Abu Dis. What about Bethlehem? I had a lot of friends there, and it was only about twenty minutes from campus. But Bethlehem came with risks. If the PA police caught me there, they would turn me over to the Israelis. This was unlikely, however; there were plenty of foreigners living in Bethlehem, and chances were that the PA police would assume I was one of them. There was another issue: I'd have to go through the Container every day on my way to campus, but it was relatively rare for the Israeli soldiers to stop a servees there, and when they did, they usually only checked the men's IDs.

Yes, there were militants in the West Bank. But they attacked settlers, that is, Jewish Israelis living in Israeli-only settlements and I wasn't a settler. I was going to live in a Palestinian city, among the Palestinians. Militants didn't look for Israelis in Bethlehem or in the servees running between Bethlehem and Abu Dis.

Bethlehem was the city that made the most sense to both of us. I would go back.

15

Another Bethlehem-based international friend, Matt, was headed out of town for six weeks and offered to sublease his place to me. It was another temporary living arrangement, and I was increasingly feeling like I couldn't keep bouncing around from one short-term place to the next.

As a nod to the fact that I would likely stay in Bethlehem, I contemplated buying a car from my friend Hadas, an American Israeli academic who herself had lived in a Palestinian area of the occupied territories and who was returning to the States. I couldn't afford a car, but because a family member had gifted her the very used car, she was willing to sell it to me for next to nothing.

Were I to stay in the West Bank, a car would be necessary for so many reasons. Because this was an "Israeli" car—that is, it had a yellow Israeli plate—it meant that I could move more or less freely through all areas of the West Bank, even Palestinian areas, and through most checkpoints. While there are indeed separate roads for Israeli settlers and Palestinians, and Palestinian movement is severely curtailed—being completely forbidden in some areas and restricted in others—there are parts of the West Bank where separation isn't complete and segregated roads merge with larger, unsegregated roads. In the West Bank, there are stretches where it's normal to see both yellow-plate cars and white-plate cars, which are registered under the PA, driving side by side. As Palestinians from East Jerusalem get yellow plates for their cars, just like Israelis, it's also fairly normal to see yellow-plated cars in Palestinian areas of the West Bank.

The infrastructure of the occupation is dizzying, as was moving through all these spaces constantly. The point was this: a yellow plate would allow me to move through the West Bank more or less freely. It would also make it easier for me to enter Israel, allowing me to go through many checkpoints without stopping, making Jerusalem more accessible. An Israeli car also meant that, if I was brave enough to take the risk, I could drive Mohamed—or any of my Palestinian girlfriends—into Israel with me.

But there was subtext to all of this, something that Hadas, who was fiercely pro-Palestinian, didn't articulate but that we both knew and that hovered over our conversation: the car could also be an escape hatch for me should I end up in any sort of danger. It would be a way to get out and get out fast, if I needed to.

So I bought the car, but I didn't take it to work because the drive from Bethlehem to Abu Dis was too overwhelming—not because of the soldiers and settlers but because of the road itself, which was carved into the side of a mountain and included all these hairpin twists and turns. I left the car parked on the street, in the Old City, outside of Matt's building and fell into a rhythm: living in Bethlehem, waking up to the light streaming in through the windows, walking across the plaza to the bus station—listening to the Arabic singer Fairouz blasting from the speakers of a café, her silky-smooth voice bouncing off the limestone walls—working in Abu Dis, going to Arabic classes, spending my weekends with Mohamed.

He would usually arrive late Thursday afternoon, and we'd sip wine and talk as we made dinner together in the tiny kitchen, the wind from the Judean Hills rolling in through the windows. Or sometimes the breeze came from the other way, from the direction of the coast, and I could smell the sea, the same as I had in Tel Aviv. Sometimes the air came from both sides, in and out, like we were in a pair of lungs and the place was breathing around us.

I had Arabic class on Friday mornings, so, after dinner, Mohamed would check my homework, making sure I'd gotten it all right, gently correcting what I'd gotten wrong, and ensuring that I was ready for tomorrow's lesson. I also talked a lot about the classes I taught at the university, my students, and their lives. Mohamed loved how much I cared about my students; he loved how passionate I was about teaching and empowering them. And then we'd finish dinner and take to bed, where I would leave Mohamed sleeping on Friday mornings when I went to class and where I would join him when I returned.

One weekend, we broke our routine: Mohamed's best friend, Ramzy, came from the nearby village of Dar Salah and was spending the weekend there at his parents' house. Could we have him over for dinner on Thursday night? Mohamed asked. Of course.

I'd already met Ramzy in Ramallah; he was the first friend Mohamed introduced me to. But this would be a big step. It would be our first time hosting one of Mohamed's friends.

Ramzy, a lawyer, was stubborn, loud, and argumentative, and he never stopped talking. He reminded me a bit of a rooster, noisy and blustery, puffing out his chest and proverbial feathers, squawking, letting everyone know he was there all the time. True to form, he put on quite the performance when he came for dinner. After a taste of the salad, Ramzy cleared his throat, tugged at the collar of his button-down shirt, theatrically adjusted his black-framed glasses, and then used his fork to pick through the vegetables.

Finding the culprit, he speared it and held it up on a tine for all to examine.

"Onion!" he cried, in Arabic. Ramzy, by the way, didn't speak a word of English. "Who puts onion in salad?!"

After going on for a while about the onion, Ramzy turned his attention to the apartment, which he complimented, in an attempt to redeem himself.

Mohamed gestured to the hand-painted floor tiles. "Look," he said, pointing out the Star of David and menorah that were parts of the pattern.

"*Ya bayyeh* [Wow]!" Ramzy exclaimed. He mused aloud as to how the tiles had gotten here. The building had surely been built during Ottoman times. Mohamed guessed that the tiles had been put in during a British Mandate–era renovation.

"Maybe a Jewish family lived here?" Ramzy wondered.

I shifted uncomfortably in my chair. Ramzy knew that I was American, of course, but he didn't know that I was Jewish or had an Israeli ID.

"There were no Jews out here in Bethlehem," I said, in my clumsy, stiff Arabic, hoping to bring the conversation to a close.

"Maybe there were," Ramzy argued. "There were Jews in Hebron. This place *is* Bayt Lechem. That means 'house of bread' in Hebrew."

I played dumb, like I didn't know a word of Hebrew. "*Laaa* [Nooo]," I responded, in Arabic. "The name comes from the Arabic: Bayt Lahme [house of meat]."

Historians hadn't worked it out, and we weren't going to, either. Ramzy dug in his heels and continued to insist on the Hebrew name; I cleared the table.

When Ramzy left that night, Mohamed shrugged it off. "*Ta'amari*," he said, grinning. The Ta'amari were a Bedouin tribe that had left behind their seminomadic ways and settled in the Bethlehem area; other Palestinians stereotyped them as quarrelsome and hot-blooded. But Ramzy hadn't bothered me, despite the fact that he hated my food and argued with everything I said. In fact, after that dinner, I felt a warm affection for the guy. I liked his energy, even if it bordered on obnoxious. He was sensitive, emotional, and wore his heart on his sleeve. There was no guessing with Ramzy.

* * *

Though Mohamed and I were a little world of two suspended in this apartment that overlooked the Old City and the land beyond, though we lived in the land's lungs, in the fragile breath that moved between the river and the sea, though we were living in an impossible dream, our relationship felt real. My life with Mohamed and at the university and in the West Bank felt sustainable. Until one afternoon.

A student, Iman, lingered after class, waiting for everyone to clear out. Like Neda, Iman was from Hebron and dressed conservatively, wearing the hijab and abaya and no makeup. Unlike Neda, Iman often wore jeans and Converse sneakers that peeked out from the hem of her robe. Something about those shoes reminded me that she was still very young—a child, really. So I didn't know how to react when, after the last student had left the room, Iman said, "I heard you're a Jew, and I just want to tell you—you're so brave to be here. Anyone could bring a gun to campus and shoot you."

Her Converse sneakers squeaked on the tiled floor as she turned and walked out of the room, leaving me alone, a smile frozen on my face, my hands shaking as I tried to shove a pile of student papers into a red tote bag emblazoned with the words "Keep calm and write."

When I'd finally managed to get those papers into the bag, I stood there afraid to walk out. Was Iman paying me a compliment? Or had she issued a warning? Should I mention this to my boss?

I decided against it.

I didn't feel like I was in imminent danger, and if I told Sarah what Iman had said, not only would Iman likely get into some sort of trouble, Sarah and the rest of the administration would probably question my ability to continue teaching. I loved my job, and I loved my students. I wanted to keep doing what I was doing. So I would keep quiet.

But that was the first sign that the mood had shifted on campus. That was the first indication that, soon, I would no longer be welcome in the place where I had, just a year before, begun to feel at home. Among Palestinians, the "anti-normalization" movement was gaining momentum; the thinking behind the movement was that any contact at all with Israeli "occupiers"—a category that even included people like me, despite my politics—constituted "normalization" that would allow Israelis to feel okay about the occupation. Where would anti-normalization leave people like me, people who were opposed to Israel's oppressive policies, people who believed that Palestinians and Jewish Israelis could and should live together in peace, people who were increasingly less welcome in Israeli society? I wasn't sure. Already, I felt like these tenuous footholds I had out here in the West Bank were disappearing.

* * *

And yet, on another afternoon, I felt the complete opposite: I stepped out of class and into the hallway to find Ibtisam, a student I'd had the first year, waiting for me by the door. She greeted me with a hug, and then, from a tote bag, she produced a white envelope. An invitation. This is the custom in Palestine—the bride and groom or their family members distribute invitations in person; the closer you are, the more likely you are to get it from the bride or groom her- or himself. So it meant a lot to get the invitation from Ibtisam, and she let me know that by explaining the custom to me, taking care to mention that she *could* have had some random cousin deliver the invitation, but she'd wanted to do it herself.

Handing the envelope to me, she said, "I'm getting married, Professor Mya. And I want you to come to the wedding."

"Oh!" I said, looking down at the invitation in my hand. "You're getting married."

I didn't have to explain my feelings to Ibtisam. She'd been one of my most promising students the previous year, her freshman year. She'd been eighteen, so I was guessing she was nineteen now. I was concerned that she wouldn't finish her degree and that she was being forced into a life she wasn't choosing for herself. But I couldn't say any of this because it was her culture, her life, and it wasn't for me to pass judgment or comment on.

"And who is the groom?" I asked, avoiding her eyes.

She explained that he was a cousin who lived abroad. It was an arranged marriage, but she'd gotten to know him on the phone over the past year. "He's a good man, Professor Mya," Ibtisam said. "He's promised to let me finish school. It's part of our marriage contract. I wouldn't be marrying him otherwise."

Let you finish school? I thought. It reminded me, of course, of Miguel. But I couldn't explain all this to her. And, obviously, it wasn't my choice anyway. So, instead, I promised her that I would be there. Inside of me I felt tears gathering, but I looked up at her and smiled. "No matter what. I will be there," I said, tucking the invitation into my purse, taking both of her hands in mine, shaking them, and swearing that I wouldn't miss her wedding for the world.

Ibtisam hugged me then. As she turned to head down the hallway, I touched her shoulder. "Wait," I said. "Can I bring a guest?"

* * *

We schemed via email. There was no way her very conservative family would allow me to bring a boyfriend to the event, which would be in Ramallah the following Friday. But Ibtisam wanted to see this man who had captured my heart. We would have to say that Mohamed was my fiancé, at least, she explained. We probably shouldn't say that he was my husband because that was too big of a lie, and if, God forbid, someone from his extended family ended up there and word was circulating that we were married . . . well, that would be scandalous.

I felt guilty about lying, of course, but I increasingly understood that in this culture, this was the way things were done, the way things were smoothed over, so everyone could get on with the business of living.

Once Ibtisam procured her parents' permission for Mohamed to come with me, and Mohamed had agreed to come, I got to work finding an appropriate dress for the wedding. Despite the fact that Bethlehem had a growing Muslim population, the best stores in town were still geared toward the city's Christian minority, and their dresses weren't modest enough. I would drive to East Jerusalem, where, I figured, the styles would be appropriately modest for a conservative Muslim wedding and the prices probably wouldn't be too bad. I found a shop close to Salah a Din that carried gowns from Turkey, and there, among the racks, was a gorgeous black, silk sheath dress. It was sleeveless, but I would put a little cardigan on, and it would be plenty modest. I would be covered from neck to toe and elegantly so. The dress was slightly expensive—three hundred shekels, about eighty dollars. But the event was bigger and more symbolic than Ibtisam's wedding—it would be the first time Mohamed and I went to a large event as a couple. I coughed up the cash, settled the dress in the passenger seat next to me, and drove back to Bethlehem.

* * *

But a week before the wedding, I got sick. This wasn't just a little cold. I couldn't hold anything in my stomach. Eating left me doubled over in pain; the only relief was the horrific, watery diarrhea that expelled everything from my system. Even sips of water left me running to the bathroom. Once there was nothing in my stomach or intestines, I would feel fine and certain I was ready, finally, to eat and drink—only to get sick again.

Still, I was intent on going to this wedding.

But I had no idea how I would get there. Driving, in my condition, seemed risky. If a spasm came—if the pain, which was completely debilitating, struck—I wouldn't be able to continue. I would have to pull over on the side of the road in the middle of the West Bank, which wasn't safe for any number of reasons: soldiers, settlers, Palestinians. Pick one. Depending on where I was, I could be in different types of trouble. And if I needed to go to the bathroom, well, along the road, there would be no bushes to squat behind, no trees to conceal me.

Delegating the driving to someone else—taking public transportation—would be easier. But what if I got sick in a servees and I shit my pants on the way to the wedding?

The obvious question: If I was so sick, why didn't I just go to a doctor?

Well, what if, at the clinic in Bethlehem, they asked for ID and I handed them my American passport and then they checked for a visa and there wasn't one? What would happen if the people at the clinic realized I was Israeli?

Like every other Israeli, I had state-sponsored health care. So, going to the doctor meant driving back to Jerusalem, to the Israeli clinic I went to in Kiryat Yovel. Between the trip in and sitting in the clinic waiting for God knows how long, I would lose half a day, maybe more. And I was busy with my Arabic classes and teaching.

So I made a decision: if food and water were the irritants, well, then I would fast to ensure that I wouldn't get sick on the way to Ramallah. I was going to this wedding. I'd promised Ibtisam. And Mohamed would be waiting for me, too. In a way, appearing before hundreds of people—Arab weddings are huge, numbering as large, sometimes, as a thousand—as an "engaged" couple was like a wedding of our own. It cemented our status.

Though Mohamed had agreed to go with me, the closer the wedding got, the more he expressed his reservations about attending such a public event. Still, the night before the wedding, I put the black dress I'd bought in Jerusalem in a bag beside the door, along with a pair of high heels and a black cardigan. I couldn't wear such clothes on public transportation. I would have to change when I got to Ramallah. That, too, would be an ordeal—Mohamed was concerned about me walking into the office in one outfit and emerging in another. Someone was always watching, and the owner was a conservative Muslim who wouldn't approve of a woman changing inside of a place he owned. So I would meet Mohamed at his office, and from there, we would travel to Professor Tomas's apartment—he'd left Abu Dis and the burj, too—where I would be free to change and put on my makeup. Everything here felt impossibly complicated all the time.

* * *

The morning of the wedding, I got up and, without a sip of water or a bite of food, got ready for Arabic class as usual. Thinking ahead to the servees ride, I dressed modestly in jeans and a black turtleneck and rushed off to class. Afterward, I stopped back by the apartment, with the intention to take the bag with the dress from its post by the door. Slightly dizzy, a headache creeping in, I dropped my Arabic books and notebook on the desk, added my makeup bag to my backpack, and left, racing toward the servees stand, where I grabbed a seat to Ramallah.

The servees set out, flinging itself down the mountainside and then racing through Beit Sahour, past Shepherd's Field, flying past Ramzy's hometown of Dar Salah, its buildings scattered haphazardly across the hillside and glimmering white, its mosque pointing toward the sky.

After passing Dar Salah, the road narrowed sharply, becoming a two-lane "bypass road"—a nice way of saying that it's a Palestinian-only road that routes Palestinians away from both Jerusalem and the nearby Israeli settlements. This particular bypass road was often referred to as Wadi Nar, "Valley of Fire," because the road is cut into the side of the mountain that forms one side of the wadi. This road was also the only route connecting the south of the West Bank—that is, the Bethlehem and Hebron areas—to the north of the West Bank, where Ramallah and other major Palestinian cities stand. Because this road is bisected by the Container, if the Israelis shut the checkpoint down, they can literally cut the West Bank in half, severing the north from the south. This bypass road—which didn't exist before the First Intifada and which was created by Israel's civil administration—is part of Israel's system of separation.

The servees began its steep upward climb, passing a USAID sign reminding passersby that the organization had recently repaved the road. The windows were cracked, and the familiar smell of burning trash filled my nose. There was an odd comfort to the smell—after all, this was the same route I took to campus four days a week. And though it was nerve-racking, I knew every inch of this journey. After we cleared the Container, I knew, it would be a short ride to the university and the adjacent taxi and servees stand. From there, the minivan would turn and head toward Ramallah.

Once we'd made it up the mountain, the servees began hurtling down the other side. It was quiet because it was a Friday, but on a normal day, not only would the driver be riding the brakes all the way down the steep decline—which also included hairpin turns—but he'd be trying to pass people, as well, including enormous trucks. Sure, there was a guardrail to the left, where the mountain dropped off, but the trip was terrifying.

We rounded the last corner, and there, ahead, stood the Container, its watchtower looming. As always, the servees was filled with the sound of seatbelts sliding through the metal guides and the *click click* of them fastening. Many Palestinians don't wear seatbelts, but they put them on as they head into an Israeli-controlled area or a checkpoint—wearing a seatbelt, a visible sign of compliance, is one less reason for a soldier to stop them.

And then came the next familiar sound, a routine part of the commute to Abu Dis—that sound of the servees tires bouncing over the tire spikes, *caduk caduk*, and that familiar jerk as the minivan lurched over the spikes. The soldiers didn't even look at the servees. That was it. We were through.

I was always tense the whole way to the Container. The ride through Wadi Nar was treacherous and terrifying, and passing through the checkpoint was, too. Every time we cleared the checkpoint, my whole body relaxed. The same was true that Friday. The sounds of the seat-belts unclicking, the fabric whooshing back reminded me of a sigh of relief. As I settled into my seat and became aware of my hands clutching my black backpack on my lap, I realized that something was missing.

The bag.

The dress.

Oh no.

In my mind's eye, I saw it all by the door of Matt's apartment, and I saw myself breezing out, pounding down the stairs, as I'd hurried to the bus station.

I sent a frantic text to Mohamed: *I left the dress at Matt's.*

Go back and get it, he replied.

I can't. We've just passed the Container.

Get down in Abu Dis and go back.

That Friday morning, the roads were empty, and the servees was tearing through the village, bouncing over potholes, speeding toward the center where the driver would turn toward the open road that would take us to Ramallah. The farther we went, the farther away I got from the dress, the longer it would take me to get back to Bethlehem, the later I would be to the wedding.

I knew that, if I was going to go back to Bethlehem, I'd better do it now. Once we were out on the open road, there would be nowhere to stop and no servees for me to take back. There would be no choice but to continue on to Ramallah and either show up to Ibtisam's wedding in jeans or not at all.

"*Law samaht* [If you please]," I said to the driver, in Arabic. "I'm sorry, but I forgot something in Bethlehem, and I need to go back."

As if by magic, a servees—white and unmarked, different than our official yellow one—appeared on the road, heading in our direction.

Our driver stuck his arm out the open window and waved at the oncoming vehicle, which stopped. Idling in the middle of the road, my driver asked the other if he was headed to Bethlehem and, if so, did he have room for one more?

I was in luck. He was headed to Bethlehem and he had one empty seat left.

"Yalla [Let's go]," my driver told me.

I thanked him profusely as I got out.

"*Allah maik* [God be with you]," the driver responded.

I boarded the white servees—which was a gypsy cab—and found that it was full of men. They looked like workers, presumably on their way back to their homes after spending the week on a construction site, possibly inside of Israel. They all seemed to know each other, and they chatted boisterously and amicably over the Arabic music blaring through the speakers as we continued forward—that is, heading back in the direction I'd just come from.

The Container was again in sight.

16

Just moments after I'd cleared this very checkpoint headed in the other direction, the soldier stopped us and collected IDs. And we were stuck here, between a mountain and a wadi, with the windows rolled up.

Ten minutes passed, and I felt the temperature climbing. Already dehydrated from days of diarrhea and the fast, my head was pounding. I could have heatstroke here and die, I realized. A few more minutes passed, and my stomach seized up. I began to retch and choke, and I pulled at my turtleneck, trying to get it away from my body. But with my head exploding, even that irritated me—as I pulled at the turtleneck in the front, I felt it straining on the back of my neck. I rolled the turtleneck down, exposing my throat, and then I pushed the sleeves up, feeling them tight around my elbows. I didn't care about modesty. I needed to cool off.

"I'm sick," I said aloud, in Arabic. "And I need water or I will die."

It was a little bit dramatic, but that was the best I could do in the language. And part of me really did think I would be in serious trouble if we sat here much longer.

Fuck it. I was getting out of the servees. Either I was going to die from dehydration or the soldier was going to shoot me.

I opened the sliding door and got out, my legs shaking.

"*Slicha* [Excuse me]," I said in Hebrew to the soldier standing there. I didn't care anymore. Arrest me. Whatever. I just needed water.

He looked at me. I took that as permission to speak.

"I'm very sick and I need water," I said in Hebrew, gesturing to the water cooler on the bench behind him. The cooler was orange, with a white tap at the bottom, like the ones you would see at a college football game. Here we were suffocating inside a servees with the windows rolled up while this soldier was in the shade with all-you-can-drink water.

He didn't respond.

"Please," I continued, in Hebrew, "I really need water. I'm dizzy. I'm going to die if I don't drink something."

"OK, you can have some," he told me. "Bring a cup."

"I don't have a cup."

"Then get back in the vehicle," he said, jerking his gun toward it.

I climbed back in and began to cry.

"He's saying that I need a cup," I reported back to the driver, in Arabic. Without a word, the driver got out of the servees and, with his hands up, approached the soldier. And then he argued with the soldier in fluent Hebrew, not letting up until the soldier brought a paper cup from the guard booth and filled it with water.

The driver came back to the car and presented the cup to me. I thanked him profusely and then held the cup with both hands, worried I would spill it. I sipped it slowly, swirling the water around my mouth to wet my dry gums and tongue, and then swallowed. It burned on the way down. I would be sick again soon.

About half an hour later, a soldier came to the servees, opened the door, and tossed the stack of green IDs in, onto the floor.

No explanation, no nothing. Just like that, we were free to go.

As we pulled away, heading toward the treacherous Wadi Nar road that would lead us back toward Bethlehem, everyone opened the windows. The air flooded in, and I rejoiced as the wind caressed my face. We were moving! Again I could smell burning garbage. That meant I was alive!

A man picked up the IDs off the floor and distributed them. For a moment, no one said a word. And then the driver broke the silence.

"You," he announced in Arabic, turning to glance at me before putting his eyes back on the road, "are an angel."

"*Ana* [Me]?!" I asked in Arabic. "*Lesh* [Why]?"

"It would have been much, much worse if you hadn't been with us," one of the men answered. "Much worse." I assumed he was saying this because he'd seen my American passport, and he felt that, if the car had been full of Palestinians only, the soldiers would have felt free to do whatever they wanted. In the driver's eyes, as a foreigner, I was a witness who made the soldiers feel more accountable.

Spending forty-five minutes in the blistering sun in September with the windows rolled up seemed horrible enough to me. I couldn't imagine how much worse it would have been. Would the soldiers have held the men for hours, until someone really did have heatstroke or die?

The driver put the radio on—another Arabic love song—and the men began to shout their conversations again over the wind and music as though we hadn't all just almost died on the side of a mountain.

* * *

The second ride to Ramallah went without incident, but I was still rattled by what had transpired at the Container—more so, perhaps, because when I passed it for the third time that day, it was completely quiet. From the window of the servees, I looked for something—a sign, some physical trace, anything at all, that those men and I had all just been rendered powerless by an eighteen-year-old kid with a gun. For some of those men, I realized, that boy was young enough to be their own child. How humiliating. I looked for a sign of that indignity but could find none.

The injustice visited upon us was invisible. Of course, as a journalist, I knew plenty about all of the horrible things happening all over the

West Bank every day. But what about moments like this—that left no trace on the land and that didn't show up in the written record? Moments that didn't get reported to some nongovernmental organization, that didn't end up in a press release? Moments the only traces of which resided in the soul.

Of course I didn't need to explain any of this to Mohamed. He had lived through countless moments like this. When I burst into his office finally, the black dress tucked inside a paper bag hanging from my arm, he stood up and rushed over to me, gathering me in his arms, kissing my head.

"I was so worried about you," he whispered into my hair. "That something would happen to you at the checkpoint."

He squeezed me harder then and told me he loved me and began to rock me, as one would a baby.

Mohamed was, generally, a cool, restrained guy. He didn't call me *habibti*, "my love," or call his friends any terms of endearment, either, as most Arab men did. He wasn't like Ramzy—loud and attention seeking and prone to emotional outbursts about finding raw onion in the salad—and observing the two of them together, the way Mohamed just laughed and laughed whenever Ramzy was around, I realized that he enjoyed the way other people displayed their feelings because he struggled to do so himself. So this was one of the biggest shows of emotion Mohamed had given me. As he continued to rock me, I buried my face in his armpit. He rested his chin on my head. And we stood there, swaying like that for a while even though it was hot and he was in a sports coat and this turtleneck was strangling me and even though, at this point, it was hard for me to stand at all with my head throbbing and my legs aching from dehydration.

And then I pulled away.

"Come on," I said. "We can't miss Ibtisam's wedding."

* * *

We were very late to Ibtisam's wedding. When we entered the hall at the hotel—one of Ramallah's finest—the bride and groom were already ensconced in elaborate chairs on the stage as was the tradition, and they looked out silently over the crowd. Ibtisam had just the tiniest hint of a close-lipped smile on her face. She looked serene, content.

I remembered then sitting out on the plaza at the end of the spring semester with Ibtisam and some of my other female students, who were sharing with me, for an article I was writing for the *Los Angeles Review of Books*, what it meant to be a young Palestinian woman. She and some of the other girls had explained to me then this piece of wedding etiquette that revealed so much: "You're not supposed to smile too much at the wedding because then everyone will think you're excited to go to bed and that you're a *sharmouta* [a whore]," Ibtisam said.

The other girls roared with laughter.

"But," Ibtisam continued, "you can't look, like, upset, either, because then it will seem like you don't like your husband or that you're disappointed with the match."

Everyone laughed again, nodding.

"In other words," one of the girls chimed in, "you're not supposed to look like you want to have sex with your husband, but you're also not supposed to look like you *don't* want to have sex with your husband."

Their words echoing in my head, I waved vigorously to Ibtisam, so she would know I'd made it. She tipped her head almost imperceptibly in acknowledgment. I knew, too, that everything she did today would be subject to intense scrutiny and gossip. She had warned me: if she showed too much excitement at the arrival of one guest, she could potentially offend another. So she remained sphinxlike on the stage.

I gulped a glass of water, knowing I would pay for it dearly soon, that I would spend the rest of the wedding in the bathroom. But all that mattered had happened already. I'd reached Mohamed. We'd made it to Ibtisam's wedding, and she'd seen both my face and Mohamed's. She'd seen us together, and she'd given me that slight nod, that little sign of approval.

Suddenly, everyone began to move toward the stage. Mohamed explained to me that now we would present gifts to the bride—mostly gold jewelry—and we would take pictures with the newlywed couple. I hadn't brought gold with me but, rather, a wad of Israeli shekels, the currency that was also used in the occupied territories. I was expecting that it would be the same here as it was at Israeli weddings—I was expecting that there would be a table decked out with a large box and envelopes for guests to leave their cash gift.

As everyone headed toward the bride and groom, I asked Mohamed, "But isn't there a box? Where's the box? And the envelopes?"

There was none. That wasn't how people did things here.

So I stood to make my way to the stage, gripping the wad of money in my hand. When Mohamed didn't stand, I urged him to come with me.

He refused, explaining he didn't want to have his picture taken.

I felt like I'd been slapped in the face. After everything I'd been through to get there, after Ibtisam's efforts to get her parents' consent for Mohamed to come to the wedding. Knowing how important her wedding was to me and knowing, too, how meaningful it was to me that he was attending this event with me.

And he didn't want to appear in a photo?

I asked him why, and he went silent, leaving me to fill in the blanks. I could only assume it had something to do with the risk involved of having such a photo circulate. If, somehow, a family member or friend saw the photo, and someone from the wedding explained that I was his fiancé, he would be in trouble, of course, with his family. But if someone else who knew I was Israeli saw the photo, there could be a whole other kind of problem: Mohamed could be accused of being a collaborator. And those simply accused of collaboration were sometimes killed by other Palestinians. During the Second Intifada, such murders were fairly commonplace, and the bodies were sometimes displayed publicly as a warning to the public: collaborate with the Israelis, and this will be your fate.

And though Mohamed hadn't been accused of being a collaborator, he was already under pressure in the West Bank. Even before he'd been beaten by PA policemen, a plainclothes officer had come to complain about a story Mohamed had worked on. On more than one occasion, as I'd taken the stairs to his office, I'd noticed men loitering in the stairwell. Mohamed had told me that he suspected they were PA henchmen. He was certain he was being watched.

Still, Mohamed's refusal to accompany me to the stage and greet the couple—and his unwillingness to explain himself—made me wonder about his intentions. What was this relationship? Was it real? Upset,

I headed toward the stage alone, feeling as though the other guests were seeing me and judging us. It felt humiliating to get in line by myself as he sat there at the table, and I wondered, too, how all this would look to Ibtisam.

And then I felt a presence next to me. It was Mohamed, there in his sports coat, standing with me. "OK. We'll do the photo," he said.

It was our turn and we mounted the stage. Mohamed went to the groom to congratulate him and I went to Ibtisam. My throat caught and my eyes filled with tears as I whispered, in Arabic, "*Alf mabrouk*," a thousand congratulations. I took her hand in mine and handed her the crumpled wad of cash, apologizing for the faux pas. I also told her I was sorry for being late. "The Container," I explained, and she nodded knowingly.

It was time to pose for a photo. Flanking the bride and groom, Mohamed and I smiled toward the camera and then walked off the stage.

We sat back down, and Mohamed, looking uncomfortable, rested his hands on the table. I knew he was thinking about the photo. I took his hand in mine—which would have been taboo if we were merely dating but was fine as an "engaged" couple—and I squeezed it, thanking him for joining me.

I knew then that we were in this together.

17

After the wedding, I finally felt confident that our relationship was on solid ground. Now my sublease was almost up, and I needed to find a permanent place to live. I wasn't moving back to Jerusalem, where Mohamed wouldn't be able to reach me. And though Ramallah would put me and Mohamed in the same city, it was too far afield—it could take upward of an hour to get to campus. I definitely wasn't going back to Abu Dis, where everyone watched our every move. Although the Container stood between Bethlehem and Abu Dis, the commute only took about twenty minutes. So I began to look for a place in Bethlehem where, we agreed, we could spend weekends together after spending the workweek apart.

Bethlehem seemed close enough to Mohamed for us to continue our relationship, for us to be intimate, for me to make sure I wasn't cutting myself off from love, but it was also far enough from him that it ensured I would have my own life. Still painfully aware of the way my relationships with Miguel and Oded had allowed me to hide from the world and myself, I wanted to make sure I wasn't getting involved with Mohamed for the wrong reasons. Yes, we'd talked about getting married in the future and, yes, this move was supposed to help us figure out if we wanted to take that step. But I wanted that choice to come from a healthy, balanced perspective: I wanted enough time with him to be confident in a decision about building a life together but not so much time together that we would be codependent or that I would be involved in the relationship as a way to avoid facing myself.

Online, I found an advertisement for a stunning place on the edge of the Old City—on the other side of the Church of Nativity, close to the village of Beit Sahour. The price was shockingly low—a few hundred dollars for the whole ground floor of an old, limestone-faced Arab mansion. The photos showed a spacious living room, a large eat-in kitchen, and two bedrooms, all capped with those soaring, vaulted ceilings. French doors opened to a garden glowing green with lemon and apricot trees, jasmine shrubs and grape vines.

But the elderly landlady—a Christian Palestinian woman by the name of Jacqueline—what did she want to show me when I arrived?

Taking me firmly by the hand, she led me to the kitchen. Next to the stove was a pair of curtains. She parted the fabric to reveal a crawl space, and she lifted a stone to reveal a hole in the floor. She got down on her knees then and insisted I do the same.

Jacqueline pointed into the hole.

"We have a well," she said.

This was the apartment's most important feature. Not those vaulted ceilings. Not the garden. Not the many windows and those cushioned alcoves. But the well. Bethlehem frequently lost water. I remembered this from the weekend I'd spent at my friend Robert's apartment, how he'd had buckets in the bathtub to collect the water that ran off his body as he showered. How he'd bottled it, explaining to me that he used it to flush the toilet when the taps went dry. Israel diverts much of the West Bank's water for its own use; the Israeli government even forbids Palestinians from collecting rainwater.[1] I wasn't sure if Jacqueline's well was full of rainwater or if it tapped into some underground supply—there were springs all over the place in both Israel and the West Bank—and I wouldn't have been surprised if it was the latter.

Whatever the case, she covered it back up and then walked me through the apartment, showing me everything she considered an advantage. The first thing she pointed out was that, as a woman living there alone, I would be very safe because the apartment was more or less hidden. From the main street, the second floor—where Jacqueline lived with her sister—appeared to be the ground floor. Only when the road made a sharp right and pitched itself downhill, wrapping around the corner of the house, were the garage and garden doors exposed. I could use these two as my entrance. There was space to park a car, if I had one, she added, and taking me into the garden, she pointed out that, with the house to my back, I had walls on either side of me. Because the house was built into the hillside, the garden was on a terrace and we were elevated, with a ten or so foot drop below the garden. It would be next to impossible for someone to climb up from the neighbor's orchard below.

So I wouldn't need to worry about intruders, she said, something I hadn't thought about at all.

Jacqueline led me upstairs to her living room to chat. One wall was nothing but windows, and when I gasped audibly at the view, she chuckled.

"Oh my God," I said. It was the same as the one I had from the garden but even more spectacular. Dheisheh refugee camp was invisible here—it was just the hills, an unfettered view of the olive terraces, and it was like being transported back in time. There was no refugee camp, no Israeli settlement looming on the horizon. It was like 1948 and 1967 had never happened. All I could see was Palestine.

Jacqueline asked me if I wanted tea or coffee, and I said I would take a cup of tea. She urged me to sit, and I did. Returning with a tray, she took a seat across from me.

---

1. See "The Occupation of Water," Amnesty International, November 29, 2017, https://www.amnesty.org/en/latest/campaigns/2017/11/the-occupation-of-water/.

"I have many questions for you," she began, explaining that, as we would be living in the same building together, she couldn't just rent to anyone. Adding that she had rejected the last person who had looked at the place because she suspected he was a Jew, she gave me a pointed look.

"Uh-huh," I said, nodding, concentrating on my tea. I took a sip.

She waited for me to say something. "What about you?" she asked.

"Oh!" I said, pretending like I hadn't realized she was waiting for me to answer her pointed look. "I'm an American."

"An American," she repeated, nodding. "Yes. I can tell by your accent. How long have you been here?"

"Six years."

"In Bethlehem?"

"No. Inside. In Israel."

"Six years inside? Long time. The Israelis don't give out visas like that. Usually foreigners stay two, three years, and then"—she wiped her hands one against the other—"no more visa."

Having no way to defend myself, I stayed silent, which only stoked Jacqueline's suspicions.

Shaking her head, she put a finger in the air, wagged it, and asked me outright, "What are you doing here? How have you managed to stay for so long?" The subtext was clear. Jacqueline suspected that I was a Jew, an Israeli, or maybe both.

"I've been working as a journalist," I said, sidestepping the visa issue. "Now I'm teaching at the university in Abu Dis."

"And you still don't speak Arabic?"

"*Bahki Arabi shway* [I speak a little Arabic]," I responded. "I studied in Jerusalem, and I'm learning here, now, too."

She nodded, took a sip of her coffee, and stared at me, letting the silence accumulate around us, letting it bear down on me.

"I have a Palestinian husband," I blurted out, in Arabic. "He works in Ramallah and will only be here on the weekends."

"No, you don't have a husband," Jacqueline answered in English. "You have a *boyfriend*."

Of course she didn't buy it. Not only was I not wearing a ring, but if I did have a local husband, chances are we'd be living with his family. Or I would have mentioned him earlier on in the conversation. I blushed.

"It's OK," Jacqueline said, reaching across the small table between us to offer me her hands. As I placed my fingers in her palms, I felt her skin, thin, papery, cool. "As long as it's only one. Some of these foreign girls have so many boyfriends. Oooo! So many men coming in and out of the house! I can't have that going on here. *Jarritna,* our neighbors. You know."

She dropped my hands then and gestured to the air around us, as though everyone was watching even at this moment.

I told her I understood and that I only had one boyfriend.

"Good. Good. I come from a good family," she added, lifting her chin proudly. "We have a good name. But I never got married."

"Why?" I asked.

"Oh," she shifted uncomfortably in her chair, glancing out the windows at the hills, "I got sick when I was young. I lost a kidney. I was skinny, like a chicken." She laughed then. "No one wanted to marry a skinny girl."

I suspected there was more to it than that. She'd put the blame on the men, but for some reason, I suspected that it was Jacqueline who hadn't wanted to marry. But I didn't ask any questions. I left it at that. And there we were, two women hiding our pasts, hiding ourselves, from one another.

"Your boyfriend," she continued, "his name is?"

"Mohamed."

She arched her eyebrows. "Ah, he's Arab? What's his family name?"

"Jaradat," I answered.

She repeated it to herself. "I don't know this family," she said.

"They're from Sa'ir."

She nodded. "This boyfriend, this Mohamed of yours," she said with a hint of conceit in her voice, and I knew right away that she wasn't a fan of the Muslims, "I would like to meet him before I give you an answer about the apartment."

* * *

That evening, on the phone, I recounted the conversation to Mohamed, who laughed and agreed that we would go see Jacqueline that weekend.

We returned to her house on Friday, after my Arabic class, knocking on the front door. This time, she came out and led us around the corner to the small door in the wall, which opened onto the garden patio. She unlocked the French doors, and we followed her in that way, into the apartment.

"Wow," Mohamed said, as he took off his sunglasses. He looked up at the vaulted ceilings and out toward the garden. "It looks like a movie set."

He explained to Jacqueline that he'd worked recently on a feature-length film with a famous Palestinian director and that he'd been a location scout and manager. Clearly impressed, she nodded appreciatively and asked Mohamed about his work. Mohamed said he mostly worked with journalists. "That's how I met Mya," he said, grinning.

She smiled, too. "Come on," she said to Mohamed, "I want to give you a tour."

As we fell into line behind her, Mohamed whispered in my ear, "I'm pretty sure she likes you."

Jacqueline took us straight to the kitchen, parted those curtains again, and lifted the stone.

"*Taal* [Come]," she said and gestured to Mohamed, and they kneeled together. "*Shuf* [Look].

"A well!" she exclaimed in Arabic.

Mohamed was impressed. He followed her around, listening patiently to the same talk she'd given me just a few days before—how secure the place was, how safe I would be there, even when he wasn't around. As I watched him listening to her respectfully, I was reminded of our first day together in Ramallah, and I thought about how much I liked the way he showed the people around him honor. He was quiet, and that was sometimes difficult for me, but that was also what I loved about him—he seemed solid, calm, steady.

Mohamed asked her a few gentle questions, and it pried open her whole story, which spilled out of Jacqueline in a mix of Arabic and English, presumably for my benefit.

A refugee born in Jaffa—one of seven children—she and her family had fled in 1948, during the war, coming to Bethlehem, where they had relatives. After her brothers finished their studies in Bethlehem, one after another, all had left for university or work abroad—either the Gulf or America—never to return. A brother who lived in California had bought the house where she and her older sister still lived today. Her older sister was quite ill and was bedridden; Jacqueline was her caregiver.

As her name hinted, Jacqueline spoke fluent French—which was not uncommon for Christian Palestinians of her generation—and she had worked for many years at a French nongovernmental organization. But to make a little extra money, Jacqueline had been renting out the bottom floor for over two decades now. In the beginning, all of her tenants had been Palestinian students who attended Bethlehem University. During the Second Intifada, with movement restrictions, it got crazy for a while, she said, as students who normally commuted found themselves stuck in Bethlehem. Sometimes she would open the door that stood between the second floor and the garden apartment and peek down the stairs only to find a dozen to two dozen people sleeping in the place.

"No more," she said. "It was too much. Chaos."

After the Second Intifada, she'd stopped renting to students for the most part and had been very careful about whom she rented to, mostly leasing to foreigners who were in Palestine working for nongovernmental organizations or an embassy or whatever.

"And now, *inti*, ya Mya," she said to me with a grin, grabbing my hand and dropping the key into it, folding my fingers around it, and patting them.

I was delighted. The place was perfect. And it was mine.

It also felt meaningful to me to rent from a refugee, to put money in her hand. I felt a tinge of guilt about not disclosing my identity to her. But I knew that she wouldn't rent the place to me otherwise, and I was technically an American, just like I told her. That wasn't a lie.

18

Mohamed had promised that he would come from Ramallah to spend my first night in the new apartment there with me. My lease began on a Tuesday, and after school that day, I rushed back to Bethlehem from Abu Dis, picked up the very last of my things from the sublease, loaded them into my car, and drove through the Old City the very short distance to Jacqueline's. The garage door opener she'd given me worked, and slowly, the enormous steel door—which had been painted mustard yellow—moved to the left.

I steered my car in, and then the door slowly slid shut behind me. When it clanked to a stop, I was struck by the silence of the place, the peacefulness of it. The garden was before me, filled with green, and there stood the large, graceful stone house. The place felt like an oasis.

Here, tucked under Jacqueline's house, hidden behind a wall, I could pretend like the outside world didn't exist.

Inside, I readied the house for Mohamed's arrival, making the bed in the master bedroom and unpacking pots and dishes in the kitchen for the dinner I would make. Before heading to the market, I called Mohamed to see if there was anything special he wanted to eat.

"I'm not coming," he said.

My stomach dropped.

"But you said you would," I said.

"I'm sick," he said.

"*Salamtak,*" I said, wishing him health. "What's wrong?"

Mohamed explained that Ramzy had shown up at his office the previous night with a bottle of whiskey. Mohamed didn't think, in his current state, he could stomach the ride from Ramallah to Bethlehem.

"So you're not sick," I said. "You're hungover."

I was getting tired of his white lies, his omissions. I was tired of being omitted from his life, too. Besides Ramzy, he'd only introduced me to one other friend at this point. And, one evening, just before I moved into Jacqueline's, his sister called to ask Mohamed if he was coming home. I eavesdropped on the entire conversation and understood that he'd told his sister that he was out "with friends" and that he would be back tomorrow. Not a word about me. I didn't push the issue; I understood that oftentimes even Palestinian couples dated in secret until they were ready to get married. Still, I couldn't help but wonder if I'd moved to Bethlehem—if I was putting myself at risk—for someone who wasn't really so committed to me.

Now, on the phone, Mohamed admitted sheepishly that he was indeed hungover. And that was starting to annoy me, too—the way Mohamed refused to show any vulnerabilities, the way he refused to admit, ever, that he'd made a mistake. No chinks in the armor. Ever.

As we said goodbye, he promised he'd be there Thursday night. Or maybe Friday.

It was like that moment at the wedding again, when he refused to take a photo with me. It was like the days following his trip to Gaza, when he disappeared on me. Here I was, making sacrifices and putting myself out there—in the most literal sense of the word—crossing the line, living beyond the wall, in Bethlehem, deep in Palestinian territory. And yet, here I was alone.

I felt like I was in the dark. Mohamed said he loved me. In Kiryat Yovel, we'd sat on that bench and talked about getting married; we'd agreed that I should move to Bethlehem so we could spend more time together, so we would know for sure that marriage was the right decision.

So where was he? If my move out here was important to Mohamed, maybe he wouldn't have gotten hammered with Ramzy the night before. Knowing he was traveling to Bethlehem the next day, he would have had a couple of drinks. Whether it was intentional or subconscious, the fact that Mohamed hadn't shown up today to celebrate the move with me felt like a message that he didn't really care and that this step wasn't all that important to him.

Wondering if I'd made this move for nothing, I looked around the big, empty space.

* * *

Mohamed showed up that weekend, and we drove to the Palestinian village of Battir, which happened to be the home of Ali—the young man we'd interviewed in 2012 whose wife was stuck in Gaza. Battir is a UNESCO world heritage site because of the unique watering system the local families still employ today to care for the village's ancient agricultural terraces. Eggplant is among the produce locals grow, and *beitinjan battiri*, "Battiri eggplant," is renowned throughout Palestine for its unique flavor.

As we wandered about the village, we happened upon a brochure that discussed the village's history—including mention that the place was once home to an ancient Judean town, Beitar. This sort of acknowledgment of the narrative of the "other side" seemed strange to me, and I pointed it out to Mohamed.

"Of course the Jews were here in Palestine," he said. "It even says so in the Quran."

"Hence," I said, "Beitar Illit [Upper Beitar]," a Jewish settlement in the West Bank.

"*Aiwa* [Yes]," Mohamed said. "But just because the Jews were here in the past doesn't mean they have a right to occupy us today."

He was preaching to the choir, I reminded Mohamed. I was on his side. According to international law, all of the settlements, including Beitar Illit, were illegal. Not just that, but they'd been built on land confiscated from either private Palestinian owners or Palestinian villages. I was entirely opposed to the occupation—I didn't think the settlements should be there, and the army definitely shouldn't be out here, either.

In the days that followed, Mohamed and I talked a lot about that brochure and the effect it had had on me. There was something really powerful to me about the mention of the ancient Jews' presence in Beitar, an admission that, in my mind, didn't undermine the Palestinians' presence on the land. However counterintuitive, pointing directly to all the layers of history, including that of the ancient Hebrews, had the opposite effect—acknowledging the counterargument rather than trying to brush it under the rug only strengthened Palestinians' claim to the place. But dare I say, too, that the brochure gave me hope? Mentioning Jews' historical connection to the place made me feel like the one-state vision that Mohamed and I shared was a real possibility.

After our trip to Battir, we talked a lot about narratives and the power that came from simply acknowledging others' stories. We discussed how when we tried to erase things, how when we tried to omit or discount others' narratives, we were opening the door to the delegitimization of our own stories. We agreed that you don't have to agree with someone to listen to them. Understanding and acknowledging their narratives, their lived truths, doesn't mean you agree with those stories or the ideas or politics behind them.

I felt ready then to share a big piece of myself that I'd been hiding from Mohamed—the story of my connection to Tel Aviv. No, I didn't have a proper family in Israel, but that city felt like a parent to me. Tel Aviv had been the place where I'd liberated myself from a marriage I found confining and oppressive; that city had given birth to the adult version of myself. There, I'd become a journalist, I'd learned Hebrew, and I'd remade myself in that old-new language. In Tel Aviv, I'd had a new necklace made—one that said my name in Hebrew, as it appeared in my Israeli ID: מאיה.

In Tel Aviv, I'd become the woman that Mohamed fell in love with; he couldn't really know me—he couldn't understand me—without seeing this place that had shaped me.

I asked Mohamed if he would like to go to Tel Aviv with me. He said yes. But getting to Tel Aviv from Bethlehem when your boyfriend is a West Bank Palestinian without a permit to enter is no small task.

I would have to drive him through the checkpoint that I used to exit the West Bank and reach Jerusalem, a checkpoint known as "The Tunnels" because beyond it were the tunnels that carried traffic underground and into the city. This trip was dangerous, of course. If we were stopped at the Tunnels, we could both be arrested. I could be arrested for helping a Palestinian enter Israel without a permit, and Mohamed would be arrested for entering without permission. Obviously, if this happened, the consequences would be far worse for Mohamed. As a citizen of Israel, I would be subject to civil law and that would put some parameters around my arrest. Mohamed, who was subject not to Israeli law but that of the military regime, could, in theory, end up in administrative detention, detainment with charge or trial.

Despite the enormous risk, we planned a Friday trip. We would walk around the city, we would meet some of my friends for a drink, and then we would hit the beach to watch the sunset and then drive back out to the West Bank. As we did all of this, I would explain to Mohamed what these places—and the people—meant to me. He didn't have to agree with the city's existence or how it came to be or any of the politics around its birth or its current status. He didn't have to agree with anything. I just wanted him to see this city that would forever be a part of me; I wanted him to see and understand me.

* * *

"Are you sure about this?" I asked Mohamed as we got into the car that Friday morning. Part of me hoped he would back out. I was nervous about going through the checkpoint. I was also increasingly worried that this trip would blow up in my face, that my attempt to share this place with him would upset him, that we would end up fighting.

"Yes. This is my land. They're not going to tell me when and where I can enter," he said, taking my hand. "If I want to go to Tel Aviv with my Jewish girlfriend, I'm going to do it."

I started the engine, and we were off, rattling over the cobblestone streets of Bethlehem's Old City, making the climb up through Beit Jala, passing the army base on the edge of Beit Jala, making a left onto the road that linked both Beit Jala and neighboring Israeli settlements with Route 60, and then making a right onto Route 60.

The Tunnels were right in front of us.

My stomach turned. We were so close there was literally no way to turn around. As the checkpoint drew nearer, Mohamed wiggled downward in his seat, until his head was barely visible, as though he was hiding from the soldiers. But I was worried that would just make things worse. I didn't know what to do—if he sat up straight, maybe they would see him and stop us. If he slouched down and a soldier spotted him, the slouching would make it obvious that he was trying to escape detection, and that would arouse suspicion, too.

It depressed me that Mohamed was hiding like that; it felt undignified. It also felt ridiculous—the Tunnels connected one part of Palestinian land to another. He shouldn't have to hide while he was on his own land.

For all these reasons, I almost told Mohamed to sit up, but as I opened my mouth to say the words, I stopped. Who was I to tell Mohamed how to deal with this moment that was infinitely more fraught for him as a Palestinian than it was for me, someone who held Israeli citizenship? It was much more dangerous for him to get caught sneaking in with me than it was for me to get caught sneaking him in.

But neither of us should have to sneak around at all.

The closer we got to the checkpoint, the sicker I felt. My intestines twisted, and I felt the urge to go to the bathroom. I slowed down as we hit the rumble strip. The car bounced over the tire spikes, and we approached the booths and the soldiers and private security forces—mercenaries—milling about. Keeping my left hand on the wheel, I lifted two of my fingers at the soldiers, a gesture I'd learned from Hadas, who'd sworn that it conveyed authority and cool confidence to the soldiers, signaling them to stand down.

And they did. They stood down. One waved at me as I passed, and that was it. We were through.

Mohamed sat up in the seat and smoothed out his white, button-down linen shirt. We entered the Tunnels—which had been built on and under privately owned Palestinian land that Israel had confiscated from two villages—and were immersed in the darkness. When we popped out into the light again, we were in East Jerusalem.

19

I drove us to my old neighborhood in Tel Aviv—not the city center, where I'd shared an apartment with Oded on that corner of Allenby, King George, and Sheinken, but, rather, my old neighborhood in south Tel Aviv, Kiryat Shalom. Parking close to my old apartment, I walked Mohamed through the place as I'd experienced it.

"There's my old balcony," I said, pointing up at the French doors and telling him how, when I'd first arrived in September of 2007—after living for six weeks on a kibbutz—it was brutally hot. So I'd slept with those French doors open, and the pigeons had flown in and out of my room all night long; terrified, I'd spent the night awake, cowering under the scratchy orange polyester sheets I'd bought at the Central Bus Station. On one occasion, a pigeon had flapped straight into the ceiling fan, and the blades had sent it flying across the room. After that, I'd tried sleeping with the French doors closed, but it was too hot. So I'd been forced to overcome my fear. I'd gotten used to the birds; eventually, I'd even come to like them.

I pointed to the neighbor's apartment, recounting to Mohamed how the Bukhari Jewish family that lived there, thinking me too skinny, had taken to dragging me into their kitchen where the old matriarch had force-fed me chicken, despite my protests that I was vegetarian. "It's not meat!" her sons told me, in Hebrew. "It's chicken!"

I led Mohamed through the neighborhood, navigating it as I had when I lived there—not by street but by sight. I knew to swing a right by a particular clump of jasmine, and I knew that, when I saw this particular lemon tree, we needed to duck into the alley and that, when we popped out of that alley, we needed to follow the brick pathway past the house with the rooster and then cross the road with the heavy name: Kibbutz Galuyot, the "ingathering of the exiles."

After we crossed, I showed him the graveyard that was hidden from the road by a retaining wall. Before I'd known what was there, I'd walked by it day after day until one afternoon, I'd noticed a mound of dirt and a path that led over the wall. Curious, I'd hiked up and been shocked to find headstones engraved with Arabic. It was the Sheikh Murad cemetery, which predated the state, serving as a reminder that this part of the city was once part of Arab Jaffa.

I explained to Mohamed how discovering this graveyard right here in the middle of the path that took me through my daily routine had started to make the nakba salient to me in ways it hadn't been before, how that moment had been a turning point for me. I'd been left-wing before, but walking through the Sheikh Murad cemetery had left me outraged. I'd been infuriated by the retaining wall that seemed like an attempt to hide the site. And as I'd stood there in the cemetery—looking across Kibbutz Galuyot Road and seeing an empty field on the other side—it had been easy to imagine this place without the road. I'd seen how what Israel had built had literally split this piece of land—and all the land—in half. I told him how the site had galvanized me to learn more and to go deeper into the history and politics as a journalist, too.

We walked through Shapira, and I stopped to point out the basketball court where I'd covered that Passover seder where African asylum seekers and Israelis had gathered around tables together.

We popped out of Shapira at the Central Bus Station. Other people hated this place, but I found it beautiful because it was a hub for Israel's migrant community, a group I'd spent years covering as a journalist.

Block after block, story after story, Mohamed listening intently, we made our way to the city center. I showed him the Shuk HaCarmel, where I'd bought my groceries and, for a time, collected free food. I pointed up Sheinken Street as we passed and told him that my old building was second from the corner and that farther up the street was where I'd picked through the bags of leftover bread on Friday afternoons when I was struggling to survive.

We went on to the beach where, sitting side by side, we watched the sunset, snapping a photo together with the sea behind us. I told Mohamed how I used to run here, along the *tayelet*, "the promenade"; I didn't tell him how, in my earliest days in Israel, I'd drilled myself in the Hebrew language as I did so, chanting newly acquired vocabulary.

From the beach, we headed to a bar to meet some of my friends, and that was when Mohamed lapsed into silence. Most of the friends I'd invited were Anglo, and all were English speakers, so it wasn't about an inability to communicate. It was an unwillingness.

I couldn't figure out why he seemed so upset. He'd agreed to meet these people. Why was he so sullen now?

"Are you OK?" I whispered to Mohamed as he sat, still, as everyone engaged in an animated conversation around him.

"Yeah," he said, and then he took a slug of his beer. But I knew this wasn't true.

I zoomed out for a moment and wondered how we looked to Mohamed, how it felt to him to be sitting here, in this place, among us. And I became uncomfortable. I knew why he was silent; I knew what he was thinking: *This is Palestine, and look at all these people, all these foreigners, on my land.* I felt guilty then in a way that I didn't when I was in the West Bank, where my presence didn't affirm the state of Israel but, rather, resisted the ideological and physical boundaries it imposed on everyone.

"What's wrong?" I asked Mohamed, knowing the answer.

"Nothing," he said, forcing a smile. "*Kolshi tamam* [Everything's fine]," he said in Arabic.

* * *

But he remained quiet as we departed the bar and began to make our way back to the car. I tried to lead the way—we would retrace the route we'd taken to the city center—but at every turn, Mohamed insisted on a different route. I did not want to argue about directions with him. And the whole thing seemed silly. I was the one who had actually lived here.

Standing on the corner of Allenby and Jaffa Street, we began to argue. Mohamed was insisting that we hang a right, but what we needed to do was go straight.

"I know where I'm going," he shouted.

"No, you don't. I lived in Tel Aviv for years."

He scoffed. "But you have no real connection to this place."

"I don't?" I asked.

Had he heard anything I'd said to him today? Had he understood what this city meant to me? Hadn't he gotten that it was a place where I had overcome so many fears, that it was a place where complete strangers had pulled me into their home to nourish me and my body, that it was a place where I'd felt safe enough to become strong and independent? I'd had empathy for him and the plight of the Palestinians. Was it too much to expect that he would extend some to me—not as an Israeli but as his girlfriend?

"Nothing I showed you today matters?"

"No," he said. "You weren't born here. You didn't grow up here."

"You didn't either," I shot back, surprised to hear myself saying this and shocked that I'd gone for such a low blow.

"I was born here."

"And then you grew up in Amman."

"My whole family is from here."

"OK, so you 'count,'" I said, using my hands to make air quotes. "So that's the measure: being born here? What about Palestinians who were born in the diaspora? Whose parents and aunts and uncles and cousins were all born in the diaspora, too? Whose whole families left even *before* 1948? Whose great-grandparents and grandparents were born in Chile or wherever? Are they still Palestinian?"

"*Tab'an* [Of course]," he answered in Arabic. "They have a connection to the land."

"And the Jews don't?"

"They *did*. But they don't anymore because they left. By their own free will, thousands of years ago."

"So? The Christian Palestinians who left *before* 1948 left by their own free will, too. Why is their connection to the land legitimate and the Jewish connection to the land isn't?"

"*Heik* [It's like that]," he said in Arabic, shrugging. "Because this is Palestine."

"OK, yes, sure, it's Palestine. I don't really care *what* we call the place. Jews can't have connections to Palestine? I've lived here for *years*. I still do. I live here. I work here, with Palestinian students. I drink the water, I breathe the air, and none of that counts? You're telling me I have no connection to this place?"

All the things we'd talked about after our visit to Battir—about listening and acknowledging—were out the window in an instant. The fight went on and on, and I found myself arguing points that I didn't even believe in. I talked about the religious connection to the land even though I'd actually long believed that the concepts of Zion and Eretz Yisrael were entirely metaphorical. If Palestinians in the diaspora yearned for the land they'd been expelled from less than one hundred years before, then imagine—the Jews had longed to return for a couple thousand years! Why was one group's feelings legit and the other's not? I talked about how my grandfather's parents had emigrated from Poland only to lose contact with all the family they'd left there, presumably because everyone died in the Holocaust. Surely, at some time, we had needed a place to go. And maybe it shouldn't have been here—maybe we should have gone to Nigeria instead, as some early Zionist leaders had proposed—but, "*Heik*," I said in Arabic, it's like that.

"*Hinei anachnu*, here we are," I said in Hebrew, before switching to English. "So, what, you want to push us all into the sea?" I asked.

"No, but you could all just *leave*," he said. "Go back to Germany or Poland or America or wherever you all come from."

"We don't all come from somewhere. Not everyone here has a second passport. There are Israelis who were born here," I reminded him. "What about *them*? Where are they supposed to go?"

"I don't know," he said. "It's not my problem."

"Jesus!" I shouted. "And what about *me*? What about *us*?"

"You're different. You can stay."

"But you just said I have no connection to this place!"

Neither of us was making any sense, and it went on and on and on like this as we walked in circles and fought in circles, and I tried to remind Mohamed how someone—how I—could love the land and the place and the people and feel deeply connected to it all and still be totally opposed to Zionism and Israeli policy. These were all things we'd discussed and agreed on before, when we were sitting in his office in the West Bank. But I realized there was a difference between talking about all this with me while we were in the middle of Ramallah and actually walking through Tel Aviv, where most people were not like me. I realized that while he believed in one shared democratic state, intellectually, it was deeply upsetting emotionally for Mohamed to see the city that had played a key role in cementing Israel on the land.

Still, I was frustrated to find myself arguing about things we'd seemed to be united about.

And there was no convincing Mohamed of anything, and there was no convincing him to follow me through the city. So there was no choice but to shut up and let him take the lead.

Of course, I knew the way back to the car. I could have just walked away—I could have just left him there on the sidewalk and let him sort it out on his own. But I loved Mohamed, and I wasn't going to just abandon him in Tel Aviv without a permit. And even if he did have a permit, they didn't allow Palestinians to be inside overnight. I knew, too, he wouldn't be able to find transportation back to the West Bank at this time. I knew he would end up sleeping in a park.

Finally, an hour into this, he stopped along a busy road—cars whizzing by—and he just stood there, eyes wide, arms drooping at his sides. He was defeated, I realized. He was lost and exhausted. But

I knew that he couldn't admit this. And I wasn't going to force him to do so.

So I tried to take his hand—to mend the rift, to guide him home—and he yanked it away. I tried again, taking him by the elbow this time, and he didn't resist. I steered him as gently as I could, leading him through an empty parking lot, across a street, along a road, across another street. Eventually, my hand slid down his arm, and we laced our fingers together. But we didn't speak. Like this, silently, we wove our way through the city until we arrived, at last, back to my car in Kiryat Shalom.

Almost as soon as I began to drive, he fell asleep in the passenger seat. I made the trip back out to the West Bank in silence—no radio, no nothing—waking him only when we'd arrived at Jacqueline's, when we'd pulled into the garden and, behind us, the garage door was safely closed.

We got into bed, and he went back to sleep right away. But I lay there, replaying our trip to Tel Aviv in my mind. I realized that we wouldn't be able to live inside together. Never mind the legal barrier, being inside together had been far too fraught. If this was how he'd reacted to a trip in, I couldn't imagine how upset Mohamed would be every day if he lived there.

I realized that, if we were going to make a life together, we would have to do it here, in the West Bank.

20

In part because I didn't have reliable internet at my place—the old street and the building, at that time, lacked the infrastructure—and because Lena, a Palestinian Christian woman who was my best friend here, lived at home and was always happy to get out of her parents' house, the two of us became fixtures at the Casa Nova, a small hotel and restaurant immediately next to the Church of Nativity. The place wasn't just for tourists. Centrally located, Palestinians often sat there, too, either on the stone terrace that was ringed with potted plants or inside, under the spectacular ceiling decorated with a brightly painted geometric molding that evoked Morocco or Andalucia. Leaning back on a cushioned bench, looking up at the patterns, I thought of Islamic

Spain—the golden age during which Muslims, Christians, and Jews lived together and learned from each other, when our cultures mingled.

Maybe that was the real reason we sat at the Casa Nova so much—we felt free, like we were in another place or another time.

There, at the Casa Nova, which we affectionately called "the Nova," we knew the lone waiter by name. We always ordered drinks but usually skipped the food, which wasn't great; I would leave Lena and dart across Nativity Plaza to get *makhlouta*, "mixed nuts," from a little place next to the mosque facing the Church of Nativity. And then I'd return with the makhlouta and we sat there, working our way through the bag, sitting not across from each other but next to each other, sometimes with our laptops, trying to work, but usually gossiping in a mixture of English and Arabic and laughter.

"Write this one down in your little notebook, ya Mya," Lena said one afternoon. "Are you ready?"

Notebook and pen in hand, I said I was.

"OK. *Shayf addik arnab*," she said.

I repeated the words back to her and labored over them in my notebook and then showed them to her, like a proud pupil.

"Is that right?"

"*Ken* [Yes]," she said, in Hebrew.

I hushed her.

She shushed me back. "*Shoo* [What]?" she asked. "*Shoo* the fuck is *hada?*" Lena said, laughing. [What the fuck is this?]

"You can't speak Hebrew in public," I admonished her.

"I can, *habibti,* because I'm Palestinian."

"Yes, but what about me?" I whispered, implying that she could blow my cover without saying so.

"*You* can speak Hebrew here in the Casa Nova, too," she said. "Every day there's Israeli tour guides in here on their phones: *Ken! Mah koreh, achi?*" [Yes! What's happening, my brother?]

I'd seen them, too, rushing out of the Casa Nova to take a call while the group they were escorting ate lunch. Her impression of them was spot-on and hilarious, and we dissolved into giggles.

Lena was making light of what was a big point of contention, of course—while Area A was supposed to be legally off limits to Israelis, an exception was made for Israeli tour guides who had permission to come in and out of Bethlehem. But Palestinian tour guides who were actually *from* Bethlehem, who actually *lived* in Bethlehem, could not do the same. Therefore, because they could not freely travel to and from Jerusalem—and what tour of the Holy Land excluded Jerusalem?—Palestinian tour guides were, by and large, excluded from this business. Add to that the fact that tours were designed to pop in and out of Bethlehem for the day and return to Jerusalem, where the tourists would sleep at hotels in West Jerusalem and the majority of the money stayed in Israeli hands. Every day, on my way to and from the bus station where I picked up the servees to Abu Dis, I would pass all the souvenir shops—open and empty, the Palestinian owners lingering in the doorway, waiting for someone to come and spend even just a little bit of money—and I would think about how unfair it was, how this practice of corralling the tourists and their dollars in Jerusalem had a ripple effect through the local economy.

It was extractive, exploitative, and yet another of the endless reminders that the occupation permeated every last corner of Palestinian life.

I tapped on the notebook and then at the phrase I'd jotted down. "*Shayf addik arnab,*" I read it aloud. "To see a rooster rabbit?" I could translate this phrase literally, but I had no idea what it meant.

"*Bizzabt!*" Exactly! Lena began laughing again. "See a rooster as a rabbit."

"OK," I said, growing impatient. "But what does it actually *mean*?"

"It's how you feel when Mr. Jaradat makes you angry."

Mr. Jaradat was how she referred to Mohamed—a nod to his stiff formalness and the fact that he never laughed at any of my jokes, something that concerned Lena and our other friends. "He doesn't get your sense of humor, Mya. This is *lo tov* [not good]," she'd once said, finishing the sentence in the Hebrew I'd been teaching her when we were tucked away in the privacy of my car. This was where we had our impromptu Hebrew lessons—in my car, as I drove us through Bethlehem, then Beit Jala, then the checkpoint, and into Jerusalem, where we often went out to dinner.

I might as well state the obvious here: Lena was not a Mohamed fan. Sometimes I wondered if, on some level, she was jealous of the pull he exerted on me and my time—time that she and I likely would have spent together. She always said that she didn't like how he treated me.

Lena wasn't alone in her concerns. Reema, my friend in Abu Dis, also had questions about the relationship.

But Jacqueline took to him, and with Jacqueline's blessing, Mohamed arrived every Thursday or Friday to spend the weekend with me. In the armoire in the master bedroom, alongside my clothing, he'd stashed some of his own—a sweatsuit, some T-shirts, a pair of jeans, a button-down shirt. In the bathroom, he had a toothbrush.

So I wasn't entirely surprised when I came home from school on my birthday, which is in November, to find Mohamed there, standing on the stairs. Behind him was Jacqueline, peeking down from her door. Using her network, she'd managed to ferret out Mohamed's phone number somehow; knowing my birthday was coming and wanting to make the day special for me, Jacqueline had called Mohamed and the two had conspired together to surprise me. Jacqueline had also gifted Mohamed with a spare key to my apartment.

I'd walked in just a moment after the two had finished wrapping colorful paper streamers around the staircase railing that led up from my apartment to the rest of the house. In the living room, they'd hung a banner that read, in English, "Happy Birthday."

From the top of the stairs, Jacqueline called to me: "*Kol am waintu bekheir* [May you be well every year]."

And then she shut the door, leaving Mohamed and me alone.

Mohamed rushed down the stairs, took my purse and backpack from me, kissed me, and then steered me toward the couch. He returned with a glass of wine and told me to just stay here and relax. He was going to cook for me.

In the kitchen, he got to work making fettuccini alfredo and mushrooms. After dinner he set a piece of cake—which he'd bought at a patisserie in Ramallah—before me, complete with a candle, telling me to make a wish.

And then came a small jewelry box.

I opened it to find a coin from the British Mandate, attached to a delicate silver necklace. In the center of the coin was an olive branch; at the top was the word "Palestine" written in English, Hebrew, and Arabic.

Mohamed told me to lift up my hair; I did, and he put the necklace on me, fastening it on my neck.

"*Bnshuf* [Let's see]," he said in Arabic, and I turned back toward him. "I like this on you," he announced.

My hand flew to my throat, and I ran the tip of my finger over the words in all the languages. Despite our fight in Tel Aviv, I understood the necklace the same way I'd read the purple mailbox—as a memento of a better time, days when the land hadn't been divided and the future was still open. I took the necklace, which included both Hebrew and Arabic, as a sign of acceptance—not of the Israeli government and its system of oppression but, at least, of the people, all the people, who lived on the land. I took the necklace as a sign of hope.

* * *

A week later, I was wearing my Palestine necklace when Brandeis University cut ties with Al Quds University over the Hamas and Islamic Jihad rallies that had been held on campus earlier in the month.

The rallies had taken place the first week of November; when I'd arrived to campus that morning, I'd found Israeli flags, made out of white poster board and markers, taped to the floor of a thoroughfare, students walking on them on their way to class. There was an effigy of a kidnapped soldier. An enormous banner extolled the actions of suicide bombers by calling them martyrs.

Intellectually, I understood that one could be anti-Zionist and not antisemitic. I also understood that the Israeli flag was not a symbol of Judaism writ large but, rather, a nationalist symbol that had appropriated the Star of David, hijacking it for the national project. So intellectually, I got it. But my heart didn't quite get what my mind did. Sure, I was with my students—I was with Palestine—but that didn't mean I was against Israel. And I struggled to hold all my conflicting feelings at once.

Then came the rally.

It took place on the plaza right outside my building. Surrounded by banners that were tributes to various Palestinian martyrs, a group of students had taken to the center of the plaza, where—clad in black, holding fake automatic weapons—they marched, raising their arms in a gesture reminiscent of the Nazi salute.

Someone on campus leaked images of the rally to the media, and a storm of controversy followed. Under fire, the Al Quds University president, Sari Nusseibeh, a Palestinian from one of Jerusalem's oldest, most prominent families, doubled down, issuing a statement offering the students who held the rally his unwavering support. In the wake of that letter, two American universities—Brandeis and Brown—cut ties with Al Quds. Bard, however, did not; our program continued.

While Iman's warning that anyone could bring a gun to campus and kill me had rattled me, the rally and the ensuing fallout was the writing on the wall. No matter where I lived, no matter who I loved, no matter what my politics were, no matter what sort of necklace I wore—and regardless of who had given that necklace to me—there would be no integrating here, not while the place was occupied. As an Israeli, my days of working at Al Quds University were numbered.

* * *

So, paradoxically, just as I'd thought I was settling into my life in the West Bank, I found myself driving into Jerusalem to do basic things—things I could have easily done in Bethlehem—like run and go grocery shopping. It would have been infinitely cheaper to buy my produce at the market in Bethlehem, but now I found myself missing the shuk in Jerusalem and the rhythms of Shabbat. It was mostly fine to run in the Bethlehem area—save for the occasional harassment from the local boys, save for the screw I'd stepped on once, forcing me to stop midstride and yank it out of my foot—but now I preferred to drive in, park in Kiryat Yovel, and let my feet fly on my old trail, the one that connected Yad V'Shem and Ein Karem. Sometimes, when I was done running, I even let myself into my old studio—Oded had taken over the lease but had urged me to keep a key, should I have an emergency—and showered before driving back out to Bethlehem.

On one of my drives in, Mohamed arranged for me to meet with a man—an Israeli fellow—who had received from the French journalists Mohamed had worked with in Gaza a DVD copy of the television episode Mohamed had gone to Gaza to produce.

We met at Mamilla Mall, a place I tried to stay away from as much as possible because it literally turned my stomach. The shopping center had been built on top of a Muslim cemetery that had been there for centuries. We found each other outside of a café; as he gave me the DVD, he asked how I knew Mohamed. I told him Mohamed was my boyfriend.

"I understand," the man said. "Do you have time for a coffee?"

I did.

"Come sit with me," he said, beckoning me to follow him into the café.

Settling in at a table, he explained to me that he was also involved with an organization that tried to help women like me—that is, Jewish girls who were in relationships with Arab men.

"Sister," he began—and I have to admit here that, as an only child, the word thrilled me. How I'd always wanted a proper family, how I'd always wanted siblings and lots of cousins, and how I'd wanted to sleep in one big bed, among a tangle of arms and legs.

"I met Mohamed," he continued, in Hebrew. "He's amazing. Sweet. I understand why you like him. But you don't know what it's like with these Arab men. They're all nice in the beginning—they seem open; they seem like they accept you as you are, as a Jew. And then the second you marry them, they take you to a village and make you put on a hijab."

"What's wrong with the hijab?" I asked, bristling.

"What's wrong with the hijab? Sister, do you want to cover all that beautiful hair of yours? Look at yourself; you're so pretty."

"It's not about that," I said, thinking about Neda and Ibtisam and my other students who had explained that the hijab was, first and foremost, about their relationship with God.

"Never mind the hijab," he said, waving me away. "The point is—*goyim,* non-Jews, they don't understand us. Years ago, I was in love with a Chinese girl, and my mother was so upset that I was going to marry her—"

"So what happened?" I interrupted. "Did you marry her?"

"*Chas vchalila* [Heaven forbid]! No. In the end, I listened to my mother. I broke up with her."

"I'm not breaking up with Mohamed."

"Why not?"

"Because I love him," I said, grinning to hide my discomfort.

"I loved my Chinese girl, too, but I didn't marry her. Look, you want to get married? You want babies? I know ten guys who would be happy to marry you and make you children."

I forced a laugh.

"Seriously."

Thanking him for the DVD and the coffee, I stood.

"I have to get going. I have a long trip," I said, "back to Bethlehem."

Dropping some coins on the table for a tip, I walked out of the café and headed toward my car. I could have taken the Tunnels back out to Bethlehem, where it was unlikely I'd have a run-in with soldiers. But I wanted to get home as quickly as possible. So I would enter Bethlehem via 300, a checkpoint that was off-limits to me, bouncing over the tire spikes, flashing my American passport at the soldiers.

21

The first night of Hanukkah, I lit my candles alone and in secret, in the pantry, where Jacqueline—who was increasingly coming down into my half of the house unannounced—wouldn't be able to see me from the stairwell, guarding them as they burned, ready to blow them out and hide the whole thing: the *hanukkiah* I'd bought in Tel Aviv my first winter in Israel, the candles I'd picked up at a store in Jerusalem recently, the matches. Once the candles were extinguished, I wrapped the hanukkiah, the candles, and the matches in a plastic bag and stuck it all under the sink, in the kitchen, under the mountain of plastic bags I kept there alongside the empty jars I also collected, two things that made Mohamed laugh and comment that I was like a little old Arab lady. I felt a tinge of guilt about treating my hanukkiah this way—it felt disrespectful. But this spot seemed like the last place Jacqueline would look for anything.

Not only was Jacqueline increasingly popping in on me, but on more than one occasion, I'd entered the apartment to hear the door above me clicking shut. She was snooping, I realized, and my key in the lock was like a bell announcing my arrival, giving her the warning she needed to get out and get upstairs just in time. On one occasion, she was still in the apartment when I came in, and I gasped when I stepped into the living room to find her. She offered me a vague excuse about watering the plants and that she'd misplaced her key to the garden.

If she didn't know who I was, I realized, it was just a matter of time until she figured it all out. In a drawer of the huge, old wooden armoire that stood in the spare bedroom, I'd stashed my Hebrew-language books, the ones I was too attached to to get rid of when I'd left Jerusalem. Among them was Eshkol Nevo's *Four Houses and Longing*, the first novel I'd managed to read in my adopted tongue. Another forbidden good: a Hebrew driving handbook. I was studying for my Israeli driver's license, and I was determined to learn the rules not in English but in Hebrew.

There were other bits and pieces of paraphernalia that, should Jacqueline stumble upon them, would blow my cover. Obviously, my Israeli ID was the biggest one, so I carried it everywhere, all the time. But going out for a run was a dilemma: Did I jog with my ID tucked in my bra or shorts and risk it falling out on the sidewalk, revealing my identity to whomever might be around? Or did I leave my ID in the house and take the risk that Jacqueline would find it? What would happen when she discovered my identity? Would she kick me out? Call the PA police on me? Would the PA, in turn, hand me over to the Israelis?

I took to locking my ID in the glovebox of my car, locking my car, and then running with my keys.

I couldn't have a Hanukkah party, but I'd always loved entertaining, and I craved some sort of winter celebration. Mohamed indulged me, and we decided to cohost a small Christmas party. Texting an invite, gathering food and supplies, winding tinsel around the handrail of the stairs—this all made my life feel so normal. Like I really could live here.

The day of the party, which was almost two weeks ahead of Christmas, a big storm dumped over a foot of snow on Jerusalem and the surrounding areas, blanketing everything in white. The roads were a mess, but one by one, people filtered in—including Jacqueline, who made the journey downstairs to join us briefly before heading back up. Many of the people at the party were internationals: Matt and Beth were there, of course, and our circle of friends in Bethlehem, which included Lena and a number of Christian Palestinians. A dear friend, a Palestinian Canadian woman who was a lawyer for the UN, came from Jerusalem; another good friend, Lital, an Israeli academic, had her diplomat boyfriend drive her out in his diplomatic-plated car—which, according to law, soldiers couldn't and wouldn't check. She was the only Israeli to come.

When she stepped into the apartment, she gasped at its beauty. I gave her a tour, and from the positioning of everything, she cobbled together a history of the house that was broader than the story Jacqueline had given us. But like Jacqueline, Lital—who would go on to write a book about Jerusalem—used the well as the starting point. The water had likely come first, she said, and the original inhabitants had settled next to the well because of the water. They might have lived in the caves in the hills at first—she pointed to the spare bedroom, which was built into the side of the mountain—eventually turning it into a small, one-room house. And then another family—probably led by a brother of the first family—built an adjacent one-room house. She gestured toward the master bedroom, where Mohamed and I slept. The well stood in between the two brother's houses, and the living room we were standing in didn't exist. It was a courtyard, a gathering point, shared by the families. People might eat here together, or the kids would play. Pointing up at the soaring ceiling, Lital explained that two homes had likely been connected later and closed into one.

This all made sense to Mohamed, whose great-grandparents themselves had lived in caves in the Hebron area before building houses out of stone. It was easy for him to envision this history, but for me, it expanded my consciousness and reminded me that even though this mansion looked ancient, it had been built on top of something and that this place was made out of layer after layer. So many stories. So many different ways of living. Everything that was happening now was just a blip on the radar—I was a blip on the radar—and that feeling of smallness imbued me with a sense of lightness and optimism.

Or maybe it was the booze.

Mohamed was the consummate host, refreshing drinks, making sure everyone had a full cup all night long. With the space heaters and radiators on, the French doors were thrown open despite the cold, and people wandered between the garden and the house with cigarettes and joints and whiskey and wine and champagne. The conversation flowed. So much so that, at some point, Lital and I slipped into Hebrew—a fairly loud exchange, too.

I felt eyes upon me. Ramzy. There he was, in a crisp, white button-down shirt, sleeves rolled up to the elbow, drink in hand. I watched as he pulled Mohamed aside, leaned his head close to Mohamed's, and whispered in his ear. Mohamed looked toward Lital and me and then at Ramzy and was silent for a moment. Finally, Mohamed nodded. Ever theatrical, Ramzy opened his eyes wide in disbelief, tapped Mohamed's chest with the back of his fingers, and then spoke to him at length before striding over to me.

"Mya, we need to talk," he said in Arabic, grabbing my hand and leading me to the guest room.

My stomach dropped. I liked Ramzy. He was one of the few friends of Mohamed's I'd met. I didn't want to lose his approval. I didn't want to explain myself to him, either. As I followed him into the room, I readied the Arabic words in my head.

Ramzy sat down on the bed and gestured for me to join him.

"Mohamed told me you have an Israeli passport," Ramzy began. "Personally, me, I don't care. I love you, ya Mya, and I understand you. I understand what you're doing here and why you live here. But not everyone is like me."

He paused.

"Not everyone will understand what you're doing here. And I'm scared for you, for what will happen if the wrong people find out you're here—"

He didn't finish his own sentence. He just shuddered. I knew that Ramzy was referring to militants, of which there were plenty in the West Bank.

"Ya Mya, I'm scared for you," he continued. "Very, very scared."

I did my best to reassure Ramzy that everything was fine. That only a few people knew my status.

"*Qwais, mashi*, good, fine. But you don't know who *those* people know. You don't know who they might have told and who those people have told." He gestured with his hand, making waves to illustrate the way gossip moves. "People around here love to talk."

I thought of Noor, my Arabic teacher, who, I'd learned through the grapevine, had speculated that I was in the Mossad after I'd accidentally slipped into Hebrew during class because the languages are so close. But eventually I'd won Noor over with my diligent class attendance and attention to my homework and with the way I hurried off to Abu Dis, to campus, to teach my own classes. She admired my dedication to my Palestinian students, and through that, she had come to understand my politics.

But, of course, I also thought of Iman and the rally on campus. And I knew that Ramzy was right. There were plenty of people out here who would be completely opposed to my presence.

I thanked Ramzy for his concern and stood to show him the conversation was over. As we rejoined the party, I found Mohamed in the kitchen. His sharing my status with Ramzy felt like a public commitment, a stand—maybe even more than going to Ibtisam's wedding—and I asked him then, "Are we really doing this?"

"We are," he said, slipping his hand in mine and squeezing my fingers.

I felt a thrill ripple through my chest. I am my beloved and my beloved is mine—so much so he was even willing to admit that he'd crossed the line and fallen in love with someone from the other side.

And yet I was left deeply unsettled by the conservation.

Ramzy's words frightened me. He'd driven home the point that this place wasn't Al Andalus; it wasn't even Palestine under the British, before the land had been divided, before the conflict simmering between our peoples had boiled over. Even if just for a moment, Ramzy had pushed me out of the fantasy Mohamed and I were living in and reminded me that I was living in the occupied West Bank, where Palestinians staggered under the weight of Israel's military might. I was living in a place where my people were standing with a collective boot upon the neck of Mohamed's friends, family—his people.

* * *

And I had other doubts. There'd been the afternoon we'd run into a distant cousin of Mohamed's as we walked down the street in Ramallah and not only had he not introduced me, but the man had called Mohamed "Abu Yasser," which meant "Father of Yasser."

Did Mohamed have a child? I'd wondered.

After he was out of earshot, I'd asked Mohamed if he had anything he wanted to tell me.

"It's a joke," he said, explaining that, as he was the eldest son, when he had children, he would have to name his firstborn son Yasser, after his father. His extended family had taken to calling him "Abu Yasser," he said, in an ironic, tongue-in-cheek way, to tease him about the fact that he was single and childless still, at his age.

"They've been wanting to marry me off since I was eighteen," he said, shaking his head.

I hadn't known what to think about it all. Maybe Mohamed had a wife and kid tucked away somewhere. How was I to know? I still had only met two of his friends. I hadn't met anyone from his family; I didn't even know where exactly Mohamed lived. He said he lived with his parents, but how could I be sure?

Feeling my friend Reema better poised to size Mohamed up, I asked her for help. Now that we were on winter break from teaching, we had the time to travel together from Abu Dis to Ramallah, where, one afternoon, we went out with Mohamed for a coffee. On the servees back to Abu Dis, Reema gave me her verdict: She liked him. She found him polite. She didn't take him to be the type who was married and running around with a foreign girl.

But, she cautioned, it was hard to tell from just one meeting.

"And nothing matters until you know his family," she said.

After returning to Bethlehem, I got on the computer. Reema was right. Whether he was married or not, I knew nothing about Mohamed's family. While I'd googled him, I'd never googled his last name alone. So I did now, and literally the first thing to come up was a Wikipedia entry: Hanadi Jaradat.

I clicked on the link and was surprised to find a photo of a woman who bore a striking resemblance to Mohamed. It was literally like someone had taken his face, plucked his eyebrows, lightened his skin a tiny bit, softened his chin, painted some red lipstick on him, and stuck it in a black hijab. Hanadi's eyes were the exact same shape as his, with that slight downward turn at the edges. She had a wide nose, like Mohamed, and her lips were plump.

And then I looked at the text:

> Hanadi Tayseer Abdul Malek Jaradat (Arabic: عبدالمالك تيسير هنادي جرادات)
>
> (22 September 1975–4 October 2003) was a Palestinian from Jenin, who blew herself up on Saturday, 4 October 2003 in a suicide attack on Maxim restaurant, a restaurant co-owned by the same Jewish and Arab families for 40 years, in the northern Israeli city of Haifa. She killed 21 Jewish and Arab Israelis, and injured 51 more. Among the dead were four Israeli children, including a two-month old infant, and five Arabs. She had been recruited by Islamic Jihad.

I was sitting at the kitchen table, facing the French doors and the garden beyond them, and over the edge of my laptop, the horizon tilted and righted itself. I realized then that I wasn't breathing, that my head was spinning, that the sky had appeared to move because I'd nearly fainted.

I read the rest of the entry. The details were gruesome. *But, no, she can't be related,* I told myself. *This woman is from Jenin, and Mohamed's family comes from Sa'ir.*

That face, however, haunted me. I stared at the photo. It was Mohamed's face. It was the face I'd kissed, I'd woken up to, that I went to sleep next to every weekend. I picked up the phone to call him—to ask him if this Hanadi was some sort of kin. To ask him how he felt about what she'd done. But the phone, I realized, would be letting him off the hook too easily. This was a conversation we needed to have face-to-face.

* * *

Under the guise of having lunch together, I drove to Ramallah, stewing the whole way about everything—that Mohamed had some cousin, however distant, who had been a suicide bomber, that he hid me from everyone, that he kept making big promises about the future, and yet I was living alone in Bethlehem and didn't see any change on the horizon. By the time I got to the office, I'd whipped myself into a rage. I pounded up the stairs and burst through the door. Mohamed looked up from his desk. Smiling, he stood and walked over to greet me as he usually did—by enveloping me in his arms. Shaking, I pushed him away and asked, "So. Are you related to that suicide bomber, Hanadi?"

I thought I saw a smile flutter across his lips.

He didn't answer. But I wasn't going to let him stonewall me this time. I was tired of all his silences and his deflecting. This time I wasn't going to let him off the hook.

"Are you?" I insisted, my voice getting louder, edging upward, tilting toward a scream. "*Are you*?" I shouted.

"I am," he said, his chin tilting upward just a hair. "She's a cousin."

"And you're *proud* of that?" I asked.

"Not completely," he said.

"*Not completely*?" I repeated. "So just a little bit proud? She killed *civilians*."

"*Your* army kills civilians *every day*."

"*My* army? It's not *my* army. I don't approve of the occupation. They're not doing this in my name. And I don't condone civilian deaths on any side. I'm upset when anyone dies—Palestinian or Israeli. You know where I stand. Where do *you* stand, Mohamed?"

"I stand with peace."

"OK, so why is it fine for Israelis to die? Why are Palestinian lives worth more to you?"

"Hanadi," he began, dodging my question, "*suffered*. Her brother was killed. She watched him die. Her fiancé was killed, too."

"So it's OK to go out and kill a bunch of civilians?" I asked, reminding him that, according to international law, just as an occupying power was forbidden from transferring its civilian population to an occupied territory, so are militants resisting occupation forbidden from targeting civilians. And that's what Hanadi had done—she'd targeted a restaurant full of civilians.

"The Israelis bulldozed her home," Mohamed countered.

"After she bombed a restaurant!" I shouted.

I couldn't believe what I'd just said. I was totally opposed to the Israeli policy of demolishing homes, and I reminded Mohamed of that now—that I didn't support demolitions or violence of any kind.

"I thought you were against violence, too," I said. "Isn't that what we stand for?"

"*Yaani* [I mean]," he began, looking doubtful, "I don't think violence helps. But I can understand it. The people here are suffering."

"And so someone on our side should suffer, too? So it's OK to kill Israeli civilians and just use a Jewish girl? We're human, too!" I yelled.

"Who's using a Jewish girl?"

"I don't know—you tell me."

"I'm not using a Jewish girl."

"That's not what Reema thinks."

"Who's Reema to me? What do I care what Reema thinks?"

"And what about your parents?" I asked. "What do they think is going on? What are you telling them when you disappear every weekend?"

"They know that there is a girl—a foreigner."

"And?"

"They're just relieved I'm not gay."

"Jesus," I said. "They don't want to know who I am? Don't they care? Don't *you* care? I can't live like this anymore. In the dark. Not knowing where this is going."

"Of course they care. It's just—"

"So? Am I going to meet them at some point?"

"Yes, yes. At some point."

"When?"

"Next month. In January."

"Why next month? Why January? Why is everything always delayed with you?"

"The timing has to be right."

"The timing will *never* be right. I'll never stop being Jewish."

"You have to understand, Mya, I come attached to a family."

"You have to understand, Mohamed, I do, too. I'm a *person*, remember. Just like all those people your cousin killed."

22

Mohamed hatched a plan. He was sure that his parents would love me if they didn't know I was Jewish.

"You want me to hide my identity from them forever?" I asked. "I won't."

"No, no," he said. He didn't expect me to do that. But we'd let them meet me, fall in love with me as a person, and then he'd be like: *"Guess what, Mom and Dad—surprise! Your future daughter-in-law is a Jew!"*

They already knew a bit about me, he said. That I worked at the university and that I was highly educated, that I was a journalist also. But he would extol the fact that I'm *maadaleh*, "thrifty," he said, to his mom, and he would also praise my cooking. His dad would be impressed by my complex political views; maybe he would read some of my articles to him, translating them to Arabic as he read. Mohamed's parents didn't speak a word of English.

After that, we tried to pretend everything was fine. We began to plan a summer visit to New York City, so we could attend the June wedding of my favorite aunt. Mohamed would meet my family at that point, including my parents and my grandfather, the one who had wanted to join the Hagana in 1948 and fight for the Jewish state. Though Mohamed had spent time in New York in 2007 while he was on a media fellowship at the United Nations, his visa had recently expired; now he was starting the process of applying for a new visa to visit the States.

Mohamed came to Bethlehem for Christmas, and on Christmas Eve, we went to Manger Square, the plaza next to the Church of Nativity, the plaza I crossed every day on my way to campus. That night, the usually open space was filled with throngs of Palestinians—Christian and Muslim alike—who had come out to see the tree and browse the small Christmas market. While Muslims don't celebrate Christmas, they revere Jesus, whose Arabic name is Issa, as a prophet, and the story of the immaculate conception and the virgin birth are both included in the Quran. Mary is venerated in Islam; her Arabic name is Maryam. And the excitement in Manger Square was palpable on Christmas Eve. Families were out, and children ran around.

When we returned from Manger Square and got into bed that night, I found something under my pillow—a wrapped gift.

As I pulled the package out, I asked Mohamed if it was from him. When he said it wasn't, I felt disappointed. I unwrapped it to find some old makeup, clearly partially used.

"Jacqueline," I said to Mohamed, and he chuckled.

I realized that she had very little money, or very little she felt comfortable sparing, and that she had likely searched her apartment for something she could wrap up for me. I was touched by the gesture. She loved me. And I felt very strongly for her, too. How could I not, seeing her day in and day out? She was also providing a space for Mohamed and me to have our relationship, and I realized that giving a young unmarried couple a place to make love was no small thing in Palestinian society.

But I also felt unnerved. That she had spirited the present down and tucked it under my pillow was yet another confirmation that she was coming into the apartment when I was gone. If she hadn't discovered all my Jewish things or proof that I was an Israeli citizen, it was only a matter of time before she did.

And then it was January.

Jacqueline, who had been brought up-to-date on everything—both by eavesdropping and through our frequent conversations—was excited. Almost every day, when she heard me enter the house, she would open the door between us and stick her head into the stairwell, shouting down, "Ahlan, ya Mya!" and then asking if I'd gone to see Mohamed's parents. I hadn't? When would it happen?

Mohamed hemmed and hawed, evasive, promising that it would happen "by the end of the month."

But as the days ticked by, it began to seem like this was yet another way to buy himself some time.

And then he invited me to attend the premiere of a movie he'd worked on, *Falastine Stereo,* the latest film by the acclaimed Palestinian director Rashid Masharawi, whose feature *Laila's Birthday* had gotten rave reviews abroad. Working with this director had been a big deal for Mohamed, who had served as a location scout and location manager, and the evening would be Ramallah's version of a red carpet event. Mohamed said he wanted me there by his side, and I wanted to support him, of course.

There was also some peer pressure for me to go: one of my best friends from Tel Aviv, Ruth, an Israeli American woman, would be attending the event with her partner, a Palestinian citizen of Israel who lived in Jaffa. (Prior to 1948, the great-uncle of that partner had married a Jewish immigrant to Palestine; when the war took place, the two fled to Jordan, where the woman converted to Islam and lived the rest of her life under the guise of being a Muslim refugee. Some, but not all, of her descendants knew that their grandmother had been Jewish. On one trip to Amman, years before Mohamed and I got together, Ruth's partner connected me with his cousin, who shared the family's story with me over dinner in downtown Amman.)

And Ruth herself had been invited by her boss, yet another Jewish Israeli woman in a mixed relationship with a Palestinian.

So despite how upset I was with Mohamed, I agreed to go. I tried to pull it together and fake it. There I was, walking down a red carpet and entering a building, where I met Ruth and her partner, and we posed with some other friends and acquaintances for photos. There I was, in a slinky, one-shouldered black lace dress, purchased especially for the occasion, and heels, taking my seat beside Mohamed in the movie theater.

The film was, in a word, bad; later, it would be panned in a review that described it as soap opera-ish and melodramatic and poorly written. But Mohamed had done his part well. He had done a magnificent job finding the perfect locations for the scenes, and it was like seeing Palestine through his eyes, projected on the big screen. Mohamed struggled with words on so many levels—just as his feelings for me went uncommunicated, feeding my anxieties about our relationship, so had his feelings for the place, for Palestine, gone unexpressed verbally. But I didn't need his words. I saw his love for Palestine on the screen before me: It was in the sweeping vistas he had picked, the scenic shots that showed the land, magnificent in all her beauty, resplendent in the morning sun and the last rays of the day, that particular gold that danced only in the Mediterranean.

Sitting in the dark theater, I remembered that afternoon that I'd driven Mohamed to Tel Aviv and how tired I'd gotten from walking in the wrong direction. I hadn't fully understood his stubbornness, his insistence on showing me the way through my own city, a place he'd only visited briefly a few times in the past. But now, with Mohamed's version of Palestine flickering on the huge screen before me, I understood. I understood that every nook and cranny of Palestine lived in his head, and that's why he'd been able to pick these perfect, breathtaking vistas. That he knew the place with an intimacy I never would and that that intimacy had started with those childhood hikes in Jordan, looking out over Palestine stretched before him, at once so close but also unreachable. The vision of Palestine that I saw before me wasn't just Mohamed's—it was his father's and his father's before him, and it went back generations, hundreds of years.

Looking at the screen then, I also understood what Mohamed meant about coming attached to a family, and I realized that his love for his family was there, too, on that screen.

The family that was absent from this event. The family I was never going to meet.

The lights came on, and we filed out of the theater. I dashed to the bathroom, where I ran into a friend—an Israeli Canadian journalist and filmmaker who was there with her Palestinian girlfriend—who invited me and Mohamed to another party. When I returned to Mohamed's side, I told him about the party. No, he said, he'd just made plans for us to go out with Rashid and some other people.

As Mohamed and I walked to the car with different destinations in mind, unable to agree, he gestured to the red carpet. "This is all for you," he said, as though he could wave the tension away, as though I was a child and he could shake a shiny object in front of my eyes and distract me from the things that bothered me.

"No, it's not," I replied, with a snort. "This has nothing to do with me."

I laid into him, pointing out that he'd worked on the movie long before I came along. And taking me to this event didn't make up for what he said was going to happen in January and still hadn't—here we were halfway through the month, and any talk of meeting his family had fallen away.

We fought in a way that we've never fought before as we drove through the empty, silent streets of Ramallah. I don't remember the words now—it's not a fight that stuck in my head like the one about Hanadi did—but I remember that he was driving and I was sitting there looking out the passenger window, looking out at the streetlights spilling pools of yellow onto the sidewalks and the pine trees and the apartment buildings and houses, their red tile roofs peeking out over the low walls that divided all of these homes from the street. As we passed the houses, I thought of the families inside and I realized I didn't want to be in the car at all going to any party. I wanted to be in there, tucked in a home, the windows glowing warm in the cold night. I ground my high-heeled foot onto the floorboard as though I was braking. And then, out of frustration, I put my feet on the glovebox and pushed on it, as though I could stop the car.

This wasn't what I wanted; this wasn't why I'd come here—to the West Bank or Ramallah. I didn't want to be stuck in a long-distance relationship that was going nowhere; I didn't want to be sitting in a car, arguing with Mohamed. I didn't want to drive through fucking Qalandia ever again. I didn't want to drive anywhere anymore. I didn't want to run away from relationships or myself. I didn't want to live separately. I didn't want all these complications.

I just wanted to be still somewhere, together.

* * *

Jacqueline's constant questions had become embarrassing. After arriving back from campus one afternoon to the usual interrogation about when this so-called meeting was going to happen, I got on the phone and said to Mohamed, "It's almost February. So I guess it's not going to happen this month, huh?"

"Give me a few more days," he said.

"You've had the whole month," I said, exasperated.

"Next week," he promised. We picked a day, and he swore he would make it work. I should plan on coming over for lunch, he said, and I should dress sufficiently modestly. "Cover that big butt of yours," he teased me, and I laughed.

I headed up the stairs, knocked on the door, and reported everything, in detail, to Jacqueline, who took my face in her hands, squeezed it a little too hard, and exclaimed that I was going to be a beautiful bride.

The day before I was supposed to meet Mohamed's family, I came home from campus to Jacqueline shouting down the stairs. "Tomorrow," I shouted back up. "I'm seeing them tomorrow."

I called Mohamed.

"Are we still on for tomorrow?" I asked.

"Yes," he said to my surprise. I expected him to cancel. I was relieved. I started babbling about some different ideas of what I would wear until Mohamed interrupted me.

"Actually, no," he said.

My heart sank. "What?"

"This morning, my father was asking me questions. After all, his eldest son is getting married. So he asked me about your religion."

"Oh no. What did you say?"

"I said that you're American."

His father, knowing that "American" isn't a religion, had pushed.

"She's secular," Mohamed said.

"Surely her people were something; they had some kind of religion at some point," his father had insisted.

"Well, her mother is Jewish," Mohamed had said.

And his father had called the meeting off.

"We'll find a way to move forward," Mohamed said. "I promise. Just give me some more time."

The phone dropped from my hand, and I followed it, sliding off the couch and onto the ground. I could hear Mohamed talking still, trying to offer me some reassurance that we would move forward. I snapped it shut.

And then I opened it again and called Lena.

"The meeting is off," I said between sobs.

"Don't worry, me and Beth are coming, *habibti,*" Lena said.

Minutes later, they were at my door, unlocking it with the spare key I'd given Beth.

They came in and sat down on the floor, placing a pint of ice cream down by my head.

"Spoons, please, ya Beth," Lena said, and Beth rushed toward my kitchen to get them.

Lena stroked my hair.

"Oh, habibti," she said. "How are you feeling?"

"*Shayf addik arnab,*" I answered.

Lena laughed. "Ya Mya, go get your notebook and write this one down, too: *Inti mashtuba*. Do you know what that means?"

I clicked my tongue to say no.

"It means 'You're crossed out.'" She held her arms up, using them to make an X, before continuing. "But, *yaani* [I mean], it's a good thing because you can do better. Fuck him, ya Mya, and fuck his family. Forget about Mr. Jaradat. Time to move on."

23

In the coming days, as I told everyone that the meeting was off, I heard countless stories from Palestinian friends and acquaintances about their parents or some family members getting a rocky start. It almost seemed like a rite of passage here. A Muslim Palestinian friend from East Jerusalem told me how her father's family initially rejected her mother because she came from the next village over. "They still call her *ajnabiyah* [a foreigner]," my friend said, laughing, "and she's *Palestinian*. From the neighboring village."

Everyone said that Mohamed's father would come around eventually. And if he didn't, well, I could—I should—just move on. But I didn't want to.

* * *

Despite Mohamed's father's stance, Mohamed's mom wasn't entirely opposed to the idea of meeting me, Mohamed told me when he visited that weekend. So his new plan was to find a way to get me and his mother together, and then his mother would convince his father, who would come along eventually.

After Mohamed left on Saturday, I dutifully reported this all back to Jacqueline, who sat on my couch.

When I told her that Mohamed's father had rejected the match and she'd asked me why, I simply said, "My religion."

Jacqueline nodded knowingly and left it at that. I was relieved that she didn't push me for clarification.

At this point, I was fairly certain she knew that I was Jewish. Nonetheless, our relationship had grown closer over the months. When I got the flu and was too sick to cook or take care of myself, Jacqueline appeared with homemade *fatayer sabanekh*, spinach pastries flavored with onion and sumac. And when I wasn't keeping the place quite up to Jacqueline's standards of cleanliness, she brought a Muslim woman to clean. As Jacqueline followed her from room to room, fussing at her and bossing her around—and as I followed Jacqueline, trying to get her to leave the poor woman alone—the woman looked from my face to hers and then asked if we were mother and daughter. We'd laughed and told her no. But just like the reporter calling after the Freedom Ride and asking me about my "boyfriend" at the time, the question had the strange effect of bringing us closer.

Now she gazed at the garden as she spent a moment digesting Mohamed's plan to get me and his mother together. Then she looked at me and waved at the space around us.

"The house," she said, "is open."

I was astounded at her words. My heart stood still for a moment.

In Palestine, the norm is for a man to "open a house" for his bride—it was very rare, if not completely unheard of, for a couple to marry without the groom providing a home. Jacqueline was suggesting that we buck this norm and live there with her, as though she was our—as though she was my—family.

Moved, my eyes filled with tears.

"But Mohamed's family is building a whole apartment building," I managed to say. "One of those floors was supposed to be ours."

"You don't need that place. You have *this* one." She patted my hand. "Bring Mohamed's mother here. I will meet her and tell her what a good girl you are."

The tears spilled down my cheeks.

"Oh, don't cry, ya Mya," Jacqueline said, reaching over and smacking me on the thigh—that strange habit of hers of giving me affectionate but hard slaps.

So I told Mohamed the plan. Jacqueline was willing to stick her neck—and her family name—out for me and stand as my family to meet Mohamed's mom. This would be a whole different kind of family meeting. No fathers. No male permission. Just the women, making decisions together.

* * *

In the meantime, my days continued as always. I went to and from campus, where I taught my classes. It was the spring semester, which is when we did our unit about Andalucia as it existed in the Muslim golden age—when Jews and Muslims mingled freely and where the cultural exchange that took place made a lasting impact. There was, of course, a great irony to teaching about Jewish-Muslim-Christian coexistence in the fraught setting of Abu Dis, where the university gates were within sight of the wall and where the campus was subjected to frequent raids by the Israeli army, events I witnessed myself. Where students were sometimes arrested and hauled off to be held in administrative detention and where windows had, on occasion, been shattered by tear gas canisters fired by Israeli soldiers.

One Thursday morning, early—I was still teaching my 8:00 a.m. class—something happened near the gate, the gate where I usually entered, and soldiers tore into campus, firing tear gas. Windows were shattered, the upper floors of the building were filled with so much gas that students and faculty couldn't breathe. Everyone began to run out, and my students and I could all hear the commotion going on outside.

But my classroom was on the bottom floor, and when Professor Tomas stuck his head in to say we needed to evacuate, I refused, explaining I didn't smell any gas here and, more importantly, I was *teaching.*

"But the soldiers—" Professor Tomas began.

I cut him off. "Fuck the soldiers," I said, slamming my hand down on the table.

My students cheered, Professor Tomas left, and we dug into our work with more focus than ever. Until Sarah, my boss, came and said, "Mya, it's really bad, and the administration has decided to evacuate all of campus."

"We're staying. I'm teaching. They're learning," I said, because I was tired of all this. I was tired of going through the Container every day on my way to campus, I was tired of my students having to go through checkpoints on their way to campus every day, I was tired of classes being disrupted by the army, and I was tired of the faculty having strikes because the PA couldn't get its act together and pay them properly. I was tired of the strikes, too, we had when there was a war with Gaza or when there was a martyr in the West Bank, and I was tired of there being wars and martyrs. I was tired of people dying.

I was tired of students being arrested; I was tired of students' family members being arrested. Neda—the student I'd adored, the young woman whose face I'd visualized when I couldn't get out of bed in the morning—her little brother had been taken away for administrative detention on suspicion of throwing stones, held without charge for months and months now. And I hated that Neda had to worry about him, that she had to persevere. I didn't want anyone to persevere. I just wanted everyone—Mohamed and myself included—to have normal lives.

And because I wanted everyone to have normal lives, I wasn't going to let a bunch of soldiers—my countrymen, for God's sake—disrupt our Thursday morning class.

"I'm staying!" I shouted at Sarah. "We're staying!"

My students cheered and pounded on the table to show their agreement.

"No! Mya, you can't just *stay*. There's liability. If something happens to any of you, we're *liable*."

Powerless, I cursed as I packed my belongings and we exited the classroom, following the crowd fleeing toward the other side of campus, streaming like ants, exiting via a gate I'd never used before.

We were on the other side of the village, a part of Abu Dis that was totally unfamiliar to me. Disoriented, I climbed into a servees headed toward Bethlehem. Batul, my colleague and friend who lived in Hebron and who always took her hijab off when we reached West Jerusalem, got on after me, and the minivan peeled out of there, speeding through the village toward the Container. The driver explained that the army would probably close the checkpoint—if they did, we would be stuck in Abu Dis, unable to reach Bethlehem or Hebron, until it reopened.

When we arrived, we found the Container open, and everyone sighed with relief as the minivan jerked over the last set of spikes and began the climb up the mountain, Wadi Nar looming in the valley to our right. But when we reached the other side and the road ran under a small bridge that was a settler road and we saw settlers and soldiers up there, looming above us, we were all gripped with fear. Settlers might pitch stones at us; soldiers could fire on us. The driver accelerated, and soon the bridge receded into the distance behind us. We flew past Dar Salah and entered Beit Sahour.

From the bus station in Bethlehem, Batul walked home with me; we cooked lunch together and ate and rested on the couch, pretending like we were two friends enjoying a leisurely afternoon together and not two professors who had just fled campus because of an army incursion that brought our classes to an end.

* * *

Later that afternoon, after Batul left, Mohamed called to tell me that his mother had changed her mind. When his parents had started to ask more questions about me, he'd admitted to them that not only was I Jewish, but I also had an Israeli ID. His mom had been willing to meet, perhaps, with a Jew. But an *Israeli*? Regardless of my politics, that was unacceptable. And that I was an immigrant who had known the situation here and had taken citizenship anyway made me even worse. An Israeli who was born here was one thing—they had been born into the conflict and had no choice in the matter. But someone like me? Well, in the eyes of Mohamed's family—and many other Palestinians—I'd chosen to be a part of this conflict, and I'd chosen the wrong side.

So now the meeting with his mother was off, too.

Still, Mohamed insisted, we would find a way to move forward. On the one hand, I trusted him. He'd gotten his visa to the States; we continued making plans to go to New York City to attend my aunt's wedding. Despite his parents' disapproval, we were still planning for Mohamed to meet my entire family, including my parents. On the other hand, I wondered what would happen after that trip. Would we return to the West Bank and to the same holding pattern? Would I live in limbo forever? Yes, meeting my family would be a step forward. But, as Reema had told me, in this culture, nothing was real until I met *his* family.

At night, I found myself unable to sleep in either of the bedrooms. They felt too empty, too lonely. Even with sheets and blankets on, my back felt open, exposed, and I craved Mohamed's presence in the bed with me, his warmth, his calmness, his steadiness.

So I took to the couch, letting the back cushions cradle me, pretending it wasn't a piece of furniture but, rather, Mohamed next to me. I struggled to sleep there, too, but eventually I would drop off with the satellite radio playing through the TV, Arabic classics going. It was Abdel Halim Hafez or Umm Kulthoum, the queen of Egyptian vocalists, rocking me to sleep. Her song "*Baeed Annak*" (Far from you) would play: *I forgot to sleep and dream. . . . The nights of longing have enslaved me. Enslaved me!*

She paused and then the strings swooped down, cascading, falling through the scale, before soaring back up. *No matter how your absence tortures me, no matter how sleepless my nights are, never will your absence change me. Nor will the days keep me away from you.*

The irony: With three years of Arabic under my belt, I could understand much of the words. But no matter how much Arabic I learned, no matter who my students were or my boyfriend was or what my political beliefs were, no matter where I lived or who I paid rent to, in Mohamed's family's eyes, I was completely unacceptable. A line had been drawn through my name; I'd been crossed out. *Mashtuba.*

24

In early March, Mohamed showed up to spend yet another weekend with me, as though nothing had changed, which irritated me. I wouldn't live in limbo like this forever, I told him; he couldn't use my house and me as a weekend retreat and then return to his real life in Ramallah. He kept saying we would "move forward." But what did that mean?

We were on the couch together, me lying down with my bare feet in his lap, discussing the possibility of moving in together in Ramallah. Yes, he would be openly defying his father, but not only would it be a way of moving forward; it also might force his father to face the music and accept the match. I pushed him to try to talk to his father again, and Mohamed turned his head to the side and raised his eyebrows, the face he always made to express reluctance.

"I mean," he began, "we have to be really careful about how we approach him." By "we" Mohamed meant him and his family. His father, Mohamed explained, had a heart condition. Years ago, he'd had a massive heart attack and a quadruple bypass surgery. Between that and his hot temper, everyone trod lightly about everything. The subject was closed for now, Mohamed said, but maybe it could be broached again in the future.

"Maybe?" I asked. "In the future? You can't expect me to spend my life waiting around for you."

But our conversation was cut short because, just then, Mohamed got a phone call. He spoke briefly and then hung up, visibly upset. His younger brother, who lived in South Florida, had been arrested by ICE and was being held in Krome Detention Center, in Miami. He'd left the West Bank in 2007 after elections; an accountant for the PA, he'd been disturbed by the corruption he'd seen with his own eyes and had given up on the place. He'd gone first to New York City and then to North Carolina, where he'd initially been arrested for overstaying his visa. After he was detained, he'd then moved to Florida, where he'd lived without problem for years.

Until now.

"I gotta go," Mohamed said, standing. "I have to be with my family now." And he walked out of the apartment, closing the door behind him.

* * *

His brother's detention gnawed at him, as did his own powerlessness. His brother, as it turned out, had married a US citizen several days before ICE picked him up and so, technically, should be spared from deportation. But the two had not yet filed any papers, and Abdullah's lawyer was rushing to take care of everything and to get Abdullah out of jail. There was nothing Mohamed could do to help, much less from the other side of the ocean.

So we continued our lives and began looking for an apartment to share in Ramallah; Mohamed had heard about a great, reasonably priced two bedroom, and we made an appointment to see the place. But when I arrived at Mohamed's office—five days after he'd gotten the call about his brother—I found him wearing the same clothes he'd been wearing when he left my apartment. He was unshaven, his eyes tired. He didn't want to go eat lunch or grab an orange juice from our usual spot up the street. And he didn't want to go see the apartment, he said. But we had an appointment with a real estate agent, and Mohamed believed in honoring his commitments, large and small.

When the real estate agent called, Mohamed answered the phone with a weary, "*Aiwa* [Yes]," and said in the flattest voice possible that we'd be downstairs in a moment. He grabbed his keys off the desk, and I followed him as he locked the door and trudged down the stairs.

The real estate agent was all smiles as he greeted us and helped us get into the car. As he drove us there, he attempted to chat with Mohamed, who had descended into a stony silence. When the real estate agent mentioned that he had some similar places in mind if "your wife" doesn't like this apartment, Mohamed snapped, "She's not my wife. She's an *ajnabiya* [a foreigner]. I'm just helping her."

My heart sank. I understood why he was saying it. Here, in Ramallah, where his family lived—where his *parents* lived—we were too close to home. He couldn't strut around town with his "wife" like he did in Bethlehem, which was farther afield, because the odds were higher that this real estate agent knew someone who knew someone who knew the family. And seeing how Mohamed's father had expressly forbidden him from marrying me, he couldn't have word spread that he was out and about with his wife just a few weeks later. I got it. But still, his words stung. And part of me wondered if this had really been the truth all along—if I was just some silly foreigner he'd been helping out while I was busy deluding myself into thinking we were in love—and now, with Mohamed under so much stress, the truth was finally coming out.

The real estate agent parked on a familiar street, which I couldn't quite place in the daylight. We walked past a familiar retaining wall topped with a wooden fence, shielding a house and a courtyard, entering the apartment building next door. The apartment itself was on the third floor, and as the real estate agent walked us through, he led us toward the large balcony. Opening the doors, he led us outside and pointed down, "Look," he said, "you know Beit Aneesa? You're right next door."

I gasped as I looked down at the place where Mohamed and I met for the first time. The place was already perfect. Living next to Beit Aneesa was the icing on the cake.

I pulled Mohamed aside, out of the real estate agent's earshot, and told him that this place was perfect and we should take it.

He didn't respond.

"What do you think?" I pushed.

"I think we should wait," he said. "There will be other places."

"What are you always waiting for? And, sure, there will be other places, but they won't be *this* place."

"I can't make a decision like this now, with my brother in jail. I just can't."

We rejoined the real estate agent, who looked at us expectantly.

"*Shoo raykum* [What do you guys think]?" he asked.

"*Shukran* [Thank you]," Mohamed said, which was the polite way of saying no.

As we followed the real estate agent back down the stairs, he asked if we wanted to see any other places.

"No," Mohamed said firmly.

* * *

Mohamed was silent as we mounted the stairs to his office. Sitting back down at his desk, he gestured for me to sit on the other side, as though we were working together again. And then he told me, "I can't rent an apartment with you because I don't know if I'm going to be here in a month or two."

His family had decided that someone needed to go to South Florida to try to help his brother or at least to run the cell phone store he owned while he was in Krome. With few commitments locally—Mohamed was in between media projects at the moment—his parents thought him the right son to send. And because we'd planned to go to New York City that summer to attend my aunt's wedding, Mohamed already had a visa. Now, using that visa he'd gotten expressly to meet my family, Mohamed was leaving.

"But you'll be back," I said. "We can take the place. I'll be fine in Ramallah for a couple of months on my own."

"Look, my father wants me to break up with you before I go. He says it's a good time, a natural way, to part."

I gasped. "You said you didn't care what your father thinks. You said we were moving forward even without his blessing."

"I'm sorry," Mohamed said. "I meant it at the time, but I guess I'm more conservative than I thought."

Sitting there on the chair across from him, I began to cry. What had changed? I wanted to know. His father, Mohamed explained, had sat him down and said that he would accept the match—he would accept me—under three conditions: If I got rid of my Israeli citizenship, if I converted to Islam, and if I wore the hijab, a headscarf.

I didn't have a problem with the hijab in and of itself. From my students, I'd come to understand that, for many of them, it wasn't something they were forced into. I knew that for some it was an expression of faith, and I knew that you could be a good feminist and wear the hijab, too. In Abu Dis, I'd gotten used to covering from throat to ankles; adding a headscarf didn't feel like a huge step for me.

As for converting to Islam, I knew women—foreigners—who had converted to Islam on paper while retaining their own faith. So this felt doable, too.

I was surprised to find that the sticking point for me was the Israeli ID. As much as I was completely opposed to the occupation and to Israel's policies in Gaza and the West Bank—and inside of the country, too, where the government set about systematically discriminating against everyone who isn't Jewish—I was deeply attached to my citizenship. This was the place where I'd become an adult; this was the place where I'd recovered all the bits of myself I'd buried in the wake of July 4. Here, I'd started to put myself back together.

How to explain all of this to Mohamed? I'd tried when I'd walked him through Tel Aviv. What I hadn't been able to tell him was that Israel was the first place I'd felt safe and strong, where I'd felt free. I couldn't describe to him the feeling I'd had when I'd held that ID in my hands and had read my own name there, in Hebrew. I couldn't describe to him how I'd been able to build my own life in Tel Aviv and what it had meant for me to see my byline, how I'd stood there on Dizengoff Street, clutching that newspaper in my shaking hands, staring at my name, in print, the voice that had been stolen from me restored. What it had meant for me to give voice to the voiceless, myself included. I knew that the Israeli ID I carried was this strange contradictory thing that left others horribly oppressed while setting me free. I was totally opposed to the state's politics, which I believed were a threat to Palestinians and Jewish Israelis alike. And yet, because Israel was the place that I had become whole again, I couldn't give that ID up.

And now that was exactly the thing both Mohamed and his father wanted me to do.

"I told you, that night in La Vie, that the ID would be a problem," Mohamed said. "But I don't want you to convert to Islam if you don't want to, and I don't want you to wear the hijab. I love you as you are."

I stood and went to his side of the desk, and we wrapped our arms around each other.

"I'll do anything," I said. "I'll do anything." I sobbed.

And Mohamed, the rock, who swore he didn't have any feelings, began to cry, too. It was everything, he said. Us. His father. His brother, in a jail cell in Florida. His little brother, who he was supposed to protect, for life. There was another time that he hadn't protected Abdullah, he said, when they were little, and they were out riding bikes, and Abdullah had ridden out in front of a car and had ended up in the hospital.

And now he wasn't protecting him again.

I told Mohamed there was nothing he could have done to stop this. He couldn't have possibly protected his brother from getting picked up by ICE.

I held Mohamed as he cried. When Mohamed calmed down, I asked him if he really wanted to break up with me and said it was fine if he did, that I would respect his wish and his boundaries.

"No, no," Mohamed said. "I don't want to lose you. We will find a way."

25

Mohamed left for the United States as winter was lifting and everything was starting to bloom. The ride along Wadi Nar was still terrifying because of the hairpin turns and everyone passing each other and the sense that, at any moment, the servees would hurtle off the side of the mountain and crash into the valley below. But now that valley was carpeted in green and looked slightly less menacing than it had when it was brown—its sharper edges made soft by the grass.

Shortly after he left, I emailed my mom. Although my parents were living in southern Georgia at the time, I wanted them to know that I had shared their number with Mohamed in case he had some sort of crazy emergency. If Mohamed had the time, I added, maybe they could meet?

My mom already knew, of course, that Mohamed's family had rejected the match. Now she expressed, again, her reservations about the relationship. Not because he was Palestinian, she said, but because—even if his father came around eventually—the relationship had created problems in the family. And that tension would always remain.

Maybe you should just move on, she wrote.

I didn't feel heard or understood or supported. I felt judged. I felt rebuked, just as I had when I was seventeen and I'd sat on the couch with my mother, silent, unable to share. While I understood that her advice came from a good place, I wouldn't heed her warning. I was my beloved's, and my beloved was mine. I was determined to make things work.

* * *

With Mohamed gone, a close friend, Isaac, offered to visit. We'd been friends since I'd done an article about the volunteer grassroots initiative he'd founded, which was known as Fugee Fridays. Volunteers went stall to stall in the shuk, asking vendors for their leftover food before they dumped the produce on the pedestrian thoroughfare; then the volunteers drove everything they'd collected down to south Tel Aviv, where they distributed the food to African asylum seekers.

Like me, Isaac had dated a Palestinian—he'd had a fairly long relationship with a woman who was a Palestinian citizen of Israel. They'd even lived together in Jaffa, a secret she'd kept from her family in the north of the country. Although Isaac had been ready to go the distance with the woman—marriage and kids and all that—she'd eventually broken it off because of her family.

I'd kept Isaac updated about everything going on with Mohamed, and rather than offering me some empty words of consolation, he was going the distance, literally, by making the journey from Tel Aviv out to Bethlehem. Because he was an American Israeli, it would be illegal for him to visit, but he was coming anyway to spend the weekend with me.

First, I would have to clear the visit with Jacqueline—who would never allow a guy friend to come stay at the house.

So I decided to tell her that Isaac was my cousin; I felt guilty about lying, of course, but there was no other way. But what would be the cover story? I wondered. If I admitted that he lived inside of Israel—that he had been there for years, even longer than I had been—that would be awfully suspicious.

"I have a cousin from America," I began, "who is visiting Tel Aviv."

It still felt like a dead giveaway that I was Jewish. But Jacqueline didn't bat an eye.

"He wants to come visit me for a weekend," I continued, "and I was wondering if he can stay here."

"Of course," Jacqueline said. "*Ahlan wasahlan.*"

Like everyone who met him, Jacqueline fell in love with Isaac. On top of being a lovely human being—the sort of guy who figured out a way to get food to refugees and didn't complain about spending half his weekend doing so—he was strikingly handsome: tall, broad shouldered, with chocolate brown hair and dark eyes. His maternal grandparents were Iraqi Jews, and it was easy to imagine Isaac—who radiated self-confidence—as an Arab heartthrob.

I cooked, as always, and Isaac and I lounged about—talking, laughing, reading. On Friday, he took to one of the alcoves in my room with a book in hand. As I lazed about in bed, I looked over at him. Isaac was so perfect, so handsome. I thought of how easy it would be to walk across the room and kiss him and then pull him into bed with me. How much easier this would be than Mohamed.

But I couldn't do it.

On Saturday, when I returned from driving Isaac into Jerusalem, where he would begin the journey back to Tel Aviv, Jacqueline came rushing downstairs.

"Why don't you marry him instead?" she asked me.

"Isaac?!" I exclaimed. "He's my *cousin,*" I said, so much in the role that I believed my own words.

"So?"

"We used to do that in my family," I told her, thinking about the genealogical research I'd done in which I'd discovered, on my maternal great-grandmother's side, the family name Raphael stretching back for generations as Raphaels married Raphaels married Raphaels. "But we stopped intermarrying at least a hundred years ago."

"Mohamed's in America now," Jacqueline said, shrugging. "And he's not coming back for you. They never do."

* * *

I had faith that Mohamed would return; after all, he'd booked a round-trip ticket. But a small part of me started to wonder if Jacqueline was right. As his time in the States went on, I heard less and less from Mohamed, and I found it harder to get in touch with him. Two weeks before he was scheduled to come home, Mohamed called and told me that he was thinking about moving to Florida.

"This place is amazing," he said. "There's no army, no soldiers, no checkpoints. You just get in the car and *drive*."

That was what he was doing when he wasn't managing his brother's store: he was studying maps, just as he had as a boy in Amman. Just as he'd ridden his bike all over that city, he was going for endless drives now in South Florida.

"But what will you do there?" I asked.

"Work," he said. "My brother is talking about opening another store. I would run it."

Part of me was shocked that Mohamed was considering moving. Despite everything he'd been through while living under Israeli occupation—and despite the beating he'd received from the PA policemen—Mohamed was committed to this place, to Palestine. He'd passed up his last girlfriend's offer to move to Spain; he hadn't overstayed his visa when he'd gone to the States in 2007. Why the change?

It occurred to me that, in the process of defying his father's wishes by dating me, Mohamed was reconsidering everything.

His father had sacrificed for Palestine and had spent his entire life serving the cause. But what had his work amounted to? Mohamed had tried, to, too serve the cause in his own way. But the occupation went on and on. Palestine wasn't free and Mohamed wasn't either. Now, Mohamed was coming to the realization that the cause wasn't going to save him. He needed to save himself.

Part of me understood; part of me felt betrayed. Didn't we both believe in this place? Didn't we believe in a shared future here? Hadn't

I moved out to Bethlehem so we could start to build a life in Palestine together?

I put these questions aside for now, though, because I was certain that when Mohamed got back, he would forget about Florida. And with his brother still in Krome, this the idea of the two of them opening a store for Mohamed to run seemed impossible.

* * *

Two weeks later, Mohamed came back to the West Bank.

After landing in Jordan—Palestinians who live in the occupied territories and hold green IDs can't fly through Tel Aviv—Mohamed made his way from the airport in Amman to Allenby Bridge, the only crossing Palestinians can use to enter the West Bank. Once he'd gotten in, he'd taken a servees to Bethlehem. Telling his parents he was spending a few days in Amman, he bought himself the time he needed to spend the weekend with me.

His birthday had been the previous week, so in addition to preparing a dizzying array of salads, I baked Mohamed a cheesecake, his favorite. When we finished eating, we sat out in the garden, watching the last bits of day fade. One by one lights came on in Dheisheh—windows glowing yellow—like stars in the night sky.

Mohamed sighed and rested his head on my shoulder. "Let's make this journey—let's take this walk—together," he said. "I'm moving to Florida. Come with me. We'll get married there."

Florida? But here was the most beautiful view in the world, and here, the air—pregnant with jasmine and apricot and lemon and the smell of the soil, of the earth itself—was the sweetest of any air I'd ever smelled. *How can I leave all this behind?* I wondered. Israel. Palestine. I didn't care what anyone called the place. It was my home.

Still. I loved this man. We'd chosen each other. And I understood that, without his family's approval, it was absolutely impossible for us to remain together here. If we were going to build a life, a home, together, we had no choice but to leave.

"OK," I said finally, leaning my head on his. "OK."

* * *

And so I started dismantling the life I'd spent nearly a decade building on both sides of the Green Line.

At least, I tried to.

Sarah, my boss at the university, was shocked when I told her that Mohamed and I were leaving together. Reminding me that decent academic jobs like mine were hard to find—and dangling a small promotion over my head—she urged me to rethink my decision before I officially resigned. While I repeated that I was, indeed, leaving, I hesitated to actually put it in writing. And I promised to honor my commitment to teach a three-week course at the end of the summer, an intensive introduction to the college known as "Language and Thinking," or LNT.

Jacqueline was surprised, too, when I told her that Mohamed and I were leaving.

We were sitting upstairs, on her glassed-in porch, with that view—with Palestine—below.

"What about the apartment?" she asked.

"The place is amazing. You'll find someone else." I said, not understanding her concern. The place was beautiful, cheap, and there was no shortage of foreigners around.

"But *inti*—you . . . You're my favorite, ya Mya," she said, and I knew then, she wasn't worried about finding a tenant. I realized that when she'd asked me about the apartment, what she really meant was "What about me?"

My throat caught.

When she asked about an exit date, I told her I didn't have one; Jacqueline raised her eyebrows but said nothing.

One by one, I told my friends, too, including Oded, who was moving in with his girlfriend. He was leaving the studio, but Kinneret hadn't started showing the place to people yet.

"There's time," he said. "If you change your mind, you can have the place back."

In fact, I still had my key.

* * *

The semester drew to an end. Even though the school year was over, and I maintained that I was leaving, I couldn't bring myself to formally resign. I just couldn't imagine myself living anywhere else and doing anything other than helping Palestinians with their writing and continuing my reporting on the conflict.

But Mohamed was moving forward with his plans. He'd told his family that he was leaving; he didn't tell them I was going with him. While they were upset about the prospect of another son immigrating to the United States—particularly their eldest son, the son who bore his father's father's name—they understood his decision. Mohamed's father, who had recently retired from the PA joked that that was the best thing he'd done while he was in the PA: retire. Yes, he had sacrificed so much for Palestine and he would grow old here. But he had also resigned himself to the fact that, in his children's eyes, the place was unlivable.

Mohamed planned to leave in mid-June, which was just over a month away. He would accompany me to my aunt's wedding in NYC and then continue on to Florida. With his departure approaching, Mohamed devoted himself to spending time with his family and friends and cleaning out his office, which was full of a decade's accumulation of papers, books, equipment, and furniture. Ramzy, his best friend, often dropped by the office to keep him company; he had an eye on a director's chair that he liked. One afternoon, Ramzy asked Mohamed if he could have the chair and Mohamed declined.

"But why not?" Ramzy pushed. "You're not taking it to America."

Ramzy was right. Still, Mohamed dug in his heels and refused to surrender the chair. The two had a huge argument and Ramzy stormed out.

Mohamed told me about all of this with a laugh. He swore he was just teasing Ramzy; of course he was going to give him the chair. What use would he have for it once he was gone?

"So why not just give it to him now?" I asked Mohamed.

"That chair is special. I want him to appreciate it."

I didn't buy the explanation, in part because Mohamed was storing some of his office furniture at his parent's house. If the chair was so special, why not just fold it up and tuck it away in a corner of their makhzan, their storage room? Mohamed didn't directly express any reluctance or ambivalence about leaving. He said he was ready to go and to start a new life with me in Florida. But his inability to relinquish this particular piece of furniture—a symbol of the years he'd spent as a journalist—seemed to say it all. It was like the chair had become a locus for all of the ambivalence he felt about giving up his life in the West Bank.

The next time Ramzy stopped by the office, the two made up and Mohamed let him take the chair.

With Mohamed busy, our weekends together dropped to one day. I worked on my book proposal about Southeast Asian migrant workers and African asylum seekers in Israel and spent my free time with my friends on both sides of the Green Line. As May passed, Sarah pushed me to formalize my decision. "I have to plan for the fall," she said, over a glass of wine one night in Jerusalem. "I'll have to find someone to take your classes." I assured her that I was, indeed, leaving and that she could go ahead and start looking for my replacement. But visualizing some faceless professor moving through the halls, entering the rooms where I'd sat with my students, workshopping their writing together, left me feeling territorial and jealous, like someone wasn't just taking over my job but my life.

June upon us, Sarah emailed me, putting her request for a formal resignation in writing. I had to respond. So I wrote back confirming that I wouldn't be returning in the fall. This decision did nothing to ease my ambivalence, however, and I made no moves to get rid of anything or pack.

A couple of days before I left for Vermont, where I would attend an artist's residency before meeting Mohamed in New York City for my aunt's wedding, Mohamed came to visit me in Bethlehem. This would be the last time we would be together in the West Bank, where we'd fallen in love and where most of our courtship had unfolded. I was filled with sadness as we walked through the Old City. Stopping before the window of a jewelry store, we looked at the dazzling array of wedding gold: large ornate necklaces with intricate designs, heaps of bangles, twenty-four-karat rings. I remembered showing up late to Ibtisam's wedding and awkwardly handing her a wad of cash while everyone else was draping gold around her neck or on her wrists. I remembered Mohamed standing by the groom as we posed with the newlyweds and smiled at the camera. As fraught as that moment was, I would have never imagined that, less than a year after we went to Ibtisam's wedding, we would be planning on leaving.

I thought we would stay here together forever.

"Let's go in," Mohamed said.

In a display case, I spied an unusual ring. The edges of the ring weren't straight but, rather, waves that resembled an undulating ocean; the surface of the ring was covered with an intricate design of circles and crescents that reminded me of the phases of the moon.

The ring made me think of the moment when, as Mohamed and I sat in Jacqueline's garden together, he had asked me to go on this journey with him. It reminded me that, like our courtship, this walk would have ups and downs and cycles. But like the cycles of the moon, we would always return to where we started. Maybe not literally—maybe we would never come back to this place—but we would always return to each other and the love that had brought us together.

I slid the ring onto my right ring finger, which signals engagement, and it fit perfectly. I switched it to my left, for marriage, and again, it felt like the piece had been made for me.

But we left the store without buying it—Mohamed said my engagement ring should be a gift, not something we bought together. He assured me, though, that he was going to swing by and get the ring on his way back to Ramallah.

Returning to my place, we took to the garden, where we plucked apricots off the tree and ate them, juice dripping down our chins, as we watched the light mellow over the hills. It was getting late, and Mohamed needed to catch the servees back to Ramallah; he surrendered his spare key to me, and then I walked him to the garden door. We lingered there on the threshold. This was our last moment in Palestine together. The next time we would see each other would be in New York City, where Mohamed would spend two weeks with me before continuing on alone to Florida; by the time I met him in the city, he would have left the West Bank for good.

"I'll see you soon," he said, leaning in to kiss me.

I didn't want him to walk away. Because walking away would end this moment and that would be it—we would really be leaving the West

Bank. I wanted him to come back inside and stay in this garden with me forever.

"But aren't you going to miss this? What if we just stayed?" I asked. The air behind him grew darker, and the streetlight flickered on. Maybe he would miss the servees and would come in to spend the night. Maybe I would just skip the artist residency. We could pass the summer here, in the garden.

"I will miss this place," he said, giving the wall a little pat. "But, *yalla*, it's time to move on."

26

After a couple of days in New York City, I arrived at the residency in Vermont. There, at a marble mansion nestled among the trees, I quickly settled into a routine of writing through the morning and running in the afternoon on the tiny two-lane road that ran through the riotous green of a Vermont summer. In the evening, we had long, communal dinners with the other residents—writers, musicians, and visual artists, among them Nurit, an Israeli artist who lived in New York City. After the table was cleared and the dishes were washed, we all took to the enormous den, its shelves lined with antique books, and spent the evening talking, laughing, and dancing.

But the last days of the residency were marred by horrible news.

Three Israeli teenagers had been kidnapped from Route 60, in the West Bank, from a junction that I could visualize in my mind's eye.

It was where I made a U-turn every time I came back to Bethlehem from Jerusalem. I had to drive past the turn and then turn around and backtrack to the turnoff. The boys, who had been hitchhiking—which is common in Israel—had been kidnapped from the exact place I made my U-turn.

As much as I opposed settlements, those boys were humans, and with the place so easy to visualize, the scene played out in my mind. My heart ached for the boys and their families. And, Mohamed and I knew right away that even though this incident had taken place in the West Bank, it wouldn't stay there. Those boys' deaths would, eventually, inevitably, lead to an escalation between Israel and Hamas. We knew that Gaza would pay the price.

But the consequences were felt immediately in the West Bank, where the army started going door-to-door in the areas close to the junction—including Beit Sahour, just down the hill from my place—in a fruitless attempt to find the boys. As soldiers raided homes, reports that they were stealing money and gold surfaced. Palestinian and international friends there in Beit Sahour messaged me on Viber and WhatsApp repeating these stories. I didn't know what to think. But I was racked with worry about Lena and everyone back home.

My friend and colleague David, who was staying at Jacqueline's with my cat, emailed me, too, saying things were extremely tense in the West Bank and that the army had been close to the house. An Israeli passport holder, like me, David could be arrested if they raided the home and found him there. He didn't want to abandon my cat, but he didn't know what to do.

The army also closed Allenby Bridge—the only exit for most West Bank Palestinians, who cannot simply fly out via Ben Gurion International Airport in Tel Aviv but, rather, must go to Jordan—to all men from the Hebron area aged forty or under. Rumors that "the bridge," as everyone calls it, would be completely closed soon began to circulate, and on both sides of the ocean, Mohamed and I began to panic. Yes, he lived in Ramallah, and his ID card reflected that. But his birthplace was Sa'ir, a village right next to Hebron. Would he be unable to exit? And then what would happen when the Israelis decided to close the bridge completely? He would make it to Florida eventually, sure, but he would miss the wedding in New York.

Mohamed decided to try his luck at the bridge. With time running out, he worked around the clock to empty out the office he'd rented for almost a decade—setting furniture out on the curb, giving his favorite chair to Ramzy, hauling books and papers to his parents' house. As Mohamed made the last preparations for his journey to Jordan, I spent the last night at the residency, where, as I walked down a set of marble stairs with socks on, I slipped and hurt my foot. Without health insurance, I wasn't going to the doctor. And I figured the injury to be a hairline fracture, anyway, which I wouldn't need a cast for.

Still, it seemed a bad omen for everything to come. Between the pain and the fear that Mohamed wouldn't make it out of the West Bank—that he would miss the wedding and would be caught there as violence escalated—I barely slept. And then a message beeped on my phone: It was Mohamed. He was out, and he'd made it to Amman. It seemed like, at last, all the uncertainty and stress was over. We were finally going to be together.

* * *

Two days later, I limped my way through the terminal at JFK airport, my fractured foot stuffed in a high heel. This was our big reunion after weeks apart—this was the moment we were finally going to be free as a couple, free from his family, free from movement restrictions, free to walk around without worrying about being caught and arrested—and I'd be damned if I was going to show up in running shoes. Gritting my teeth, I bore the pain.

I stood there, in a one-shouldered black and white dress, as close to the gate as I could get without a ticket, waiting for Mohamed to walk out, wheeling the one suitcase he was bringing with him for his—our—new life in America. Mohamed had flown from Amman to London and then, finally, JFK. People came out in waves, and Mohamed wasn't among them. Where was he? I knew he'd gotten on the plane. I wondered if he'd had a problem entering the country.

The waves slowed to a trickle, and as people filtered out, I asked them if they'd been on the flight from London. Yes, yes, yes, one after another confirmed for me. This only made me more nervous.

Oh God, is he being detained?

And then the doors parted, and there was Mohamed, in the same sports coat he'd worn to Ibtisam's wedding, rolling his suitcase behind him, a backpack slung over his shoulders. I rushed toward him, doing my best not to limp.

"*Hayati* [My life]," he said as he embraced me.

* * *

Some friends of my aunt's very generously handed over the keys to their basement apartment in Brooklyn, loaning us the place for free. It felt like a honeymoon suite—here, no one was going to bust in and demand our wedding papers. We hadn't had to seek someone's blessing to carry on our love affair here. The space was just ours, with no constraints, and we were free to do whatever we want. We settled into a rhythm of spending the mornings in bed, making love, and then exploring the city in the afternoon and evening.

And, of course, we met my family.

We made the trip to Manhattan to my grandfather's apartment in midtown, where he and my parents awaited us. We'd come with gifts for everyone. I brought my grandfather a book, *1948: A Soldier's Tale; The Bloody Road to Jerusalem*, by Uri Avnery, a memoir written by an Israeli who became a peace activist and leftist. For my parents, I'd brought pillowcases embellished with Palestinian embroidery.

The meeting was utterly unremarkable. No one talked politics, not even my grandfather. A first-generation American, he shared instead his rags-to-riches story with Mohamed, who seemed fascinated. We went to dinner at Rosa Mexicano and had guacamole and margaritas, and my grandfather kept talking. He told Mohamed a lot about the years he'd spent working as a seller for different retail companies, traveling the world to procure garments those corporations would sell stateside; he asked Mohamed a lot of questions about the cell phone business and what his thoughts were about running a store. Mohamed didn't have great answers and so my grandfather told another story: this one about the time that he tried to open a company of his own—he'd dipped into manufacturing and selling neckties—only for the business to go bankrupt. "I lost everything," my grandfather concluded.

He roared with laughter, smoothed his beard, took a sip of his vodka on the rocks, and nodded reassuringly as he told us the moral of the story: "Don't worry. There will be ups and downs but you're both smart, you're both hardworking. You two are going to be just fine."

It was as close to a blessing as we were going to get.

* * *

One morning, as I put snacks and bottled water into Mohamed's backpack in preparation for an afternoon at Prospect Park, I found a jewelry box. Unable to resist peeking, I opened it—there was the ring I'd fallen in love with in Bethlehem. I didn't say anything to Mohamed about proposing. I just closed the box and put it back where I'd found it. But I found myself preoccupied all day long. As we spread a blanket on the ground, I wondered if this would be it, if he was going to do it here. As we passed a grocery store with flowers out front and he stopped to buy me a bouquet, I wondered if the proposal was coming. When we arrived at the apartment, I thought, surely, it would be tonight. But it wasn't. And I became tense, wondering what the holdup was. He'd told me in Bethlehem that he couldn't propose to me there, under his father's nose, without his blessing. But now we were in America. So what was he waiting for?

We should have been having an amazing time, but our days were shot with tension—not only as I waited for him to propose but also as Mohamed waited for his phone to ring. Since he'd left the West Bank, tensions had only continued to rise, with the army conducting a massive military operation as they continued to search for the three Israeli teenagers. Hundreds of Palestinians were detained and held in administrative detention; raids were conducted on nongovernmental organizations and universities.

Mohamed, anxious about his family's safety, kept his phone on all the time. When it wasn't ringing, he was checking it for updates, as though the thing wouldn't ping him when it came in. Or as though he might be able to catch an alert faster than the sound and that, by doing so, he could somehow avert a disaster back home. In South Florida, his brother, too, was still in Krome, but the news from the lawyer was good. Not only had being married helped save him from deportation, but ironically, so had his otherwise worthless Palestinian Authority–issued passport—there is no real state of Palestine, and as a West Banker, he couldn't land at Ben Gurion Airport. This meant the authorities had nowhere to deport him to. The downside was, until his case was sorted, Abdullah sat in jail, in limbo.

A couple of days before my aunt's wedding, Mohamed and I went to Coney Island. While walking on the boardwalk, he got a call from one of his brothers, but the connection failed. Frantic, Mohamed stopped in the middle of the boardwalk, trying to call over and over, as pedestrians parted to walk around us, frozen in the middle of the stream of people. His eyes were on his phone, so I guided him toward a bench, where he sat, panicked, calling again and again until his brother finally picked up.

"*Shoo sar*? *Kolshi tamam* [What happened? Is everything OK]?" he asked.

It was. His brother had just called to ask him how his trip was going.

Mohamed visibly relaxed, his back, which had been stiff, slumping and his shoulders rolling forward. He stretched as he chatted with his family members, one after another—they were passing the phone around—and I had no problem understanding the conversation. He told them about everything we'd been doing—only he didn't use the word *ihna* (we); nor did he conjugate his verbs in the plural form. No, it was all *ana* (I), and his verbs made it sound like he was doing this trip solo.

They don't know he's with me, I realized. They think he's in the city alone.

Coming to America had seemed like the brave thing to do. But now I saw it as just another way of hiding me, just as I'd been tucked away in Jacqueline's house, in Bethlehem, a safe distance from his family. Now I would be even better hidden on the other side of the ocean. What would happen when we got married? What would happen if we had kids, if we started a family of our own? What would this secret, hidden family—including me—be with respect to his *real* family back home? And what would happen if there was some sort of emergency back home? It didn't necessarily have to do with the Israelis—what if it was something ordinary? A close family member got sick? Or died? Would he go running back, leaving me alone and hidden with children? I remembered the word Lena had taught me—*mashtuba* (crossed out)—as I sat there on the bench next to him and he happily chatted away with his *real* loved ones.

He closed the phone, oblivious to how upset I was. Knowing how worried he was about his family, I didn't want to add to Mohamed's stress. They were living under occupation, and that occupation was going door-to-door in the West Bank. This wasn't the time to talk about my feelings about being hidden because I knew perfectly well why he was keeping me a secret. So I didn't broach the topic.

Mohamed pointed at the Ferris wheel.

"I've never been on one of those before," he said. "Let's go."

We paid and boarded, the metal cage closed around us, and as the thing ascended, swaying slightly, I wondered how safe it was, how tightly it would hold us if a particularly strong gust of wind came. On the ground, the little enclosure had looked and felt stable. But now, dangling in the air, it all felt flimsy and insubstantial.

When we were at the top of the Ferris wheel, the thing came to a stop, and we looked at Brooklyn below us. Small, the streets and buildings and treetops looked like little toys; the shoreline and ocean looked like part of a fake, plastic model. Mohamed reached into his backpack and pulled out the jewelry box, opened it, and asked if I would honor him by becoming his wife.

I said I would, and he slid the ring onto my right ring finger—Muslims wear engagement rings on their right hand. I should have been elated, but coming after the phone call with no *ihna* and all *ana*, the engagement felt false, thin. If we could only exist in secret, what sort of future would we have?

I thought how perfect it would all be if our love existed like this—suspended in the air somewhere between heaven and earth. But below, the ground awaited us, and as the Ferris wheel jerked forward, my stomach did, too.

* * *

The day after my aunt's wedding, I accompanied Mohamed to JFK again to see him off to Florida. Our parting was tense—the bodies of those Israeli teenagers had been found, and I was dreading going back. I joked about just jumping ship on my stuff—I could leave it all at Jacqueline's—and following Mohamed to Florida.

"*Yalla* [Come on]," he said.

But I couldn't. My cat was also at Jacqueline's, and I'd committed to teaching a class at the end of the summer.

Two days later, I returned to JFK alone to fly home. After the Israeli teenagers were found dead, some Jewish settlers had kidnapped a Palestinian boy from East Jerusalem, Mohammed Abu Khdeir, as he'd walked to the mosque in the early morning dark for dawn prayers. In a brutal act of vengeance, they'd taken the boy to the Jerusalem Forest—the place where Mohamed and I had hiked when he'd stayed with me in Kiryat Yovel, the place where we'd spent the previous Eid, the place where we'd snapped our first photo as a couple—and there, among those trees, they'd made that poor boy, a child, drink gasoline before setting him on fire. I was devastated at the news—by the loss of life, by the utter lack of humanity of the settlers' actions, and by the location. I imagined my beloved trees—whose branches I'd run under, whose leaves I'd looked up at and pondered during picnics—bearing witness to something so horrible.

In the wake of Abu Khdeir's death, Palestinians had gone out to protest; those demonstrations had predictably turned into riots, and now, sitting there at JFK, waiting to board the plane, I saw images of places I knew in East Jerusalem on fire. Literally. Palestinians were burning tires and throwing Molotov cocktails in the very streets I had to drive to get back to Jacqueline's.

And then I would have to spend the summer sitting there—my foot was broken—waiting to teach this course in August as the world around me burned.

My phone pinged with an incoming email. It was David, telling me that he wouldn't be there to greet me when I returned to the apartment. He'd left enough food and water for my cat and had headed back to Jerusalem. Tensions were too high, he said, with the army going door-to-door in Beit Sahour. Without a car, he'd tried to take a

Palestinian bus into Jerusalem one afternoon and had had a close call when soldiers boarded to check IDs; luckily the driver had covered for him, saying he'd picked David up on the side of the road, outside a settlement. But it was possible soldiers would end up inside of Bethlehem, of course, even though it was Area A, and David was increasingly worried soldiers would catch him there; he was also concerned about Jacqueline's snooping. He'd opened the shower curtain one day only to find her on the other side.

It was all too much, David said, and so he'd stuck around as long as he could to take care of my cat, but now that I was on my way back, he was done.

I boarded the plane, terrified of what sort of summer awaited me on the other side.

27

Driving through East Jerusalem on my way to Bethlehem, the streets were eerily quiet. I could see scant evidence of the riots on the sidewalks and the roads. There were a few blackened garbage bins, some scattered stones, but otherwise, life went on. Similarly, the drive to Jacqueline's was unremarkable. I went out through the Tunnels and then went up past the junction where the boys were kidnapped, made my U-turn, and turned right onto the road that led past a small army base where I could either make a sharp right and enter Beit Jala, the Christian village that borders Bethlehem, or continue on and arrive eventually at a settlement.

I was relieved when I finally made it back to Jacqueline's and the steel garage door closed behind me. It was like the world was dropping away. There was the garden—still and silent and calm, as though those poor boys hadn't been kidnapped and another poor boy hadn't been forced to drink gasoline before his body had been set on fire. There was the lemon tree, and there was the *mishmish* (apricot) tree, and there was the bench where Mohamed had asked me to go on this journey with him.

I was going on this journey. I just had to make it through the summer.

A few days later, Israel started bombing Gaza.

* * *

I sat, horrified, before the TV as I watched the state—whose blue ID I carried in my purse—bombing civilians. My foot was still broken and throbbing; I didn't dare venture out. I'd made things worse by walking on it all over New York City, and now a student was sending threatening emails. From the writing style, both Sarah and I guessed it to be Iman, the girl who'd told me in the fall semester that anyone could bring a gun to campus to shoot me.

Now, as Israel bombed Gaza, the anonymous student wrote long, fiery emails and cc'd the entire student body and the faculty, saying that I was a Zionist who needed to repent to the Palestinian people, saying I'd been spotted in East Jerusalem and Bethlehem and that I'd better not dare show my face in public as children were dying in Gaza.

Sarah called Iman in to confront her; Iman denied everything. After that meeting, a new "anonymous" email went out saying that any attempts to ferret out the author of the email on the basis of their writing style or language would only invoke "our" fury. The emails—which were all written in the plural "we" and "our"—grew more threatening and more specific in their content. When students had written about the occupation and I'd asked them to include counterargument, I hadn't been teaching them the basics of argumentation. No, I'd been trying to brainwash them, the writer claimed. I'd lived in a settlement, the anonymous student wrote—a flat-out lie (though many Palestinians consider Tel Aviv to be one massive settlement). My coauthors at +972 were Zionists; therefore, I was a Zionist, too—a label that didn't capture my complicated political beliefs at all. It went on and on and on. This student was determined to whip up anger against me.

So I was surprised when I received emails of support both from former students and students that I'd never even had. One wrote that he'd heard all about me, admired what I was doing there—serving the Palestinian people—and that he'd always wanted to take a class with me; he just hadn't had the chance to do so yet. His email brought tears to my eyes. The dean of the school weighed in, too, reminding the student that her accusations were slanderous and were libel and that I could sue her.

Mohamed urged me to leave. "Forget about the class," he said. "You quit already. You don't have to stay to teach a three-week course." He correctly pointed out that I didn't need the money. With my cost of living so low in Bethlehem, I'd managed to save money in the past year.

But I refused to give up on this place. I refused to give up on the people. Still, I hid in the house.

* * *

I would have spent the entire summer in Jacqueline's house and garden if it weren't for Lena. With my foot fractured, I couldn't run with her. But Lena needed to get her permit renewed, and she asked me to drive her to the base. That was the last thing I wanted to do right now. I was scared to get on the road: scared that a Palestinian would mistake me, in my yellow-plated car, for a settler; scared that a settler would mistake me for a Palestinian. Either side could pick up a stone and throw it at my car, and, in an unarmored vehicle without a helmet, a stone could prove deadly. Or even worse—what if that person had a gun and took a shot at me?

Lena, of course, was also scared—too scared to go alone. But going together as a Hebrew-speaking Israeli and an Arabic-speaking Palestinian, she said, would mean that we could handle anything that happened on the way. Being together, she reasoned, would keep us both safe. And while I had no reason other than Lena to drive to an army base in the middle of the war, that was reason enough—not only was she my friend, but I understood that I was privileged to live in the territories with an American passport and an Israeli ID that not only granted me freedom of movement but impunity. I felt an obligation to use my privilege to help her in any way that I could.

Lena came to my apartment, and as we got ready to leave, I prepped her and myself for dealing with rocket fire while we were on the road. "If the alarm goes, I'll pull over, and we'll get down on the ground, on our stomachs, and we'll put our hands over the back of our heads like this." I showed her, then, what I'd done in the south of the country when I'd gone down there in 2012 to report for Al Jazeera English on Israeli reactions to rocket fire. I lay flat on the floor on my stomach. Lacing my fingers together, I put my hands on the back of my head as though to guard my skull.

"*Shoo fucking hada*?" Lena asked, laughing, as she repeated a silly thing I'd said once when we'd been hanging out with a bunch of Palestinians. *Shoo fucking hada* translated roughly to "What the fuck is this?"

"Shoo fucking hada?! You think our *fingers* are going to protect us from a *rocket*, ya Mya? You look like you're lounging in a hammock. You Israelis are *crazy*." And she continued laughing.

It had, indeed, felt absurd when I'd done this on the side of the road near Sderot and the other areas in the south that had come under rocket fire.

Having a plan, we headed out. I took the route we'd taken so many times—out of the Old City, through the newer parts of Bethlehem that connected the town to neighboring Beit Jala, and then up the hill where the army base stood on the corner before we would swing a left onto the road that connected the nearby settlements with Route 60.

We fell silent as we approached the base. Soldiers could be out, standing in the road, stopping people. I'd seen it many times before.

Lena was fidgeting with her phone. "Listen to this, ya Mya. A little music for your soldier friends."

And then the song began: "*Uddrub uddrub Tel Abib*!" a group of men's voices sang in Arabic. Literally translating as "strike, strike Tel Aviv," it was a call to hit Tel Aviv with a rocket. The song had come out during the 2012 war and had become popular among some Palestinians again in the summer of 2014 as another war raged.

I groaned. "Lena," I said, "shoo fucking hada? That is *not* going to help."

I knew that she didn't really want Tel Aviv—or any place—to get hit. I knew that it was all tongue-in-cheek, that she was playing the song in protest, as a way to poke fun at everyone's stupidity—Hamas, Israel—and the stupidity of war. I knew it was gallows humor. Lena believed in nonviolent resistance. "What has Hamas really done for the Palestinian cause?" she'd asked me rhetorically once. "*Nothing.* Neither has Abu Mazen or his Fatah. And don't get me started on the Arab countries. *No one* is helping us."

As much as she disliked Mohamed, this was an opinion that the two of them shared; Mohamed had spent hours railing against all the Arab countries that were doing nothing for Palestine. And that was a critique in the song streaming from her phone now: the Gulf States weren't helping.

The base was to our left, and now, as we were next to it, the tension was unbearable. We both screamed and laughed more out of discomfort and fear than anything else. When I arrived at the stop sign on the corner, I hit the brakes and checked for traffic on the settler road. It was completely empty. I made the turn, and as we passed the base, Lena waved her phone out the window, the words *uddrub uddrub* getting eaten by the wind.

And then we made it. We were on the settler road, rolling downhill toward Route 60.

Our drive passed without incident. We arrived at the base, parked, and went inside, where we found business as usual. While I knew, of course, about the permit regimes and that bureaucracy was one of the many faces of the occupation, this was the first time I'd been inside such an office and seen this side of it, and I was surprised by how much the place reminded me of any other bureaucratic office—like the driver's license bureau. Like a bank. It was the ordinariness of the occupation, the mundane details, the machine that ground the Palestinians down.

Lena quickly renewed her permit; we got back into the car and headed home.

* * *

In that same period, Jacqueline came down frequently, and she was completely unabashed about it. She no longer treated me like a renter of a separate space but more like a member of her family living inside an attached area. She came down the stairs, or sometimes she entered through the door that connected the street and the garden, under the pretense of watering the plants. When I sat before the TV, she used the stairs; when I rested on the bench in the garden, icing my still broken foot, she used the side door.

One afternoon, sitting down on the bench next to me, Jacqueline told me that she couldn't handle the news anymore, the bombing of Gaza. She'd had two heart attacks when she was younger, and the stress of watching Gaza getting pummeled was too much to bear—in part because it brought back memories of 1948, when Jaffa had been bombed and she'd had to flee.

"Boom! Boom!" she cried, clutching at her chest. No. She shook her head. What was happening to Gaza now was too much to bear. So she'd turned off the TV and joined me in the garden.

She'd brought down a pair of shears with her and a plastic bag, and she stood now and began to clip at the clumps of grapes hanging from the vines over our head.

"The crop this year," she said, "is bad. Too dry." She made a face. "What to do with these?" she muttered in Arabic. She sighed, switched back to English. "I'll make vinegar out of them."

"No," I said, standing on my good foot, plucking a grape from the vine. "They're fine. We'll eat them." I was determined to make do, no matter what was going on around us.

* * *

After driving Lena to get her permit renewed, I began to venture out of the house more. At night, under the cover of dark, was the time I felt freest to emerge. I had some close friends down the hill—Amy, an American woman who was engaged to a Christian Palestinian from Beit Sahour, Shadi—and almost every night, I limped to their house, which I could see from Jacqueline's garden. We took seats outside, cracked open a bottle of whiskey, and watched the sky, guessing which of the fiery things streaking across that inky black canvas was a shooting star and which was a rocket. Not always able to tell which was which, we made wishes on nothing.

The death toll in Gaza mounting, we sat in silence.

Late in the night, Shadi would escort me home, walking me back up the hill. I would tell him it was unnecessary. It was such a short walk! But Shadi insisted. The road went around the terraced orchards that stood between Jacqueline's house and theirs, and one night, I joked that all I needed was a ladder and the trip would be even shorter. We could take the diagonal from their house to mine rather than walking all the way around on the road—we would walk through the trees, lean the ladder on the retaining walls, and climb up, and just like that, we'd be in Jacqueline's garden.

Shadi laughed at the idea of us walking around with a ladder, climbing over garden walls, wished me a good night, and left me at my door.

As I stepped inside, entering the porch, my own words stuck with me. I looked out toward the garden, at the dark beyond the trees, and realized this place that had felt hermetically sealed, that Jacqueline had ensured me was very safe, was completely permeable. Sure there were bars on the windows, but once someone was over the wall, the lock on the French doors was flimsy. It would take next to nothing to pry the doors open, despite the lock. Anyone who wanted to get inside my apartment could do so in an instant.

Walking alone through the house—through the living room, kitchen, then the pantry, all the way back to the bathroom—my still broken right foot protesting, I told myself I was being paranoid. As I washed my face and brushed my teeth, I told myself that, anyway, no one knew I was here, no one knew who I was, and the people who *did* know were friends, people who understood my politics, people who cared about me, people who would keep me safe.

But then I thought of Iman's emails.

I reminded myself that Shadi and Amy were right down the hill. God forbid something happened, I could call them. And, yes, Mohamed was gone, but Ramzy was in Dar Salah almost every weekend—I could call him, too. But then came a little voice in my head: Dar Salah is at least a ten-minute drive. Maybe I would be able to call Ramzy if someone broke into the apartment, but I might be dead by the time he arrived.

Who was I kidding? If something went down, the only person who would be able to get there fast enough would be Jacqueline. And what was a seventy-something-year-old woman going to be able to do for me?

The master bedroom seemed too big, too empty, so I went into the guest room and closed the door, even though I knew that door wouldn't help either. I got into bed and lay there, listening, certain I heard whispers. And then a rustling—was that the wind passing through the trees? Or was it footsteps? Was it boots crunching leaves?

And then I heard a voice.

"I'm afraid for you, Mya."

Ramzy's words at the Christmas party. We'd sat in this very bedroom, on this very bed, as he'd warned me.

I looked toward the window then and imagined the barrel of a gun being slid between the bars on the window. It would be easy to shoot me as I lay here.

Envisioning various trajectories—imagining the muzzle of a rifle and all the different angles from which the gun could be fired, all the different directions a bullet could travel—I got out of the bed and wedged myself into the only space that, according to my calculations, was safe in the entire room: the narrow space on the floor between the bed and the armoire. As I lay there on the tiles, I did all the calculations again, retracing all the possible angles that a gun could be slid through the bars and fired, that a bullet could travel. There was absolutely no way anyone would be able to fire on me here. I was covered. I could keep myself safe down here on the floor as long as no one came into the house.

But it brought me no comfort, and I passed a sleepless night there on the tile floor—too afraid to even move and pull a blanket off the bed to make a pallet for myself—Ramzy's voice looping through my head. *I'm scared for you. I'm scared for you.* As I listened to the leaves rustling, I was certain I heard men whispering in the garden, passing through the trees.

And then I heard footsteps on the street, accompanied by a drum, and singing—a boy's voice, a teenager, hovering between childhood and manhood. I couldn't quite make out the words. What is this? I wondered.

In the morning, when I called Mohamed, he would explain that this was a *musaharati*, someone who, during Ramadan, went around making music and singing to wake Muslims up so they could have breakfast before the daily fast began at sunrise. The sound was beautiful, and it provided me temporary relief from my fear before fading as the boy rounded the corner, continuing up the street toward the Old City.

Not long after he passed, I watched the light change—the black air in the space above me softening into a gray and then white.

I'd made it through the night.

Telling myself that no one would dare attack me during the day, I got up off the floor and headed to the kitchen, where I made myself a cup of Nescafé. Grabbing an ice pack for my foot from the freezer, I took to the garden with my coffee and seated myself on the bench. In the morning light, I could convince myself that the world around me was just fine.

28

The war and the summer wore on.

The start date for the summer course I was teaching, Language and Thinking, was approaching; when LNT was over, I was supposed to leave. But I sat and did nothing to prepare for the move. I didn't pack. I didn't get rid of anything. I just sat in the garden, reading and icing my foot, exhausted from spending another sleepless night wedged between the armoire and bed, waiting to hear the musaharati, the only thing that provided relief, however temporary, from the memory of Ramzy's words: *I'm scared for you.*

During her daily visits downstairs, Jacqueline asked about an exit date. Had I booked a ticket to Florida yet? No. Did I know when I would be leaving the apartment? No. She needed to know what my plans were, she added, because she needed to find another renter.

"Of course," I told her. "I understand. I'll let you know as soon as I figure everything out."

Mohamed and I talked on the phone every day, mostly about the war. Things were bad in Gaza; the fighting would escalate, and tensions would rise in the West Bank, too. Mohamed urged me to leave sooner. I explained to him that I had a commitment to teach the summer course and that I'd already left the university in a lurch by quitting my full-time position. I wasn't going to back out of this class too.

"It's not worth it," he said—never articulating what I knew he was thinking, what we were both thinking: that staying in the West Bank, now, in Area A, was putting my life on the line. Before the war, Mohamed hadn't been concerned for my safety, he'd said. Even if people knew who I was, my work at the university and my politics kept me safe, Mohamed felt. I was with the people. But now he wasn't so sure, and he urged me to leave early and join him in Florida. Not wanting to alarm me, he tried to be calm and level about it all.

And then, too, there were the phone calls from friends inside Israel, concerned for my safety. Oded called and asked if I needed the place in Jerusalem.

"No," I told him in English, "I'm staying out here." On more than one occasion, I'd sat on this bench and, my voice low, had conversations with Oded in Hebrew. Now that seemed foolish.

"Don't you think you should get out of there? Come back. If you need a place to stay, you can come here. Or you can even go to my parents' house. I'm sure they'd have you."

I thanked him but said I wasn't leaving. He insisted that what I was doing was crazy. That I would end up dead.

I didn't have the words to explain my feelings to him or to myself. It took me years to figure out why I sat there that summer like that. Running out of Bethlehem the moment things got tough would mean betraying my students, the ones I had loved and who had loved me in return. It would be betraying Jacqueline and Lena and Shadi and all of my Palestinian friends—it would mean I was abandoning them to their fates as though our fates aren't inextricably bound. It would be betraying all those people I'd reported on, too, and all the villages where I'd observed protests—demonstrations that included Israelis, marching side by side with Palestinians. Leaving now was a way of saying that I didn't trust the people around me, that I wasn't with them, that I wasn't standing with them in their times of pain. It would also be a way of saying that I didn't believe in any of the things I stood for as an individual and that Mohamed and I stood for as a couple. It would be betraying the moment he'd shown me the British Mandate mailbox and the other moment in which we showed Ramzy the floor tiles in Matt's apartment and we'd all mused together about what things had been like before 1948, before the land was divided, back when Jews and Arabs were buying their floor tiles from the same supplier in south Tel Aviv, back when it was possible for tiles bearing the Star of David and a menorah to end up in a Palestinian home.

I didn't know how to articulate to Oded that leaving Bethlehem now would mean that I didn't believe that Jews and Palestinians had a future together in this land. To leave now would mean betraying the vision of Jews and Arabs living house-to-house—a checkerboard of families that would be virtually indistinguishable from one another.

And if this place, whatever it was called, wasn't my home, what was?

But I felt like a hypocrite. Because as I told Oded and Mohamed and everyone else, "No, I'm not leaving until I teach my course" and as I was spending my days confidently in the garden, I was cowering on the floor every night in the bedroom, waiting for the musaharati, waiting for dawn. If I really had faith in the land and the people, I wouldn't have been hiding between the bed and the wall, imagining the trajectory of bullets zipping overhead and listening for an intruder's footsteps.

* * *

I began to venture out into the world beyond Jacqueline's garden, even with my broken foot. For Al Jazeera, I covered a Palestinian protest against the war. I walked through Bethlehem, no longer afraid of being spotted, as Iman had put it. With my engagement ring on, I bought hand-painted Palestinian dishes and embroidered pillowcases as though Mohamed and I were opening a home together here, as though I was never leaving. I told myself that they were souvenirs, things for me to take to Florida, but I didn't box them up. Rather, I put the dishes in the cabinet as though Mohamed might appear any time, as though I was going to serve him up a meal of stuffed eggplant, his favorite, just like I had the previous summer in Beth's apartment. As though he would kiss my palms again when he finished eating, as he had last summer, saying, "*Yislamu ideki* [God bless your hands]."

I had done nothing to prepare for the move to the States. I hadn't booked a ticket to Florida. I hadn't packed or gotten rid of anything. Here I was accumulating more things. I began to doubt I was going to be able to leave at all. I toyed with the idea of asking Sarah for my job back.

Language and Thinking hadn't started yet, but there was other work on campus to be done. We were interviewing potential students. And so I boarded a servees, knowing that would mean sitting next to people who might know who I was, knowing that security would be tight at the Container, knowing that I would be showing my face on campus when these menacing "anonymous" emails had warned me not to.

In Abu Dis, I got off the servees at the usual place, close to the wall, and walked across the street to campus. The guard at the gate gave me a little nod as I entered. I went into the faculty kitchen, as always, and made coffee just like I had every morning there for the past two years. I went into the shared office, where I met Professor Tomas and a Palestinian colleague. We chatted a bit and then began interviewing, in English, potential students. Everything felt normal.

It felt good to be back at the university, and between that and the trip to the army base, I was left feeling that I could navigate this place; I could exist here, even during a war. This conflict wasn't sharpening my sense of myself as a Jew or an Israeli but, rather, my feeling that I was someone who lived among and contributed to the Palestinians. To their society, to their well-being.

At least, that's how I felt during the day. When night fell and I went to bed, I found myself on the floor, Ramzy's words echoing around me: *I'm scared for you.*

And then, one night, as I lay on the floor, awake, I heard the familiar sound of the musaharati coming. Throughout Ramadan, the sound had become increasingly soothing—I'd come to associate the musaharati's rounds with safety. By the time he made it to our street, I knew the night was almost over; I knew I'd made it. His voice, his drum, banged away the chorus of *I'm scared for you,* pushing those words out of my brain, and provided reassurance that no one was coming for me, that no harm would come to me, that I would be OK.

On this night, I listened to his words carefully. The musaharati was telling the faithful to wake up. And so I did, figuratively. I saw myself there and realized that, night after night, I'd been fine.

The musaharati was telling us to get up, and so I did that, too. While Muslims, of course, would take the instruction to get up and go eat, I got up and went not to the kitchen but got into bed, trusting then not just in this young boy singing and drumming his way through the streets, not just in Jacqueline, sleeping above me, not just in the neighbors and Amy and Shadi down the hill and Lena over in Beit Sahour and Ramzy in Dar Salah but in everyone: in my students and their families. In the people I passed on the street. In the man who owned the grocery down the street and the other who drove the servees to Abu Dis and the people who sat next to me in those seats. In all the people of Palestine.

* * *

I'd spent a couple of days on campus that week, working alongside Professor Tomas and our Palestinian colleague without a problem, and no fiery letters decrying my presence arrived in my inbox.

So I was shocked when, on Saturday morning, I received an email from Sarah explaining that the administration had decided, during this incredibly fraught time, that it was best for me not to come to campus anymore. Mindful of the fact that I'd already resigned and that I'd returned for the sole purpose of teaching the course—and grateful for my commitment to the program—the college would pay for my return ticket to the States.

The ticket I still hadn't managed to book.

As I stood there, staring at my email, absorbing the news, my phone rang. It was my colleague David, distraught. He'd just received an email informing him that he was being dismissed from his position. David, who was beloved by his students and had been teaching there for years.

I thought of the conversation I'd had with a Palestinian colleague and friend in the servees, months before, during which he'd told me that our other Palestinian colleagues wanted all the Jewish Israeli professors gone. I wondered if the coworker I'd interviewed students with this week—a coworker whom I liked and respected, who always chatted amicably with me, who had smiled at me and been as warm and friendly as he'd always been—had been one of the colleagues who complained about my presence there. Had he felt uncomfortable sitting next to me this week? Had he gone to the administration, in protest, after he'd spent the day smiling at me?

My chest literally hurt, and I clutched at it.

I understood then that it was time for me to leave the West Bank.

And yet I made no move to do so. I didn't book a flight. I didn't pack. When Jacqueline came down that afternoon, I told her, tears in my eyes, that I wouldn't be teaching the summer course after all.

"Why? What happened?" she asked.

I couldn't tell her that it had to do with the war because that would open the door to questions about my identity. And if there was ever a time to come clean with Jacqueline, it wasn't now, as my people were bombing Gaza and she was reliving the trauma she'd experienced in 1948. So I just shook my head and wiped my eyes.

"When are you leaving?" Jacqueline asked.

"I don't know. Look at all this *stuff*," I said, trying to lighten the mood, waving my hands around, laughing. "What am I going to do with all this *stuff*?"

It occurred to me that I'd been accumulating things because, really, I had no desire to leave. I didn't want to follow Mohamed to America. I wanted to stay here.

Jacqueline offered to buy my radiators and space heaters from me.

"Not today," I said.

"Why?" she insisted.

"Because it's Saturday," I said, "and I'm not going to deal with this on a Saturday."

"Because you're Jewish?" Jacqueline said.

We stared at each other for a moment. Of course she'd figured it all out. She was in my apartment—her home—rummaging through my stuff every day.

"No," I said, "because it's the weekend. And I'm tired."

My stomach lurched as I watched her mount the stairs and return to the second floor. I didn't feel sick from fear. It was guilt. I knew I should tell Jacqueline the truth. But at this point, I couldn't bear it.

* * *

When I told Mohamed on the phone what had happened with the summer course and with David, he wasn't surprised. "It was going to happen sooner or later; it's good you're leaving," he said. He repeated a version of what my Palestinian colleague had told me on the servees. My presence would have been tolerated or even welcomed in the past but, as the occupation ground on, Palestinians were increasingly skeptical about the role someone like me played in everything. According to some Palestinians, what I was doing, even if I meant well, was "normalizing" the occupation. Mohamed didn't agree with this assessment, but he understood how some might read my presence on campus as normalization and how it would be especially inflammatory during a war.

But something good had come out of this, Mohamed said. Now I could join him in Florida sooner.

"I can't go yet. I just paid August rent. And besides," I added, "I can't miss Amy and Shadi's wedding."

I was making excuses to myself because, as much as I loved Mohamed, I couldn't bear to leave. Mohamed applied no pressure beyond saying that he was waiting for me; I wondered if I would keep him waiting forever, if that paralysis I'd felt in all my previous relationships was setting in, if, now that I was engaged and about to make this big step, I was building a barrier between myself and love.

I wondered if I would make endless excuses to Mohamed and myself. I wondered if, at the end of August, I would find myself paying September rent and telling Mohamed I would spend just one more month here.

29

The evening of Amy and Shadi's henna party, which took place just a few days before the actual wedding, I donned a tight pink lace dress that I'd bought in Bethlehem, piled my hair into a chignon, slid my feet into a pair of black high heels, and got into my car and left the confines of Jacqueline's garden, heading downhill toward Beit Sahour, armed with only the name of the restaurant and a street address. Not everything in the territories was in Google Maps, and when I'd tried to enter the place in my phone it hadn't shown. I was on my own to navigate.

The crescent moon signaling the end of Ramadan hung in the air, like an earring dangling alongside the graceful curve of a woman's neck. It was dark, and my tiny car bounced over the poorly paved road. I found myself navigating not by intent but by instinct: my feet knew these streets; I'd run them with Lena many times, and I'd also run them alone.

And then I discovered myself farther out in Beit Sahour than usual, in a place where I'd never run, on what had started out a familiar street but suddenly looked unfamiliar, where the road grew even thinner and bumpier. Suddenly I wasn't so sure I knew where I was going. At a crossroads, I looked up at a simple plastic sign that had been nailed to a wooden pole; in Arabic only, the sign said the name of the restaurant and had an arrow pointing to the left. Unsure if I'd read it correctly, I made the turn anyway. Soon the restaurant was in front of me, on the right-hand side of the road.

As I parked, I awoke again, just as the musaharati had implored me to, and I saw myself: arriving, alone, navigating in the moonlight, reading signs in Arabic only. No Mohamed, no translation, no Google Maps.

Just me.

I can do this on my own, I thought. I can stay here, alone, if I want to.

I stepped in, and Amy and Shadi greeted me, hugged me, and pulled me onto the dance floor with friends and family. The party went on for hours. Dressed in traditional Palestinian garb, Shadi's father danced, balancing a bottle of arak on his head. The men gathered on the dance floor and danced the *dabke*; a few had wooden batons, the sticks serving as both percussion and exclamation points. "We're here!" the movements and the thumps seemed to say. I knew Amy and Shadi had debated whether to go forward with the wedding amid the war, but now, as the men moved as one around the dance floor, their movements synchronized, their sticks hitting the floor, I felt that they'd made the right decision—this was a celebration of life, the founding of a new family that would bring children into the world. It was an act of defiance as Israel was bombing Gaza to death.

As I moved with the crowd, I felt like a part of this place, a part of the people—*all* the people on both sides of the Green Line.

Taking a break, I sat at a table, sipping a drink. As I watched the crowd move as one, I saw connections: Amy and Shadi, Amy's parents and brother, and Shadi's parents and his siblings. I saw aunts and uncles and cousins.

I was the only person there who had come entirely alone. I realized I'd taken all these physical risks to be with Mohamed, to be with the people here, and that I'd made my body vulnerable, but I'd been protecting my heart. But now I was ready, finally, to force myself to take the biggest risk of all: I would leave this land and build a life with Mohamed.

* * *

The next day, sitting at the Casa Nova with Lena, I booked a ticket to Florida. August 19. That gave me three weeks to box and ship the few things I wanted to send back to Florida—the dishes I'd bought that summer, some of the books I couldn't bear to part with—and to get rid of the rest of my belongings. Lena was sad and still had her doubts about "Mr. Jaradat." But she was supportive.

When I returned to Jacqueline's house, I raced up the stairs and knocked on her door. She opened.

"August 19," I said.

I hadn't cried when I made the ticket with Lena, but now, with Jacqueline before me, my eyes began to leak.

* * *

In the days that followed, over and over, I loaded my car with clothes and bedding to take to the YMCA in Beit Sahour, where they were collecting donations for Gaza. Onto the pile went the red wool winter coat I'd bought when I was a newlywed and that I'd worn on so many reporting trips. Onto the pile went the black pants I'd found on the bench outside my apartment on Reines Street, pants I'd often worn while I was grieving my first marriage.

And then, my windows down, the heat and dust flowing into the car, my back sweating, I drove it all to Beit Sahour and added it to the mountains of things that would be sent to Gaza. I looked at my things there—that red coat, those black pants—and found myself unable to turn, unable to walk back to the car. It felt like I was throwing myself on the pile. Forcing myself to move, I felt something ping inside me, like a little cord being cut inside my heart. Then I would get into the car and head back to Jacqueline's and feel flooded with a sense of relief. Each time I took a carload to the YMCA, donating almost all of my clothes became a little bit easier.

But my books were another matter. I sat there on the floor of Jacqueline's house, the tile floor sticking to my bare legs, piles of books before me. I'd sorted them into a discard pile and a keep pile. And then I would look and transfer one title to the keep pile, and the discard pile would shrink. Some would come with me—there were books like *Four Houses and Longing*, that Eshkol Nevo novel, the first book I read in Hebrew, which I just couldn't let go of. The rest I would bring to Jerusalem and sell at a secondhand bookstore. I had other business in Jerusalem—I had to get government permission to take my cat to the States with me.

My stomach aching, I loaded the car. I dreaded the trip into Israel because I knew it would throw my identity and sympathies into conflict just as commuting to and from Abu Dis had every day when I lived in Kiryat Yovel.

And that's exactly what happened. As I exited a grocery store in Jewish West Jerusalem, where I'd stopped to buy a bottle of water, I couldn't help but glance at the Hebrew headlines: "Goodbye, my love," one read. The words sat below the picture of a smiling young couple; the headline reminded me of an epithet on a headstone.

In smaller print, I saw the subhead: "The last messages on WhatsApp, the shared dreams, the big hole that's left in the heart."

Standing there, at the threshold of the grocery, holding a cold bottle in my hand, feeling the heat of the summer day radiating toward me, I gasped for air at the thought of this boy who had died. He was someone's boyfriend, someone's son, someone's grandson.

He was human. And now he's gone.

I wept.

Later the same afternoon, I found my breath knocked away again when I heard a small boy boast to his mother, as he gripped her hand, "We have almost destroyed Gaza."

It was a strange thing being in Jerusalem that day—there was nowhere else in the world I wanted to be, and I felt this strong desire to just sit down on a bench and never get up.

At the same time, I wanted to be anywhere but there.

30

And then it was the evening before I was supposed to fly, though I wasn't 100 percent sure the flight would happen. In recent days, Hamas rockets had landed close to Ben Gurion Airport, prompting many carriers to cancel flights, including mine. I'd scrambled to rebook and had continued carting things to DHL to ship to Florida, and I'd continued putting my possessions out on the street, and I'd gone into Israel and sold my car (to one of the Filipino families I'd become close with years before as I covered the government's threat to deport them), and I'd called a taxi driver from East Jerusalem who was willing to illegally drive me in from Bethlehem and on to Ben Gurion Airport. I'd done all of this, not really sure if I would actually be able to leave.

With just twelve hours left, Amy, Lena, and Beth came over for a final goodbye. One last dinner together.

I made a simple meal of salad served alongside pasta tossed with local olive oil, fresh basil, fresh garlic, and the al Juneidi brand salty white cheese that came packed in brine. Knowing I wouldn't be able to find this particular brand in America, I rolled the cheese around in my mouth, savoring it.

Beth, Lena, Amy, and I all ate and drank as though it was a normal evening. But when I washed the last dishes, that's when it sunk in that I wouldn't be putting them away. After I dried them, we began the task of portioning out what remained of my things. They picked over my kitchen supplies. It was like watching people go through the house of someone who had died. It was like I had died, but I was there to witness it.

I walked everyone to the door, saying goodbye one by one, watching them leave my place with dishes, glasses, my colander, the food that remained in my fridge, packets of tea—bits and pieces of a human life.

And then it was time to say goodbye to Lena.

"I know you're gonna be back, habibti. You can't stay away from this place. It's a part of you."

"*You're* a part of me, ya Lena," I said.

"Oh, Mya," Lena said, pulling me into her arms. "Now you're gonna make me cry like you always do."

She held me tight, rubbing my back, murmuring, "Habibti," and then we separated.

"I can't say goodbye," I said.

"It's not goodbye. We'll see each other soon."

And then Lena turned and walked out the door for the last time.

Alone, just hours remaining between me and my flight, I walked through the house, thinking about how all traces of my existence—the evidence that I'd lived and loved there—were all gone. Except for one place—my closet in the master bedroom. There was clothing I still hadn't packed, and now, I stood before the armoire, contemplating these last things. I still had clothes here, and though I didn't have a job, I had eight thousand dollars in my bank account.

Even if I can't have my job at the university back, I'll find something. I'll be fine. I'm going to stay, I thought.

What if I did that? What if I just got into bed and went to sleep? I wondered. I stood before a mirror, seeing myself in the place, reminding myself that I was really here; I was alive. I touched my own face and felt my skin, smooth, slightly moist with sweat—it was a hot summer night. I sat down on the floor and texted Mohamed:

I'm very sorry but I can't do it, I can't leave. I can't move to Florida.

I didn't know how to explain to him what I felt with my bones—that I just couldn't do it—and so I told him something ridiculous in a bid to break up, saying that I knew he preferred women with dark hair and my natural color was auburn, striped with gray now. I couldn't dye my hair forever. It made my arms tired.

I'll never be what you want me to be.

And then I continued, reminding him that, after his family rejected me, I quit studying Arabic.

You really want to share a home with a Hebrew speaker? I love singing along to Dikla and I'm not giving that up—occupation or not!

Mohamed called then and told me that he loved my hair, reminding me that I wasn't dyeing it when we met, and he'd fallen in love with all of me, including the messy auburn bun on my head.

Looking for something, anything, I told him that I didn't look like that woman anymore. I'd gained weight that summer, between the war and my foot and Amy and Shadi and their whiskey.

"I love your curves," he answered.

"And what about my Arabic?" I asked in English.

"You speak good Arabic," he said in Arabic.

"No, I don't," I protested. "And if your people reject me, I reject your language!"

"*Beseder* [OK]," Mohammad answered in Hebrew.

As we went on like this, I found myself taking the clothes from the closet, folding them, rolling them up, and putting them in the suitcase. The next thing I knew it was 3:00 a.m., and I was packed.

My excuses gone, I told Mohammad the truth. "I just can't leave."

"Get some sleep," he answered. "You'll feel better in the morning."

I told him I wouldn't. I couldn't leave this place.

"I'll see you soon, dear," he said as he hung up.

* * *

My alarm went off two hours later. I made Nescafé and went out to the garden for one last moment on the bench, overlooking the orchards and Dheisheh.

Jacqueline came downstairs without knocking. We'd promised each other to have one last coffee together. But my cat, who had been scared of Jacqueline from day one, hid under the bed. Panicked that I wouldn't be able to get the cat out from under the bed and into the carrier, I asked Jacqueline to leave.

"No," she insisted, "I have to see you off and lock the door behind you."

"You can come down and lock the door after I go," I pushed back. "I have to get the cat into the carrier."

We went back and forth like this, fighting about the cat because we didn't know how to say all the other things—how to say that she'd loved me despite the fact that I'd lied to her, how to say that she knew the truth, how to say that I was sorry that I'd been dishonest, how to say how touched I'd been by the way she had cared for me, that I'd grown used to the constant snooping and intrusions and that I didn't even mind. How to say goodbye.

"You don't respect my boundaries—" I began, only to be interrupted by the phone ringing. It was the taxi driver; he was outside.

My cat was still under the bed. For a second, I saw the irony of it all—once I'd finally committed myself to leaving and had packed the very last of my things, I would end up missing my flight because of Jacqueline and the cat.

I begged Jacqueline to leave, just for a second, so I could get the cat out and go. "Then we can say goodbye," I promised.

By the time I managed to coax the cat out from under the bed and get her into the carrier, the taxi driver was calling for a second time. Worried he would leave without me, I shouted up the stairs, "I've gotta go!"

"OK!" Jacqueline yelled back down.

And that was it. I began to walk out.

The carrier dangling from one arm, my laptop bag and purse hanging from the other, I wheeled my two suitcases through the porch—passing the bay where I'd parked my car—and I opened the door that Mohamed used to have a key to, where he entered so many Fridays, and I exited to the street. There was the hill that led to Beit Sahour, the hill I'd run down so many times on my way to meet Lena or to run on my own along Shepherd Field. The road that had taken me to Amy's engagement party the night I'd realized it was time for me to go.

I got into the taxi, greeted Karim, and texted Mohamed: *I'm on my way.*

* * *

This wasn't the first time I'd paid Karim to take me in from Bethlehem to the airport, and as we headed toward Beit Jala, we agreed on a cover story in case we got stopped at the checkpoint just before the Tunnels. My ID still said that I lived at Kinneret's place in Kiryat Yovel. If a soldier looked closely and saw the address, they might ask what I was doing coming in at this early hour.

"You stayed at your cousin's last night," Karim instructed me.

I began to worry, of course, that they would ask me for that cousin's name and where in the settlement they lived. I wouldn't have an answer.

We rolled past the small army base on the corner between Beit Jala and the road that led to the settlement, and we turned left. We tumbled down the hill to Route 60 and made a right. The checkpoint—the same one I'd driven Mohamed through on our way to Tel Aviv—was ahead of us.

There was that familiar shaking and grumbling as the car went over the rumble strips just before the checkpoint. Karim eased the car through, nodding authoritatively at the soldiers, who nodded back at us.

And just like that, I exited the West Bank for the last time.

Getting past the soldiers was a relief, as always, and I felt that familiar sensation as the adrenaline subsided and my body relaxed and sank into the seat. I loosened my grip on the cat carrier I held in my lap. And then I was immersed in darkness as we entered the Tunnels.

We exited the Tunnels, and the sun hit me. As we began to make our way through East Jerusalem, I realized that I was in a taxi full of the few remaining things I'd had at Jacqueline's house. I realized I no longer had a key to any place—not Jacqueline's, not Kinneret's—and that my job was gone and that I was boarding a plane to take me to the other side of the planet.

Pain surged through my ribcage. My chest began heaving. I wasn't crying, I realized; I was sobbing.

Karim looked at me in the rearview mirror. "Oh, please don't cry," he said in Hebrew.

He was silent for a moment, keeping his eyes on the road, and then, at a red light, he turned and looked at me. "It'll be OK," he said in Hebrew. "Aren't you excited? You're going to America and getting married!"

What ran through my head, what I didn't tell Karim, was that America was a place I'd left for so many reasons. It was haunted for me. After having been gone for almost a decade, I had few contacts and even fewer friends.

And my wedding with Mohamed—who would come? Not his family. None of my friends from here would be there to stand with me and celebrate; no one would dance with a bottle of arak on their heads. No one would lift us into the air.

But I didn't say any of this to Karim. I just cried harder.

And I couldn't stop.

Poor Karim listened to me cry the whole way to Ben Gurion. By the time the airport was looming on the horizon, he was talking to me like I was his school-age daughter.

"Who's a big girl? Who's a big girl?" he asked me in Hebrew, glancing at me in the rearview mirror.

"*Mish ana* [Not me]," I groaned in Arabic.

"*Ken at ken! Ken at ken* [Yes, you are! Yes, you are]!" he insisted in Hebrew.

As we approached the checkpoint outside the airport, Karim warned me that we could have trouble because he's a Palestinian from East Jerusalem. So I blew my nose into my shirt and pulled my unruly hair back in a bid to look a bit more put together. And then we cobbled together another story—one that made sense given my Israeli ID—with Karim quickly memorizing my old address in Kiryat Yovel and the two of us agreeing to say that, if we were questioned, he'd picked me up there.

He repeated my address to himself as we pulled up to the checkpoint.

We cleared it without a problem and pulled up to the curb outside of departures. Karim put my suitcases on the sidewalk, and I knew that meant I would have to get out. I couldn't just stay in the car. So I slid out, bringing my cat, laptop, and purse with me. I paid Karim, and he tucked the money in his wallet. And then he offered me his hand.

I put my right hand in his large palm and felt it—warm—as he squeezed my fingers, then covered my hand with his other hand, both his hands embracing mine.

"Good luck," he said in Hebrew. "And may God be with you," he finished in Arabic.

I looked into his brown eyes, and my chin quivered. I knew that if I tried to talk, I would start crying again, and hoping he understood this, I nodded.

He nodded back and let go of my hand and returned to his car. As he opened the door, he punched his fist into the air and said in Hebrew, "Remember—you're strong!"

I nodded again and watched him drive away.

After loading my luggage onto a trolley, I checked the departures board and then joined the check-in line. As I prepared to hand my flight confirmation and passports—both American and Israeli—to the security guard, I started to cry again.

"*Nu*, what's your problem?" the security guard asked me in Hebrew, casting a suspicious eye at all the stuff piled before me.

"*Ani ozevet* [I'm leaving]," I answered.

He shrugged. "OK, but you're returning, right?"

"I don't know," I said. "I don't think so."

Understanding my tears then, the security guard softened, his face taking on a look of sympathy. "Don't worry, miss, we're not going anywhere," he said. "You can always come home."

Epilogue

September 2024, North Palm Beach, Florida

After I arrived in Florida, Mohamed and I lived for a time with his brother. Then, we got our own place on the intracoastal waterway—a tiny, one-room apartment in an old, subdivided house. In November 2014, Mohamed and I married at a small park in South Florida, just a couple of blocks from our little apartment. A Jewish cantor performed the wedding—which was attended by Mohamed's brother, my parents, my grandmother, some friends of the family, and one of my best friends—and she sang the seven blessings in Hebrew. Mohamed's brother read a passage from the Quran at our ceremony. He was the only member of Mohamed's family to attend. At that time, Mohamed still hadn't told his parents that he was marrying me.

In April 2015, I found out I was pregnant with our first child. Soon thereafter, Mohamed finally told his family in the West Bank that he had married me. When I returned to Israel alone in the fall of 2015 to spend six weeks doing some additional research for my first book, which was about migrant workers and African asylum seekers in Israel, one of Mohamed's brothers came in from the West Bank to meet me. He'd already started reading my articles to their father, translating them from English to Arabic as he did so, in hopes that my journalistic work would speak for itself. Mohamed's brother promised to continue doing so, and he promised to fix the problems in the family. He did, and two days before I flew back to Florida, heavily pregnant, I traveled to the family's home in the West Bank—the home Mohamed and I were supposed to live in—and met his father for the first time.

As we sat on the couch together—me, a Jewish immigrant to Israel; him, a PLO man—Mohamed's father apologized for rejecting me. In Arabic, he told me, "You're like a daughter to me now, the same as my own."

During my pregnancy, Mohamed and I compiled a list of baby names that would work in Hebrew and Arabic; from that list, Yasser helped pick our daughter's name. She was born in early 2016. Whenever Yasser returned to Sa'ir to visit his extended family, he walked around the village showing everyone pictures on his cell phone of our baby girl, his first grandchild.

But he never got to meet her because, just two days before Yasser, Fatima, and Mohamed's sister were scheduled to fly to Florida to spend Ramadan with us, Yasser had a massive heart attack and died.

Mohamed and I had a second child, a boy, in 2017, who we named after his father.

However, for reasons too numerous to list here—none of which were political—our marriage didn't survive, and we divorced in late 2022 after eight years of marriage. It was a good run; Mohamed and I remain close, and two years after the divorce, it still devastates me to write those words.

But someone got their happy ending: Ali and Rihab, the young Palestinian couple who had been split between Gaza and the West Bank. The two were finally reunited, Ali told me via email, after a high-ranking friend of his met Palestinian officials from the Civil Affairs Committee in Russia, where this friend presented officials with a bottle of whiskey and an invitation to a luxurious local bar. Shortly after that meeting, Rihab's address was updated in the Israeli-controlled population registry from the Gaza Strip to the West Bank. Rihab was granted permission to travel to the West Bank to reunite with Ali; the two had a baby, a girl they named Sofia. The family lives together in the West Bank still today.

In the wake of October 7, Mohamed and I found solace in each other and the vision we still share of a peaceful life together on the land we both hold so dear. In a way, our children embody that vision, and we remain committed to raising our children together. I don't know yet how I will explain my Israeli identity to them—how can I explain that my people are occupying their father's people?—and I don't know what my Israeli identity will mean to them. Will they identify as American-Jewish-Israeli-Muslim-Palestinian? Will they take only a part of that hyphenated identity and identify with one side more than another? I don't really believe in "sides," and I hope that they won't either. I hope that they will feel, as Mohamed and I do, that we have sided with humanity.

MYA GUARNIERI is a writer and award-winning journalist who spent nearly a decade covering Israel and the occupied Palestinian territories. Author of *The Unchosen: The Lives of Israel's New Others,* which was short-listed for a Jewish Quarterly Wingate Prize, her reportage, commentary, essays, and short fiction have appeared in a wide variety of international publications, including the *New York Times, The Guardian, The Nation,* the *Washington Post, Haaretz, Le Monde Diplomatique, Foreign Policy, Slate, Guernica, Narrative Magazine,* and the *Kenyon Review Online.* She holds an MA in journalism with a focus on politics and global affairs from Columbia University, where she was an international reporting fellow.

For Indiana University Press

Sabrina Black, Editorial Assistant
Lesley Bolton, Project Manager/Editor
Gary Dunham, Acquisitions Editor and Director
Anna Francis, Assistant Acquisitions Editor
Anna Garnai, Production Coordinator
Katie Huggins, Production Manager
Alyssa Nicole Lucas, Marketing and Publicity Manager
Dan Pyle, Online Publishing Manager
Jennifer Witzke, Senior Artist and Book Designer